From Yu...

I. Allan Sealy was born in
Allahabad, and has taught at
universities in the USA, Australia
and Canada. He is the author of
The Trotter-Nama, which won Best
First Book (Eurasia) of the 1989
Commonwealth Writers Prize, and
Hero (1992). He divides his time
between India and New Zealand.

Also by I. Allan Sealy

The Trotter-Nama
Hero

I. ALLAN SEALY

From
YUKON
to
YUCATAN

A Western Journey

Minerva

A Minerva Paperback
FROM YUKON TO YUCATAN

First published in Great Britain 1994
by Martin Secker & Warburg Ltd
This Minerva edition published 1995
by Mandarin Paperbacks
an imprint of Reed Consumer Books Ltd
Michelin House, 81 Fulham Road, London SW3 6RB
and Auckland, Melbourne, Singapore and Toronto

Reprinted 1995

A CIP catalogue record for this title
is available from the British Library
ISBN 0 7493 9843 4

Printed and bound in Great Britain
by Cox & Wyman Ltd, Reading, Berkshire

For my sister
Janet

Turn eastward and look at the Western Land;
face south and the North Star is pointed out there!

Yung-chia   *Song of Enlightenment*

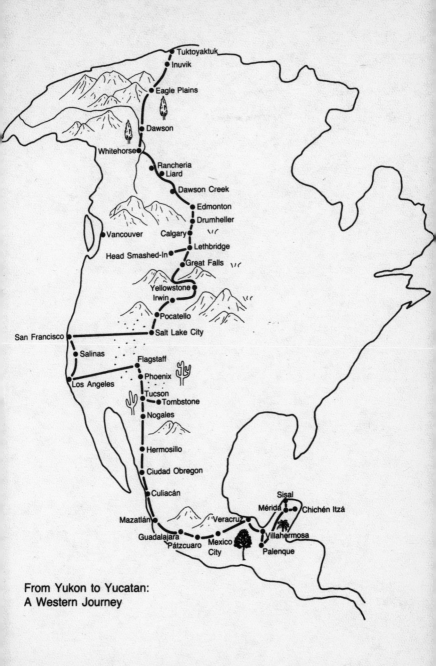

Tuktoyaktuk
Inuvik
Eagle Plains
Dawson
Whitehorse
Rancheria
Liard
Dawson Creek
Edmonton
Drumheller
Vancouver   Calgary
Head Smashed-In   Lethbridge
Great Falls
Yellowstone
Irwin
Pocatello
San Francisco   Salt Lake City
Salinas
Flagstaff
Los Angeles   Phoenix
Tucson
Tombstone
Nogales
Hermosillo
Ciudad Obregon
Culiacán
Sisal
Mérida   Chichén Itzá
Mazatlán   Veracruz
Guadalajara   Villahermosa
Pátzcuaro   Mexico   Palenque
City

From Yukon to Yucatan:
A Western Journey

Contents

The Mallee Fowl

"Siete menos cuarto," the boy in Honolulu said when I asked the local time. A quarter to seven. He was the first person I addressed on North American soil and he spoke Spanish.

Back on the plane to Vancouver a team of zoologists was returning from Australia, where they'd gone to study the Mallee fowl.

"Mallifowl?" I said to the girl beside me.

MALLEE FOWL, she wrote out on her paper napkin. The Mallee fowl is a reclusive bird that lays its eggs before it builds a nest. The team had spent two weeks watching a Mallee fowl mound – the nest goes over the eggs – but had come away without spotting the bird.

I thought of Matsuo Basho, my guide. He once walked a hundred miles to watch a full moon rise over a certain mountain – and on the night it rained. I was carrying his *Narrow Road to the Deep North*; the title seemed to fit my own journey. Basho returned home from his travels in 1691, so I was commemorating a 300th anniversary, besides anticipating a 500th, Columbus' arrival in the Americas.

There was still another anniversary to celebrate. Twenty years before, I had made my own discovery of the Americas. At the age of twenty I came out to the United States from a small town in India as an exchange student. Now, at forty, I was going back. Not back to Kalamazoo. (Rule 1 was: *Cover no old ground*.) But back to that New World to see what had changed. There were other ground rules:

(2) *Start at the top.*

1

(3) *Keep West.*

(4) *Keep down — no planes, and no more than eight hours on any bus or train.*

(5) *Leave the route to chance.*

(6) *Take three months, one each for Canada, the United States, and Mexico.*

(7) *Travel alone.*

1
Point Grey

The Point Grey taxi was a big American car with the speedometer in miles. The driver was Indian – *East* Indian. From now on *Indian* meant something else. It was night. I sat in front, democratically, but we maintained a stolid silence for the entire drive, the sort of silence men of the same race will sometimes impose on each other for fear of appearing racially minded. When the darkness grew onerous he switched his radio on low and hopped from one station to the next; for the rest of the journey he continued this nervous grazing. There was a small pile of papers beside him, his work pile, not quite on the passenger seat but not in the centre either. Was I sitting on his desk? We reached Point Grey.

"Make it twenty-four dollars," I said, rounding off the cents.

He fished in various coin holds and came up with the change.

"You *did* say twenty-four dollars, sir?"

"Yes." (*Where do you come from? Where were you born? How did you end up here? Perhaps you know my home town, Dehra Dun?*)

"Then it's just twenty cents short, sir."

"That's OK." (*Look, how old are you? When did you come out? Married? Children? Are your parents here? What language do you speak at home? What did your wife cook for dinner?*)

He heaved my gear bag to the sidewalk. There was an untried tent in there.

"Would you like me to help you carry something, sir?"

(*Bugger your sirs!*) "No, that's fine, thanks."

And there the interview ended, in my head. I'd been too long writing fiction. With novels you sat at your desk for years together talking to yourself.

3

The University of British Columbia conference centre was over-booked. There was a Milton symposium on and a Burma Star veterans' reunion coming up. The man at the desk looked like a ravaged rock star. When I got to my room there was a hair on my pillow. I took out my own little pillow from the gear bag, my one piece of luxury, and the handkerchief-sized pillowcase my wife had made for me. I was asleep in seconds.

Morning scent of pine as I stepped out into Canada. I'd lived three years in this city, on this damp northwest coast with its forests of spruce and red cedar. There was forest on four sides of the campus. In its cool gloom the ground was springy with fallen needles, the air spiked with resins.

I had two friends I wanted to look up in Vancouver. One was Maria Tomsich, who taught in the Spanish department at UBC. When I was a student we walked the woodland trails together. A refugee from the Italian coast of Yugoslavia, Maria had come to Canada as a child. When I left Vancouver she had just adopted Sheeba, a little girl from India. Sheeba was now in high school.

We had dinner at the familiar table in the familiar pink roughcast house overlooking the bay. I told them I meant to find out how Canadians, Americans, and Mexicans got on as neighbours in the new North American bloc:

"Tell Allan about your history teacher."

"What about him?"

"What he says about Canadian history."

"What about it?"

"You know, how he shows the whole history of Canada to be a defence against America."

"Ya." A hard look at her mother.

I put out a feeler. "How do your friends feel about America?"

"Oh, some of them really like it."

"How many?"

"Oh, maybe five per cent. It's a good place to visit but they wouldn't like to live there. There's one guy who'd like to but he's not real popular."

"What does his father do?"

"He's got some kind of business there. He's East Indian."

After dinner Sheeba played classical guitar for us – from her

4

room. At the end of the evening we switched to Spanish, my first conversation in ten years. I missed a lot of nouns and had trouble with simple verbs.

"Tell Allan to go to Fourth to catch his bus."

But Sheeba would not use her Spanish. "Go to Fourth," she said, and stroked her Siamese cat, Silicon. She was going to be a biologist, and vowed to quit guitar at nineteen.

"You'll regret it," I said at the door.

"No, I won't."

"Hasta la vista."

"Hasta la vista."

The other forest friend was long dead. She'd been dead when I first made her acquaintance, dead before I was born. Emily Carr was the great painter of this coast. She died in 1945. Her paintings form the core of the Vancouver Art Gallery and I felt I'd neglected them while living there. I wanted to spend a day in her company and this time I did.

The day was wet, West Coast wet, well suited to her sombre canvases. There is a sculptural simplicity to Carr's work. It's the outward sign of a singleminded quest: the pursuit of an idea – of *the* idea of this corner of the world, with its rich, slightly rotting fertility. The forms bulk and brood; a succulence fills even the dead roots that curl up from a driftwood log. Totem poles recur, the stock artefact of this coast, but the poles have become trees again, and the trees grave totems. In *Forsaken*, a derelict pole tilts right back, set upon by the forest; the totemic creatures, among them a howling wolf, gaze upwards into an immensity of blue space. Carr said she wanted to capture the "ferocious strangled lonesomeness of the place". The whole coast is sitting for its portrait; Carr's subject is the land itself.

There was a special exhibition the day I went, on Carr's French years. The one piece with any passion was a pen and ink Christ among French trees – crucified on his totem pole. The young Emily did not last in France. In 1911 she fell ill. "She cannot live in cities," the doctor said. Emily herself was more precise (she had just come home): "I am a Westerner and I'm going to extract all that I can out of this big glorious West. The new ideas are big and they fit the big land."

5

There's a programmatic edge to the voice here. People in new worlds, or newly awakening worlds, tend to stridency. But the declaration, the statement of intent struck a chord in me. This West touched me too. I was now on a journey to see what was left of it, out there and in me. It started with Cowboys and Indians – in India; untroubled by ironies of nomenclature, we played the frontier game. That West was a real country, with all the strengths of fantasy. Later the historical West arrived with its battles and treaties and its scarred Indians. The word *reservation* entered our vocabulary. It was only after I travelled to the United States and read American literature that a third West appeared, an abstract West – not the West but the idea of the West.

It was a useful idea. Without it Carr would have lost her way, painted French forests. With it an outsider could make his way through American literature and sift out an "Eastern" remnant that looked backwards nostalgically at the Old World. In this sense the West was that living part that didn't look back, that worked the new land. For close on two centuries the patrician East wrote disparagingly of the West and its works. For half a century *Huckleberry Finn*, a barefoot Western, or Sou'western, went unsung in the East – to which the author himself migrated. The canonized novelist of the day, Henry James, migrated still further east, back to the Old World. James's novels, says the Argentinian Borges, in a wiry little book on American literature, are finely crafted, but they suffer from one major defect: they lack life. It is a devastating indictment; whatever else *Huckleberry Finn* may lack, it's not life.

A late arrival, I was interested in the history of American arrivals – and departures. Departure was always easier, more tempting, from the East. James found himself more English than American; T.S. Eliot buried his bones in Westminster Abbey. "Dead England" was Emily Carr's verdict. It was not cities but the Old World that she found suffocating. Her abbey was the forest at her door, and in her later years she bought a caravan so she could go deeper in. Stepping out every day with her brushes and her pet monkey and the rat Susie tucked under her chin, she is like some real-life Robinson Crusoe, not quite rid of the past (there's a useful wreck nearby) but turning to the new land and working it with a lonely passion.

"There's no there there," Gertrude Stein, another refugee,

complained of the West. And yet there were faithful toilers on the far shore. "Make Westerly" is the title of a short story by one of them, Jack London. It was a motto I took to heart before I ever read the story. As it happened I found another West, but the idea of the frontier survived my Caribbean thesis and three winters in Canada.

In Canada the frontier is not the West but the North. Living in Vancouver I was always conscious of the weight of that North. It is impossible not to be. There are snow-capped mountains across the bay, Northern mountains, and beyond them more mountains, and after them still more, stretching to the Arctic Sea.

But another lure lay to the south. In Michigan a German-American family introduced me to sangria. It was an introduction, that dark Spanish punch, to Spain and the Spanish world. That there was more to Europe than England could still astonish a colonial; that there was more to North America than English and French was another awakening.

Sitting in Vancouver, dreaming alternately of the cold North and the warm South, it was only a matter of time before I linked the two. Let this thesis once finish (please God) and I will go from the Arctic Sea to Mexico's farthest shore.

I didn't. I went to Mexico and fell ill. I returned to India, two books intervened. Then I was forty and in need of a special celebration. I had been ten years writing. *I will arise and go now.* And finally I did.

The first human arrivals on the continent of North America are thought to have come from Asia across what was once a land bridge, Beringia. Many proofs, racial, linguistic, and technological, link the North American Indian with his Siberian forebears. Starting at the top of Canada it occurred to me that I would be following the track of that early human dispersal. The last glacial sheet, the Wisconsinan, left certain corridors as it retreated: through these passed the first Americans. About where the present Alaskan Highway begins (or ends, if you're starting at the top) was one such corridor. So when I came down from the Rockies onto the plains of Alberta, I would stand just where the first arrivals stood, and consider which way to go.

It is reckoned that the earliest Americans took some 500 years

7

to cross North America from top to bottom, and perhaps another 500 to reach Tierra del Fuego in the far south. This journey is thought to have been made between ten and twelve thousand years ago, some say much more. Travelling by bus and car I would cross the continent rather quicker than people who had no use for the wheel, and who managed without the horse for the greater part of their residence in the Americas. And in a matter of months I would cut across a much longer evolutionary journey, passing from the igloo to the pyramid.

The next wave of Americans came by water: the Vikings to the north, and some 500 years later, other Europeans. My own journey, which began roughly where the Asiatics dispersed, would finish where the Europeans arrived. In the long run the peopling of the Americas seems simply a matter of land arrivals and then water arrivals.

There were three water incidents the week I arrived – water dramas, properly, since all three showed a sense of theatre. The first was the commemorative docking, at the other end of Canada, of the Viking ship *Gaia*. The captain swore he didn't intend to upstage the 1992 Columbus celebrations; it was purely coincidental that he would put in at Washington on Columbus Day.

The other two were West Coast dramas, Westerns after a sort. First, Canada claimed harassment of her fishing boats by US vessels in the west and threatened retaliation against American fishing boats in the east. And then there sailed into the tranquil bay on 6 August the nuclear battleship USS *Missouri*.

Greenpeace were waiting. There were tussles and megaphones and rubber dinghies and water-cannon. In the morning I went down to Granville Island before the ship arrived to get details. The market stalls brimmed with fat peaches, Okanagan apricots, BC cherries, even Mexican mangoes, but I could get nothing on where the *Missouri* might lie. I bought a mango and went looking for a jacket: I had no idea how cold the Arctic might be.

That night I asked a Canadian writer about the *Missouri* visit. Keath Fraser lived down by Kitsilano beach, where he'd written two collections of stories, *Taking Cover* and *Foreign Affairs*, and edited (for a charity, the Canada–India Village Association) a collection of notable travel misadventures called *Bad Trips*.

Was this a bad trip, I asked him.

"It's a little PR work, but they got the timing wrong."

"You mean the day?"

"Yes, Hiroshima Day, but also I think the general mood of Canadians. If there were a plebiscite today on US nuclear warships, they would not be allowed in."

I said I'd got the impression from Canadian newspapers during the Gulf War that Canada was behind the US all the way.

"The newspapers, sure, but did you look at the letters to the editor? We're not that chummy. My father's no radical, but I think today even he would be suspicious. And there I am standing on Kits beach and this great sucker just comes sailing in!"

"You've just signed a trade agreement with the US."

"You mean they've just signed a trade agreement with us."

"Couldn't it be rescinded?"

"There'd be a price to pay, but it would be paid willingly by Canadians if they thought they were going to be swallowed up."

We talked about history. There'd always been skirmishing, he said. And there was 1812.

"What happened?"

"I'm not sure — we won!"

"*We?*"

"The British . . . Canada. I think what you fail to see is that there is a strong sense of Canada among Canadians which has been developing historically. What's growing now, as the country comes of age, is a counter-balance to the old defensiveness. We're defining ourselves not as anti-American but as pro-Canadian."

What about regionalism, Quebec?

"This stuff is just adolescent acne — it's the country coming of age. Right now in the West the Reformist party is just as big a threat to unity."

"If the West were to separate would you go with it?"

"I would. But you must understand that regionalism in this country is conditioned by our size. It has more to do with our resistance to bureaucracy. And that resistance is a re-imagining of ourselves. It makes us more interesting to ourselves, more complex. Resistance to the centre, to that abstraction, Government. It's not

9

a matter of 'shouldering my rifle' as it would be in the States. It's a sort of cat-and-mouse game."

"Is resistance to Free Trade like that?"

"Free Trade is another abstraction. It lets us re-imagine ourselves vis-à-vis America. At the moment we're asking ourselves: 'Why did we bother to negotiate?' "

A few months later the Canadian negotiator was calling the Americans bastards.

We talked about Canadian nationalism. "It's less onerous," Fraser said, "than American nationalism. It makes fewer demands on you. That's why immigrants from Hong Kong, say, prefer to come to Canada. This is the ideal half-country. You can keep half your allegiance. You can keep your passport."

What was needed to make it a full country?

"We need to see ourselves as a place that's interesting in itself. The Australians have done that. I envy Australian writers their sense of disproportion, their sense of being exotic to themselves, exotic enough to write about. I think we lack self-exaggeration, we don't trust the imagination enough. Our novels are too close to naive autobiography. We need to be able to tell more stories, to lie about ourselves. Look at Peter Carey in Australia. My mission as a writer is to understand what we mean by this marvellous place, this landscape, this ocean, this rain forest, the dry hinterland, to give voice to that topography, to a virgin territory. We're still a microcosm – unlike America, which has become a macrocosm: it has sufficient depth in terms of population, sufficient density in terms of culture."

"Is it a matter of numbers, then?"

"To some extent."

"Will immigration change that?"

"It should. We need more Ondaatjes, more Mistrys. A richer cultural mix. You've probably heard of the difference between the American melting-pot and the Canadian mosaic."

"I have." I was to hear more in the months ahead. Immigrants to the United States simply melted down and came up American, the theory went. In Canada they kept their shape and colour, fragments in a larger design.

The next day at lunch fresh greens disappeared under my dutiful

10

fork: I had a long journey ahead, and the last time I'd fallen ill. It was on this coast that Captain Cook experimented with greens for his scurvy crew. Quantities of "green stuff", records a diarist on board, were "Boiled Amoungst the pease Soup . . . and it was no Uncommon thing when Swallowing over these Messes to Curse him heartyly". I was lunching with Bill New, professor of English and editor of the journal *Canadian Literature*. Bill was thesis supervisor and friend; I wasn't going to talk shop. I posed a single literary question, got my answer, and that was that.

> Q. *What's the difference between Canadian novels and American ones?*
>
> A. *American heroes light out at the end. Canadians go home.*

Bill sent his tea back three times; I demanded more Greek salad. There was another anniversary to commemorate, a 250th, and it was a grim one. It was of Captain Vitus Bering's death, not far from his famous strait, of scurvy.

Greek, Thai, Lebanese, Mexican: Broadway bristled with restaurants. This was not the Vancouver of Malcolm Lowry, who found, sniffily, "a sort of Pango-Pango quality mingled with sausage and mash and generally a rather Puritan atmosphere". Both diet and morals had changed, probably together, I reflected that night as I dodged the chatty hookers on Davie Street and found a Jamaican restaurant.

Had Vancouver forgiven Lowry? Forgotten him, more likely. In my years there I never came on any memorial to him. (He is said to have rewritten *Under the Volcano* in a shack across the bay from a refinery whose illuminated sign – SHELL – had lost its S.) My ackee and fiery codfish was served by an East Indian West Indian as the dead Marley wailed from an ancient speaker. A man of Lowry's generation, in a hat of the Second World War, glanced in at the new Canada and wavered, then pushed off in search of the old.

The old Canada lingers at the grubby edges of downtown Vancouver, and in the mansions along King Edward Avenue. One block from Gastown (pre-Lowry and prettified for tourists) Lowry's city reappears, gone to seed. There, in a scruffy grey park, drunks and beggars shore up a grey war memorial. I watched two glazed-eyed Indians put off a bus at that corner. They'd given the fare to a sober woman friend and tried to sneak in at the back as she paid at the front. The bus driver didn't scold excessively – he'd done that route for years – but he wouldn't move till they got off. The Indians obeyed as if they hadn't expected the trick to work anyway. The bus moved on. Only the woman looked concerned, but she stayed on the bus.

It was a woman at a bus stop who told me about the fireworks. As she got out her fare she found some American coins among the Canadian. I asked how often she went down to the States. She thought for a few seconds before replying. Maybe four times a year. But there were people down Surrey way who did their shopping across the border. Things were cheaper there. Gas cost half what it cost here. In that case, I said, I was surprised more people didn't go shopping there. "Well!" she laughed, mumbling because there were now other listeners, "some people would say that was not patriotic."

I saw one Canadian flag flown off a house on a forty-minute walk through Point Grey. It was staid, moneyed ground, but the fact is Canadians are not flaggy. And yet the bus-stop woman's sentiments were shared by most people I talked to. Even those who said they would shop across the border admitted to a twinge of conscience. That was five million consciences on a good day – one fifth of the Canadian population. Ten years ago American coins used to jam Canadian phones. Public telephones carried assorted pleas and warnings. All that had been sorted out. The new phones will take American coins. The shops will too.

The fireworks were down at English Bay, another water drama, hobbled with music. There was a pop song whose chorus – *Bang, bang* – was meant to go with the bangs in the sky. It was about as jolly as synchronized swimming. I shifted my attention to the crowd. New Canadians stood packed close about me, their languages filling the night air with colours to match anything the fireworks barge might offer: an old couple wearing red jackets that said FILIPINO SENIORS CLUB; an Arab and his blonde girlfriend; an Italian with four lively Spanish-speaking girls who wore blue and green fluorescent chaplets in their hair.

"They'll pinch you on buses," said the Italian. He demonstrated on his girlfriend, who shrieked *"Madre mia!"* I detected Spanish disbelief. His voice went up. "Really! They'll rub right up against you." And he showed how.

12

In the scuffle someone trod on my shoulder bag. Next morning I remembered the eggs I'd bought. The glair had leaked and run around the carton and hardened in the other cups, a miracle cement. I had to break the eggs where they sat. The day after I gave up and boiled the whole carton. I was perforating the new detachable egg-cup (Biodegradable, Choice of Millions) when I received a summons to the desk.

"You owe us for another day." It was the rock star.

"But I paid in advance!"

He checked the computer and came up with the same information. And then it dawned on me. I'd overstayed – the International Dateline's sport – and missed my flight to Inuvik.

At the time my plane was taking off I was sitting in the offices of the Vancouver *Sun*. Trevor Lautens did a column for the paper and was willing to talk. At fifty-six, he could just remember the old Canada. He still wore its glasses. When he said the face of Canada had changed he was not just talking about multi-culturalism.

"I mean literally: the white European *face* has changed. It's become dowdy, indifferent, beaten. And it's not just an outer dowdiness. You'll find a whole generation of slack-jawed, spiritless youth grown up without jobs. And if the system gets poorer you'll get *three* generations of doing nothing. It's not just an economic underclass. You get louts driving four-by-fours with a case of beer yahooing the streets of Surrey. I don't want my children growing up in that sort of world."

It was a different world when he grew up out east in Ontario, but it had its own drawbacks.

"In the nineteen-forties the pub was typically a small brick building with venetian blinds. The sign said Baltimore Hotel and there was a door that said MEN and a door that said WOMEN & ESCORTS. Round tables, a dirty waiter, draught beers at ten cents: this was drinking in Canada. After the War the Europeans came and said: 'This is a pub?'

"So as a young man the US was the glamour spot. I identified much more with the States when I was younger. The thing to do was to get into the car and drive over to the fleshpots of New York, even if it was just for a movie. Guys and dolls, colour in the streets. Even the black parts of town were not dangerous in those days."

Now there was danger right here in Vancouver, and colour in the streets. "The Asian gangs here – Chinese, Vietnamese – are dealing in drugs. They're not like the black underclass in the US. They wear twelve-hundred-dollar suits and drive Porsches at twenty-two. And you get open daylight jewellery store robberies. The Wild West. And you have the Sikhs and their Khalistan. And the Hindu dowry system: the daughter who defied her father, the sister whose honour was stained – these things are beyond our understanding. The father put dynamite in her tea-kettle – our hair stands on end."

It did sound – as I reflected on that *our* – a long way from Shakespeare, Ontario, where his maternal grandfather was born of English stock. On the father's side there was a Viennese, Franz Lautenschalger, luteplayer, who came out to Canada in the 1890s with his Russian wife. Their son, Joe Lautens, a mechanic noted for his spotless white shirts, dropped the Germanic ending during the First World War. "We were not so hot on multiculturalism then," said Lautens drily.

I asked him about Canadian unity.

"The fact is," he said, "we've always been in danger of collapsing. Canada's history is one of pulling the apple out of the fire. In 1867 [the year of Federation] we got together because Canadians were afraid, ambivalent about America. There were families who'd made money out of the Civil War – some of those fine old farms in southern Ontario – so when one of the US presidents said Canada could be taken in six weeks, that it was just a matter of marching, we got our act together.

"Now it's Free Trade. But you'll see, in just the same way as they got the better of us, Mexico will get the better of them. Wages are sixty cents an hour down there. They're going to cost us jobs but they're going to cost Americans jobs too. The Americans will need a sense of humour – but that's one thing they lack. If you look at the past fifty years, Canadian leaders have generally been wittier. I mean, Trudeau, whatever else you may say about him, was smarter, wittier, than any American president since Roosevelt. And Diefenbaker was even better."

"What do you feel distinguishes you from an American?"

14

Lautens hesitated for the first time, grew jocular. "Our taxes are higher – but we have Medicare. In America you get sick, you sell your house. We have no ghettoes. Mind you, Dick Gregory used to say: 'Canada's very kind to its negroes – all thirteen of them.' But we have a Canadian voice, in film, on radio. We have a literature: Robertson Davies, Margaret Laurence, Alice Munro . . ."

It was too involved a question, the dots implied. I said: "Who are these people who shop across the border?"

"Any Canadian within shooting distance of it. He'll wear an old suit over and come back in a new one. I can't be judgemental. We were down in Seattle the other day and eleven dollars filled up the gas tank. Dairy products are cheaper too – and so they should be. We bought some Wisconsin cheese. It was like eating a candle!"

I had some shopping to do myself, Canadian shopping. I'd been warned that food was outrageously expensive in the far North (north of another border) so I stocked up on small tins of Canadian salmon. And I bought a half-price leather jacket in a spot sale at Eaton's downtown, built on the site of the old Vancouver opera house. An older Canada still. There would be few Vancouverites alive who went to Sarah Bernhardt's farewell performance given from a wheelchair in 1917, and none who would recall from 1912 an unknown Charlie Chaplin at the Alhambra up the road.

I heard their voices before I saw them.

". . . lost more men after the monsoon started. Wingate *promised* us, 'No more than three months,' but . . ."

Downstairs the lobby swarmed with silver-haired old soldiers in blazers and their wives in gowns. The Burma Star quota had arrived. Toby Thompson and Kevin Joyce were my new neighbours. They came to the door and edged in, a little high.

"My wife's birthday is the fifteenth of August, the War ended on the fifteenth of August, and India's independence was on the fifteenth of August." Thompson was English, army, settled in Australia. He was tall but weighed down by a belly and had a florid, slightly puffy face. Another drink, I felt, would make him mean. He began to tell me how he took his wife back to India to show her his war.

"I've probably seen more of India than you have," Joyce butted in, a small, square man with a Puckish face an↗ a Scots accent. He named all the ports he'd put in at, a navy man. "You know," he said, "this may go against what you think, but I think in the long run the British helped India."

"Rubbish!" Thompson said. "They helped themselves. Now I'm not a commie, I'm a normal man, but you look at China today and you look at India . . ."

Joyce nodded at me. "He's got something there."

"Once," Thompson said, "in Bombay we had to help the police. We were in a cordon to clear away some demonstrators and this guy stood up to me. I held back. I didn't want to smash him with my butt so I stopped and the cordon became a V and my commanding officer shouted at me. But this man he just stood there and defied me. I could see he hated me. I could have knocked him down 'cause he just stood there and did nothing, just looked at me. And to my dying day I'll remember his face."

"Now there you see," Joyce said. "If he had been French or Dutch that man would have been dead. We didn't want to be there. Once, we grabbed the QUIT INDIA banner from some Congress marchers and carried it ourselves. We wanted to go home."

"You'll be here for a couple of days?"

It was my last night, but I couldn't bring myself to say so.

My last day in Vancouver, my extra day, was wet and grey, museum weather. The lofty concrete-and-glass anthropology museum sits on the edge of Point Grey and, on a fine day, looks out across the bay at a blue wash of islands and peaks stippled with snow. Vancouverites like to boast that you can ski at Mount Whistler and swim in the bay on the same day, "The prettiest major city in North America!" the fireworks DJ had announced, expecting a cheer that didn't come. The crowd either felt that he was stating the obvious or worried that it should need stating. Divided between complacency and concern they had subsided into a melancholy trance from which they emerged to gasp at the showers of light above, each one more extravagant than the last, as if the pyrotechnicians, sensing the general mood, would not trust any other arrangement.

Out on Point Grey, enclosed by forest and a low, leaking sky,

16

the melancholy descends without warning. V.S. Pritchett once wrote an article about this coast called "The Pacific Sadness". It's a little faded, like Lowry's Pango Pango jibe, but caged in the anthropology museum with its mute wooden beasts, glum totem poles, and drawer upon drawer of pilfered souvenirs of other times and places, I began to succumb to the coast's darkling humour.

Bill Reid's massive creation sculpture, a raven and a giant clam in blond wood, was the only living piece in the museum. It told the Haida story of the trickster raven and the clam from which the first humans emerged. Hands, almost reptilian, thrust out of the slime, forcing the Original Shell. With its perfect case, its vulva-like tissue and its oceanic secretions, the common clam deserves copyright on all creation; after this Mother-of-all-versions the rest of the world's creation stories look coy. After Reid's sculpture the endless drawers of artefacts had an academic numbness to them. I peeped in one, a perfect Joseph Cornell box of Africa, and slid it back, satisfied.

I jogged through the drizzle to a hot meal: clam chowder with carrots and celery emerging from the primeval stew, a forest of mushrooms and garbanzo beans, a square of delftware bread glazed and sprinkled with oregano, and a piece of fried fish that the US Coast Guard might well covet.

The taxi driver who took me to the airport marshalled his facts like a professor of sociology. Of British extraction himself, he told me there were more German than British Canadians in British Columbia. He could tell me when the Lebanese began to arrive and how many of them there were in Vancouver. Likewise for Kurds, Koreans, Japanese, and Hong Kong Chinese. He knew Baha'i theology. He'd read the Koran. He had grown up next door to East Indians and preferred chapatis to bread.

"You know the Chinese built the Trans-Canada railway," he said, "at this end."

I said I'd heard something of the sort.

"Well, right at the end, just before the two ends met — you know about the Golden Spike, right? — well, at the last minute the Chinese went on strike. So you know who they called in?"

"No."

"They called in the Sikhs! It was the Sikhs who finished the Trans-Canada railway."

17

I wondered who would have finished the railway if I'd been Chinese – or a Kurd.

They called in the Kurds!

We flew across the Rockies as the sun was going down. Somewhere down there was the railway the Sikhs built. I imagined I saw the Golden Spike glittering in the dusk.

2

The Deep North

Flight CP 444 from Edmonton to Inuvik, north of the Arctic Circle, goes via Yellowknife on the Great Slave Lake. A straight line drawn between Edmonton and Yellowknife passes over no cities or towns. It crosses the high prairies, the Birch Mountains, and the Peace River valley. And then it goes over the Great Slave Lake.

When I was nine years old my father drew a map of North America in Indian ink. It was not a straightforward map. He had coloured in various features and stuck on certain symbols, say, a tuft of surgical cotton for the American Deep South. In the top half, the Canadian part, he stuck on – where the prairies would be – a few grains of wheat; I can feel their rough husk to this day. Higher up were two lakes, the Great Bear and the Great Slave, coloured in pencil a vaguely menacing navy blue. It was an indelible blue: the lakes became an obsession. For years I dreamed of them, large and cold and navy blue, and all through my student years in Vancouver, they lapped at the back of my mind.

I woke up over the Great Slave. We might have been passing over the sea, it was so wide, its blues so many and changing. Tears came without warning. I repeated *Great Slave! Great Slave!* like a mantra.

Yellowknife, capital of the Northwest Territories, sits on the northern shore of the lake among rocky islands spiked with trees. Across the aisle from me an intent-looking Levantine prepared to disembark. I imagined him cornering the cellular-phone market in Yellowknife, but when we took off he was back in his seat.

*

11.30: *In the air again. Ground covered in glacial lakes, here round, back there long parallel grooves. Screen of red algae drawn over many, others simply rimmed with red or green or outlined in pink chalk. As we climb the lakes petrify: jade, topaz, slate.*

High broken cloud, the mackerel pattern repeated in cloud shadows on the earth far below. Earth a lunar sea, pitted and cratered and going from umber to ash. Lakes blue again, now regularly spaced like holes in a grater, now with matching jigsaw-puzzle edges. Yellow sandpit knifes into pale-green lake. Depths darken water, relief darkens land.

Going down, bumping into clouds.

Then: a curve of the great Mackenzie River, wide as a coastline. The green nap focuses, boreal forest with long straight cuts across it. Smudges on the valley floor, deep rose.

Individual trees, spindly firs.

Sandy riverbeds skid straight down off the hills into the valley.

Half an hour at Norman Wells. The runway one long crazy-paved walk. Frost damage, not camouflage, fixed with ribbons of tarseal. Norman Wells a small oil town on the Mackenzie. Plain timber-frame houses and caravans on streets that run along the river. Graded gravel mounds on the river banks with giant orange shoeboxes on top. Burnoff flames on silver chimneys. Airstrip runs along river too. Life follows the great river.

12.40: *. . . take off . . . dead conifers . . . cloud judder. White cliffs, the valley walls. Lakes now flat ochre. Pencil leads of cloud up at our level, 30,000', lint scrolls below. Minutely veined features on the ground, red and yellow capillaries, like my eyes in the bathroom mirror just now. Long sleep coming. Where is the Great Bear?*

Three men in baseball caps across the aisle, workers, reading fat paperbacks. Hardly a word passes between them, though they were boisterous in the departure lounge. The Levantine with us still: he will corner the Inuvik snow-tyre market.

Again the Mackenzie cuts a cocoa-coloured swathe under our feet: grand, clean curves — seen through broken cloud — unlike its insinuating tributaries. Still the odd button-blue lake, die cut.

Ten minutes from YEV, Inuvik. Have left the mountains behind, skipped the Great Bear. Oval looking-glass lake holds a single white cloud.

Trees sparse. Our shadow races us down below, snagging on conifers. Touchdown 1.29 p.m.

The Arctic air was cool and fresh and, I fancied, a little thin. Eskimo faces peered through the glass at the terminal, but the general mix conjured up Eastern Europe. Ungreeted, disoriented, I expected my taxi driver to speak Hungarian. Only after did I see why: I was looking at the same blend of European and Mongol that occurred on the far edge of Europe when Genghis Khan's raiders swept across the steppes.

In Inuvik there is a monument to a more peaceful modern encounter – and mixture – of three races: Eskimo, European, and Indian. The tree-line in the western Arctic goes virtually down to the sea, so the forest people – the Indians – did actually meet the coastal people – the Eskimos – about where the monument stands. And it was the Europeans who decided to move the eroding town of Aklavik, in the heart of the Mackenzie delta, to Inuvik, "Place of Man", in 1957.

The Chuk campground was in the forest, in Indian (or Dene) territory, on a rise overlooking the east arm of the Mackenzie. There was a lookout tower from where you could see the delta and the town of Inuvik four kilometres further north. There was another campground right in Inuvik, in Eskimo (or Inuit) territory, but I wanted to be out of town. It meant a hike in and back every day: every day I crossed what for thousands of years would have been an uneasy frontier, now a skirmish line, now a trading line, between Inuit and Dene.

You forget the lakes the moment you are on the ground; blue gives way to green. I forgot the Great Bear and the thousands upon thousands of lakes and ponds that give the ground the look of a sponge. That sponge holds ten per cent of the world's fresh water, and it is drunk by mosses and algae, wildflowers and wild beasts.

I picked a site near the top of the hill. It was built up two feet above the ground, a mound of packed earth and stones that raised you well above the permafrost but made driving in tent pegs a problem. The tent was Korean, with a single collapsible fibreglass rod arched along its spine. Viewed from the side it made a half-disc, and that and the silver tent cloth gave it the look of an igloo. It was, with one exception, the only igloo in Inuvik.

I'd saved the airline food from the second hop (the Levantine did too) and that was supper. The sketch of my new home, with my plate and mug and knife before me on the rough-sawn table, looks downhill. Above the igloo is a stand of birch and beyond that a darker belt of conifers whose tops barb a bright strip of river. There are rainspots on the page.

I awoke at midnight. The sky at my feet, at the tent door, was light. Unless I was mistaken I was about to witness a midnight sunrise.

I was mistaken: it was two weeks past the midnight sun. I ran in Hawaiian sandals to the lookout tower. The sun was setting, not rising; the delta was molten glass. When I woke again the sun was well risen.

My tent was afloat in a pool of purple fireweed.

Beyond the purple was a low cover of cranberries, the little leathery leaves turning bright red, the berries pinned on like small white apples. There were rose-hips on a wild rose that grew everywhere and a satin pod on a kind of wild pea. Scattered through were blue lupins and a lacy dill-like weed with a tall green stem that exploded at the top into points of yellow light.

I waded downhill to the highway through masses of feathery pink barley-grass. The last few feet I let my knees buckle, and rolled.

"You should hitch a ride," three boys on bicycles advised me. I walked all the same. It grew warm. I got to town tired and trudged up the unpaved main street, Mackenzie Road, past the Mackenzie Hotel (the Mackenzie River two blocks away). At the Visitor Center I sank into a chair and looked up to see the Alexander Mackenzie School. The Dene prefer the name Deh Cho for their great river and I was beginning to see why.

The girl at the desk was Indian, home from college in Ontario. "There *is* a college here," she pointed, through the window. Things were better for native people, she said, since affirmative action started – last year.

I pointed to the post office. "Do any native people work there?"

"Never saw a one," she said.

I went across to buy stamps, and the faces were all white. It was the same in the bank. Native people have a different sense of time, I was told; punctuality, regularity, office virtues, were foreign traits. The natives for their part saw whites as birds of passage – as did the whites themselves. On the flight from Hawaii I was seated beside a white woman who'd been a nutritionist in Inuvik and hated it. "But it looks good on your résumé," she said.

There were native people in the street, moving slowly or standing still or sitting down. It was easy to overtake them, and I noticed how often whites did.

At The Roost Albert Kadri from Lebanon got my caribou burger. He wrote his name for me on the back of the docket.

"Christian name?" I said when he wrote *Albert*.

"No, Muslim. Do you want me to write my real name?"

"Yes."

"What do you do?" he asked as he wrote (AHMAD) in brackets. I said I was a writer.

"You want an assistant?" he shot back.

"How would I pay you?"

"If you write two books you should make . . ." He made a pile with his hands.

I wobbled a hand back. The truth would have alarmed him. His older brother came in, elegant in a black silk shirt.

"He's a writer," Albert/Ahmad told him.

"You want an assistant?"

Another Lebanese walked in familiarly and when asked what he would like said, "Anything." He helped himself to coffee.

"Why don't you sell gyros?" I asked Albert/Ahmad.

"No demand. I just break even with this." He spoke it as *breakeven*, one word he'd stocked up on.

"How do you like it here?"

"Not a good place for social life. People" (his thumb jerked to his mouth) "drink too much. The other day a man made a pass at my wife when she was down here working. I said" (he said it quietly) " '*You* go out; you go upstair.' So now she's upstair with two small children."

Drinking must be easy in the long winter. While I ate my burger by the river three native drunks paused to ask for coffee money. I saw them later outside the liquor store, and over the next few days I passed them again and again, stepping carefully, three abreast, like shell-shocked soldiers.

23

In the supermarket, where there were fresh pineapples from Hawaii, I ran into a friend from the morning. It was Buck McLeod of the Visitor Center, a benevolent giant busy in retirement.

"Just a snack," he said, heaping groceries on the check-out belt. "I'll be putting on some coffee later."

"I'll be there."

I walked to the end of Mackenzie and back up Franklin. Northern houses stand on stilts driven into the permafrost; everyone lives upstairs. Joining all the dwellings are what look like corridors for dwarves. These are the utilidors, which house the water and sewage pipes that would otherwise freeze and burst in winter. Every house used glass extensively; heating was no worry. Inuvik sits on huge quantities of oil, waiting for the next boom. There were other signs of optimism: sundecks crammed with pot plants, and functioning gardens with flowers and vegetables in the ground. Flourishing lawns too, with mowers parked defiantly under the stoops. But no sunflowers in the land of the midnight sun; because, Buck explained, they would twist their own heads off.

The only igloo I saw was the Church of Our Lady of Victory. The church is all dome, capped with a second much smaller dome. There was a blond Jesus on the altarcloth but the stucco medallion in the centre of the ceiling was Inuit in style, a stylized sun or flower or perhaps sunflower. I coughed to test the acoustics and the dome coughed back. The curving walls were painted to resemble blocks of ice, and there were twelve spars of white pine – the pine of the pews – that ran up the sides to become roof beams, said to stand for the twelve apostles.

"The only church designed after it was built," said Buck McLeod over freshly brewed coffee. His Visitor Center is the church's nearest neighbour, and he had heard all the hermetic structural interpretations.

Buck had worked for a tour company after retiring. From what? I asked him.

"——patch," he said. He spoke softly and breathed hard, a big, doughy man who made his clothes look small. He wore a peak cap, a summer festival T-shirt with polar bears on it, black slacks and white tennis shoes.

"Pardon?"

24

"Oilpatch," he repeated, no louder than before. Before that he'd been an electrical lineman for many years in BC.

"I have an East Indian friend," he said, "Brian Jesudasan. He's been living up in Resolute Bay for twenty-five years. Runs a tour company taking people to the pole. Speaks six languages. Cooks good too. The way he cooks curries, fish tastes like fish, and beef tastes like beef, and chicken tastes like chicken — and *man*! . . . "

"Tastes like man?" I ventured, and he liked that.

When I went back he was watching TV on the verandah. It was seven, newstime, and the sun was high in the sky. He got up, emptied the urn over the rail and put in fresh grounds.

"Don't expect this treatment every time," he warned. "Where did you have lunch?"

I told him.

"You should try the musk-ox burger." His eyes lit up.

I asked about Arctic char, a celebrated delicacy.

"Overrated," he said. "Except when fresh out of the water. You go over to the Husky Lakes — Eskimo Lakes, whatever you want to call them — in July just when the ice breaks and then they're *s-super*." He gave the last word a sibilance that spoke of past indulgence. But he had a heart condition and had to watch his diet. Cayenne-pepper-and-garlic was his nostrum.

"My eggs are *red* with the stuff."

After the news there was a documentary about an anti-alcohol drive that succeeded in one native community on the Great Slave Lake.

"I'm part Cree on my mother's side," Buck said. Where he came from Indians would marry Scots and French but not English. "You've got to draw the line somewhere," they said. Buck had had a hard childhood: they bartered furs for food in northern Alberta.

"When did it change?"

He looked down a private tunnel. "After the War, pretty much. Pretty much after the War. After that it was never a matter of survival."

It was ten when I got back to the campground, but the sun was a good way up. I opened a can of fish and ate what was left of my Lebanese fries cold because I couldn't be bothered lighting a fire. The cold meal left a painful lump in the throat that tap-water did not wash down.

The next day showed up a range of blue mountains on the far side of the delta. There was a squirrel on the toilet roof looking down fearlessly at me when I came up, chattering and twitching its tail. When I went in it raced continuously up and down the wooden laths to let me know that whatever deposits I might leave the territory was not mine. I made it a deep bow on leaving, to acknowledge suzerainty, and it made no further sound. I was less polite with the Arctic mosquito.

"Beedles are attacking," I heard an old man call. Father and son were camping together (once again, a North American ritual) a couple of sites downhill from me. "It's an interesting fact," his voice continued, through the screens of young birches, "that but for those mountains this place would be a whole lot colder. I guess God put them there for a reason."

Thanks to the shield of the Richardson Mountains, the Mackenzie delta, north of the Arctic Circle, can have summer temperatures on a par with Vancouver's, a thousand miles to the south. I sat and painted, a light breeze playing with the sun on the tent. There was some broken cloud to the north, but overhead the sky was clear. A white bird beat a measured track above the river. Beyond the shifting birches, their leaves turning yellow, was dark, still forest – the olive-green taiga – and at the horizon the mountains, pale blue. Fireweed burned in hollows, the breeze combed the barley-grass, and bees roved among the stalky flowers.

I was painting weeds. On my second morning I'd begun to notice the less flamboyant plants around my tent: one that looked like basil but grew to waist height with downy, spear-shaped leaves and tough stems; an Australian-looking bush with a brown, bark-like cladding on branches that turned crimson at the tips; a low podding plant with graceful leaf fans, nine leaves to a fan.

After lunch I made for town. I hadn't gone far when a car slowed down for me. I climbed in. It was driven by Harry Elias, an Inuit student. He drove like a man with time on his hands, taking in the taiga. He said more and more Inuit of his generation – 15–25 years old, he specified – were going to college. "This generation is going to change things for native people," he said. He braked suddenly in front of the hospital. An Inuit friend was sitting by the roadside. They chatted a while, then we moved on. Another friend appeared; we stopped again. He let me out at the shops. When I asked what tribe he belonged to he looked at me blankly.

"Inuit."

"Aren't there different kinds?"

He didn't seem convinced.

"Inuvialuit?" I prompted, using the name by which the western Inuit go.

"Inuit," he repeated, as to a hair-splitter.

Up the road I walked into Buck McLeod, who took me to the Chicken Chef. John Blatz, the owner, came over and joined us, expansive in his own restaurant. He said he was the second-biggest bullshit artist in town – after Buck. Blatz was a Mennonite, one of the reformed Mennonites. He grew up in Steinbeck, Manitoba, the middle one of eleven children.

"I was the different one. The others were content to do the usual things. They're not curious about the world outside Steinbeck. They wouldn't know the difference between an MP and an MLA."

Blatz grew up during the Second World War; his father grew up in the First, appalled at the waste of life. The idea of waste – lives were just one sort of waste – seemed to trouble the son too. He tried various things as a young man and quit to move on. He tried the police force and quit that, quit a management job in Whitehorse. The family watched and shook their heads.

"What do they think of you now?" I meant now that he was well off, a success. But I'd misunderstood him. There'd been no change in his fortunes: he'd always been a success. He'd come up here to get away from Manitoba, from those weekly gatherings, those (he waved a hand, a gesture of pushing back, back South) homecomings for Christmas, for Thanksgiving, for whatever.

"We sell restaurants," he said. "We find one that's not going anywhere, we bring it up to scratch, we sell it."

The Blatzes had come to Inuvik in March, five months ago, and got the Chicken Chef moving.

"You'd have to be crazy to run a restaurant at a loss. If you do it right it just takes off. And that's what we do. We find a sick restaurant and turn it around. But then the government steps in. Just when I had the accounts all worked out they introduced GST,

27

the goods and services tax. I sent them my return and said: 'This is how it works, now you work out the 12½%.' It's crazy, and it's corrupt. We're becoming a corrupt, wasteful society. People don't want to work: they go for the easy cut.

"In this business you work hard, you make money. I've taught my children that. That's my son, he's twenty-four. Then there's a daughter, and then there's that one. She's the youngest, she's nineteen."

"Have you brought them up as Mennonites?" I asked.

"Yes, but we're not strict with them. The problem here is people have to finish the bottle. I say, 'Moderation.' You know lately we're becoming like Americans, shopping by phone, buying, buying, two, three of everything. It happened to us. I said to my wife, 'Take a look around. What're we doing with two of everything?' We even had two new axes. So we put it all together and got rid of the lot. We sold everything and came here."

The talk turned to politics.

"I predict this will be an election which will see the West coming to the fore. It will be" (he spoke with quiet assurance, his pale grey eyes fixed on a point between Buck and me) "a government in which the West will hold the balance."

If Quebec went its way what would happen to the West?

"The West would have to consider its options." It was the first oblique statement he'd made.

"Would it break away?"

He considered that. "If it did I'd be with it."

Buck agreed. He'd fallen increasingly silent as Blatz moved in with his Panzers. Now he had a Lions meeting to attend. It occurred to me as he went that he looked like an old lion. (Crewcut Blatz looked like a hare.)

"You know it always struck me as strange," Blatz said. Then he looked up. His son was at the counter looking harassed. He went immediately to the rescue, and for twenty minutes they were busy.

". . . that the orthodox Mennonites," he continued, coming back and sitting down in one seamless motion, "weren't plagued by a shrinking gene pool. You'd hear they recruited young men for breeding."

"How would they manage that?"

"They don't shut themselves away. We had dealings with them. We'd go and buy produce off of them. But they prospered – and we prospered – through hard work. There are places where work doesn't have the same meaning."

"Where do you see that?"

"You see it where white blood was diluted."

Blatz's wife joined us. She'd been wiping tables within earshot. A little later his son and daughter came over too.

"You know," Blatz said, "there are still Germans here who talk of 'the Führer'. But I'm not an admirer of the old Germany. We're Canadian."

I had to go. The Arctic Tour Company might be closing, and they ran the only bus service out of Inuvik. I bought a ticket south for the next day. And I bought a ticket north for that evening, to Tuktoyaktuk.

Tuktoyaktuk is as far as the continent goes. Inuvik is on the Mackenzie; Tuktoyaktuk is on the Arctic Ocean proper. If I wanted to start at the top I had to go there. The thing was, the road, a snow road, existed only in winter, when the delta froze over; in summer you had to fly. The flight was at eight.

I had a couple of hours so I looked in at the offices of the Gwich'in Tribal Council. The Gwich'in (the "G" is not sounded) are a Dene splinter looking to negotiate a separate claim in their traditional homeland, the lower Mackenzie. Formerly known as the Loucheaux or Squint-eyed, they are culturally closer to the Inuit (formerly known as Esquimaux or Eaters-of-raw-flesh) than are other Dene. More to the point, they have seen the Inuvialuit negotiate a $17-million deal with the federal government (there are 3000 Inuvialuit) and would like to do the same.

In the hallway hung a map of the territories in question. I studied it and asked a passing woman a question. She looked at me and laughed. I entered an office. The woman at the desk would not look up but managed to look deeply affronted at the intrusion. I stepped back out. In a little while the second woman crossed to a room on the other side of the hall, smiling to herself.

"Liz, did you fax Yellowknife?"

"Yeah."

It sounded like a game. There was a radio on in there turned up loud, playing old hits. I went in. The girl who'd laughed was in there too. She grinned again and turned to a young man. He turned a brief smile on the women but fossicked about and came up with copies of the community newsletter, *Gwich'in Seasons*, a copy of Treaty Number 11, and a summary of the current claim.

Treaty Number 11 was concluded in 1921 between His Most Gracious Majesty George V and the Slave, Dogrib, Loucheaux, Hare, and other Indians. By it the Indians ceded, released, surrendered, and yielded up forever all their rights, titles, and privileges whatsoever to a territory several times the size of Britain. For this they received $12 apiece. The chiefs and headmen got a little more, and in addition every third year "a suitable suit of clothing". A present of $32 in cash for each chief – not exactly thirty pieces of silver – in "extinguishment" of all past claims.

In this way the British treated their way across Canada (the Americans had a shorter way with their Indians) till they reached the sea. A treaty map of the Canadian West resembles a giant jigsaw puzzle; not a very difficult one, and one which a spoil-sport has systematically numbered.

I went out into the street. Every pickup truck that passed raised clouds of dust so fine it hung in the air for minutes after. I sat with a cold drink outside a store. At the next table – on the next table, with their feet on the bench – were three Inuit girls eating corn chips and drinking Dr Peppers. The three drunken soldiers went by. The girls giggled, then looked coolly at them and went back to talking. I liked that mixture of sympathy and distance.

"You going back to school?" one asked.

"College," the other corrected her.

I went back to John Blatz's Chicken Chef, this time for chicken. He gave me three pieces and charged me for two. It was too hot to eat right away. I walked back up Mackenzie looking for Navy Street. The in-town airstrip, for small planes, was down by the river. Our pilot, a young man in blue overalls, had us gather around a wall map for a briefing. The plane was a small plane (all twelve seats were taken), built in an era when comfort was not a consideration in air travel. According to plan we should have circled back over Inuvik, but the briefing was war-movie glamour and the plane headed straight for

Tuktoyaktuk. We flew low, the delta features below in sharp focus.

8 p.m.: *Tundra at last — moss pincushions — bleached cabins on jade river channels — scarlet markers — ponds with bevelled mirror edges — still some trees — mirrors, mirrors — no birds, animals? — two pure white water-birds! — red and blue oil drums — Early Warning Station — algae ribbons in dark pools — two more snow geese — four more — fish jumping — six, eight geese, two on wing — stunted trees — foam edge to lake — alien honeycomb patches on grass, sun-spotted — floodline of driftwood — beached bleached logs — cabins, houses —*
— the Sea!

Tuktoyaktuk — known as Tuk — has a population of 2500, so it's not much smaller than Inuvik, which appears more regularly on maps. Three out of four residents are Inuit: *Here be Eskimos*, an old map said. The town is strung out along a finger of land that juts into the Beaufort Sea and crooks back to enclose a placid harbour. Oil is the town's mainstay, but there are still Inuit who hunt the *tuktu*, or caribou, for a living. Out on the lonely point, among decaying wooden buildings, are the old churches, Our Lady of Lourdes and Our Lady of Grace, and the tomb of a French padre who made Tuk his home. The new Tuk — concrete, steel, and glass — has moved away: gleaming fire station, post office, community arena, spanking new school. Food comes in by barge in the summer (in winter the sea freezes over up to 80 miles out) and it is stored in the town ice house, three underground halls dug out of the permafrost with pick and shovel forty feet down.

The bus let us out on a stony beach, the northernmost point. I walked to what I saw as the tip of Canada and dipped my hand in the sea. It was not cold. Where the water lapped I gathered some small, smooth stones, pink, yellow, maroon. Then I sat facing the North Pole and ate John Blatz's excellent chicken.

We drove back through the straggling town. There were no trees, and the rough dirt roads with shocks of tall grass and clumps of daisies by the roadside gave the place a casual frontier look. On one vacant lot was a miniature town that turned out to be dog kennels. The huskies, a whole team, sat waiting for the first snow. (We got out for a closer look, and immediately, thanks to Jack London, the dogs took on personalities: the meek, the thrusting, the slavish, the sly.) The first snow flies in October; I imagined the town coming into its own then, the people, like the dogs, in their element again, the streets shaping up, the blemishes covered over.

But one couldn't be sure. What was certain was: an open-air swimming pool; a baseball game in progress, the bleachers full; a bulldozer at work in a ditch, close to permafrost; fillets of orange fish sunning on racks — at half past ten; spray-can graffiti; three lovely schoolgirls who might have come from Beijing but for their fancy parkas; an old woman sitting on her front steps.

We flew back at 11. The sun was low and a mauve haze suffused the delta. The evening sky shaded upwards into a pale virgin blue. To one side was a crystal sea; to the other all the braided delta channels took the sun's gold. Bare bones of dwarf conifers ruled long shadows across land and water. We circled over two pingos or frost hills (ice volcanoes, I heard them called) and then flew across Buck McLeod's Husky Lakes, hopping with char. A cloud about a mile wide came between us and the sun and began to rain a golden light on the delta. On either side the sky was perfectly clear: just that veil of radiance suspended from a black tower of cloud.

We were coming down too fast. It was a co-pilot landing. The pilot looked hard at the co-pilot as we struck the ground with a jarring bump, then bumped a little more, veered horribly, and rolled to a stop.

It was fitting, in a way, after that brush with heaven.

There were children in the streets at 11.30. The sun shone straight up Mackenzie Road and glittered on their bike reflectors. My back ached from leaning forward at the plane window. Mexico seemed a long way off.

At the start of his journey Master Basho had a queasy moment too. He took to the road at first light, darkness lingering in the sky, the moon still visible, a few friends at hand. Then, he says, "the thought of the three thousand miles before me suddenly filled my heart," and town and friends dissolved in tears.

I thought about my own journey and felt a twinge. It would

32

not be a feat, I knew, and perhaps for that reason I grew morose.

The Dempster Highway, the first of my highways, commemorates the exploits of one W.J.D. Dempster, a police officer whose prowess as a winter patrolman was legendary. The frozen North was fertile ground for exploits: it called for feats, not just actions, for deeds more than simple doing. Extreme conditions required special exertions, and those who made them – Franklin, Mackenzie, Dempster – got their rewards: a bay, a river, a highway. The rest drew consolation out of thin air: they told stories, tall stories, fishermen's yarns. I began to see why boasting (in the meadhall by the hearth) was a vital winter sport with the Vikings. It helped you endure the waiting, it lent heat, it sparked courage:

> *I fancy my fighting-strength, my combat fettle*
> *at least as greatly as Grendel does his;*
>
> *and therefore I shall not cut short his life*
> *with a slashing sword, too simple a matter . . .*

Well, maybe. But even Beowulf needs to brag. He will fight the monster with his bare hands. How, one wonders, did the women manage?

But if the Norse warriors raised the yilp to an art form, the Eskimo at least kept a sense of proportion. "I, little man," he sings in *Anerca*, a collection of poems from early in the century:

> *Here I stand*
> *Humble, with outstretched arms*
> *For the spirit of the air*
> *Lets glorious food sink down to me.*
>
> *Here I stand*
> *Surrounded with great joy.*
> *This time it was an old dog seal*
> *Starting to blow through his breathing-hole.*
> *I, little man,*
> *Stood upright above it,*
> *And with excitement became*
> *Quite long of body,*

33

Until I drove my harpoon into the beast
And tethered it to
My harpoon line!

It was more than modesty. It was reverence, of which one part is fear, acknowledged to oneself and confessed to the world. The danger that besets the hunter, as well as those left behind, was keenly felt; in winter it was all-encompassing. It bred that spirit of watchfulness that pervades the poems. The drawings in *Anerca*, by one Enoeesweetok, are in pencil, the graphite point so sharp as to make them virtual etchings in paper. Tiny stick figures – a man, a sled, a bear – score the white page, presences, no more, in a blankness of sky and snow. The blankness might have bred desolation, but because skill and courage are also human responses, the result was that precise etching, firm but not overweening. There was, besides, affection for that world: the other part of reverence is love. That the Eskimos loved the creatures they killed is plain from their carvings of seals, of bears, of walruses, of whales, in stone and bone. Theirs was a perilous but alert passage through the world, not a blowsy striding over it. My first ride in the Deep North was with an Eskimo, and he had driven slowly, looking out at the land.

I walked up Mackenzie (or Deh Cho, Great River) Road. A taxi pulled over. The driver was Salvatore, from Italy.

"If you can take this winter," he said, "you can take anything."

He drove me right up to my tent site. One side of the tent was bathed in red from the setting sun, the other gleamed silver. I had a moment of house-pride. "My home," I said grandly.

He smiled. "I expected the North to be a strange place full of kayaks and igloos, but I haven't seen one. Until now."

I took a photo of the igloo with the last of the sun. Then I climbed the lookout tower for a parting look across the delta. I caught the sun again and watched the clouds change colour. There was a new tent in the campground below and three teenage boys playing out a private challenge. They were taking turns at running around the oval, downhill one way and uphill the other, to see who gave up first. The weakest-looking of the three was having a hard time of it. His breath came and went in rushes, he slowed to a crawl, he looked as if he might burst, but he was going to match them round

34

for round. And even after I was zipped into my tent and dropping off, I heard him plodding past in the twilight, his breath coming and going as if his life was leaking out, but he would not for the life of him stop.

3

Eagle Plains

I woke at six. The bus was coming at nine, and I had to strike camp. A simple matter in fine weather, but it had rained during the night and there was still a light drizzle out of a grey sky.

The bus was late. Or rather, it was waiting on the highway at the foot of the hill. At 9.15 it came into the campground looking for me, a minibus.

"I almost left without you," the driver snapped.

I said, "I told the girl I would be waiting in the campground. I even gave her the site number."

"I *never* pick anybody up in here."

He opened the back door. I stowed my gear bag.

"But I told the girl."

He stowed my tote bag. "I almost left without you."

And we left, with me.

Fabio was from Spain, a sailor turned bus driver. He said no more about the delay; we'd each had our say. The other passengers were a woman not yet sixty, Canadian, and a man past seventy, English, with fine white hair that he combed all one way so it hung in a fringe on the left. He looked mildly eccentric; the woman looked poised; Fabio, in a black leather jacket with epaulettes and black curls under a black cap, looked baleful.

The woman was happy to talk. The Englishman, in the next row, had less to say, and I, in the last, felt free to look out at the taiga. I spread myself out over three seats. I felt wildly happy, on my way at last.

The Dempster Highway runs from Inuvik to Dawson City by

way of Arctic Red River, where it crosses the Mackenzie, and Eagle Plains, a saddle at the halfway point. The first half is unpaved road, very rugged.

Fabio was a good driver. He'd been driving the Dempster for four years — four summers — three times a week. The bleak terrain suited him. He hung over the wheel glowering like Heathcliff, an attitude I thought his forward passenger fancied. I never saw a driver so driven. The gloom welled up out of some bottomless fury. Later I learnt he was building a boat, in his back yard, to sail back to Spain.

An hour into the journey it began to rain in earnest. Fabio's spirits lifted a little. He slapped on the wipers and flashed down the highway. The road was built up above the ground level, but there were still frost heaves with dips where the water collected in broad pools. The rain came down harder. Fabio grinned and speeded up, smashing a way through sheets of water, raising wide fans of caramel-coloured slush. Whenever a truck passed the entire minibus was drenched: there was a moment of total hurtling blindness, every window plastered in yellow mud. Then the wipers recovered and cleared a space and the rain beat down and light, grey light, returned. The back door was dripping slush from the roof onto my new canvas gear bag. I took it as baptism and left it there. Fabio's mood had infected me.

Then the rain eased. The road ran straight across the plain towards the Richardson Mountains. All around us was low, sparse taiga; some white birch, some brush, but mostly grey-green conifer. Spruce, the Englishman said. Someone had told him these little trees were 200 years old. They looked it. Not only were they ragged, they had trouble standing up straight. Drunken forest is the local name, and the crazy angles are the work not of age but of frost.

"Of course this would look very different on a sunny day," the Englishman said. He had a soft upper-class voice that age had further refined.

A white-tailed deer broke cover, then turned and ran back into the brush. Fabio said it was the first he'd seen in four years' driving. He turned the talk to the land.

"Who owns the land?" he asked the lady, and after hearing her out, said, "The land belongs to everybody, whites, reds, gringos,

Apaches, whatever. No one has the right to say 'This is my land.' The Indian can say 'This is my part,' but the land was given to everybody. That bloody government say to them 'This is your land, you were here first.' No! That's a lie. You killed someone to take over the land, like the man who was here killed someone else, and the first man killed the animals, and so on and so on and so on. Nobody have a right to say 'I was here first.' That's my personal opinion."

But later he said, "They're always talking about espirits, this espirit, that espirit. Who were these espirits? They was nothing but the white man. So that proves that the white man was here before them."

The rain returned. At one point the road widened into an emergency airstrip. A huge campervan came lumbering towards us and stopped, a suburban house on wheels. Fabio advised the driver to turn back while he could.

"I think so too," the man agreed. "This is *disgusting*. Just disgusting." His wife looked fraught.

We moved on. "Disgusting!" our lady laughed. "What does he expect? He must be an American." She turned to look at the licence plates but the whole camper was covered in mud. "Gumbo," she said. "We grew up with prairie mud."

In Margaret Atwood's novel, *Surfacing*, the noisy American boaters on a tranquil lake turn out to be Canadian after all. I wondered what secret the gumbo hid.

At Arctic Red River there was a ferry over the Mackenzie. We purred across a river that wobbled like green jelly. At the other end a native woman in a raincoat flagged us off. Ferry and highway are major employers at the settlement; for the rest the thirty or so families trap, fish, and hunt. Ratting season starts in early spring. Muskrat skins are prized, but also the flesh, especially the tail, grilled.

Before the Dempster there were only dog tracks in the far North. The Eskimos used them for migratory hunts and the Royal North West Mounted Police ran patrols along them carrying mail and dispatches. You could lose your way. In the bitter winter of 1910 four RNWMP men bound for Dawson City went astray and perished in the mountains. They were not traced until three months later (GOD BLESS ALL, one had scribbled on a cigarette packet) when Corporal Dempster came upon them a day's trek from Fort Macpherson.

After Fort Macpherson (pop. 700; I bought a lettuce and bread and cream cheese because there would be no shops at Eagle Plains) the Dempster climbs steeply and keeps climbing until the Yukon border. It's still a tricky road: delta mud gives way to friable shale, the surface going from yellow to black. The upland grass was moss green, the birches already yellow. Wherever soil had formed on the rocky slopes there were spread soft carpets of tundra flowers: pink, vermilion, crimson. On the sheer rock face geometric patterns glittered, like facets in hard coal. White torrents foamed in gullies; their sound filled the quiet pass and rose to meet us.

"Look!" Fabio pointed. On a crag overhanging the road was a nest, some twenty feet up. In it sat a young eagle. "It's about eight weeks old." The bird flapped its wings, releasing a downy white feather that floated down and caught on a rock.

Then we were over, on the other side. Immense yellow plains stretched before us, unreachable unless you slid a thousand feet down a scree of flinty rock. The road clung to the mountain, vanished behind a ridge, and reappeared a long way off, a crease in the valley floor. Down there, Fabio said, the permafrost was a foot below the surface.

We were a week early for the Porcupine Herd of caribou. When they crossed the road you waited hours, travelled millennia. For 10,000 years the Indians hunted the caribou, and the woolly mammoth and the camel and the dawnhorse. In the process they made the first technological breakthrough on the new continent: a simple fluted spearhead.

The Fluted Point People introduced a groove on either side of their spearheads so that the haft of the spear (or the shaft of the arrow) slotted in and was bound more truly than before. It meant more work for the armourer, more chipping away at the hard stone, more time spent with obsidian and less with some soft-hearted maiden, but Ben Franklin would have approved. With less play to it, more deadly earnest, the thrust went home deeper and surer and quickly brought the caribou down. A small step for mankind in the Americas, on the road to the intelligent missile.

39

Just short of Eagle Plains, the Dempster crosses the Arctic Circle. There is a marker there, a wooden arc set in concrete, and by it sits a rocking chair. The chair belongs to Harry Waldron. For seven years its occupant has sat there alone on the Circle, issuing certificates like any bureaucrat. There is a difference, though: Waldron wears a coat and tails and a black top hat. And he sits under the sky. He was waiting for us, the Keeper of the Circle, with his brass-tipped cane, and after the ceremonial greeting he stepped into his caravan to fetch our certificates. For years he drove a grader on the highway and paid for the certificates himself; now in his retirement, the government keep the Keeper.

Eagle Plains is just down the road, a hotel and a garage in the wilderness. Here Fabio had a lunch break before picking up his new passengers from the relay bus and driving back to Inuvik. At one end of the hotel, on a rise, is a campground, and after we let out the other two, Fabio offered to drop me there. He drove me around the sites, his lunch waiting. There was no one else there. I picked the site with the best view, a hundred miles to east, west, and north, and he helped me with my bags.

I pitched the tent in shirtsleeve weather, but a sudden thunder-shower came up and I went into the hotel to get warm. My travelling companions were there, waiting for the connecting bus to Dawson. Brought face to face after four hours' travel together, we introduced ourselves.

They were Norma Scobie and Jack Morris. Morris was a Londoner, of the City, and belonged to an exotic travel club. Scobie was Manitoban, of Icelandic stock. Her parents, now in their nineties, both spoke English with an accent, she said. They had just visited California. Americans, her mother reported, walk with their heads held up high and smiles on their faces. "You go out there and see," she said to Norma, and Norma did, and sure enough (she got up to demonstrate, a tall woman) Americans walked like this, and Canadians walked like this, with lowered heads and straight faces. When she did the Canadian walk it was not a caricature; the droop was so subtle it could only have been real.

I asked Norma how else the two nationalities differed.

"It's hard to say," she said, sitting down again. "But if a group of Americans walked in here" (she jabbed a finger at the invisible group) "you could tell."

Morris wasn't so sure. I said, "Would it be a look or a manner?"

"A manner. They would just . . . *take* over the place." She paused. "For instance, I would never call across the room, but they would. '*Earl! Oh, Ear-rl, we're waiting!*' " (She made waiting sound like *wading*.) "They come here and use words like *quaint*, or *pretty money* or *Monopoly money*."

"What else?"

"They tend to be more flag-conscious. We're a bit more . . ." (she wibbled a hand) ". . . not quite so . . . I tend to become more Canadian in the presence of Americans."

"How do you do that?"

"I become quieter, more reserved. I think we're halfway between the British and the Americans."

A chuckle from Jack Morris, who would not have said *half*way.

Their bus was ready. I had dinner in the restaurant. While I ate a second storm came up, with a display of lightning that had the guests looking out of the picture window. I began to worry about my tent. Why hadn't the Koreans provided a fly? There was a clap of thunder that shook the table and rattled the plateglass. And then there fell rain such as I had not witnessed in any monsoon.

One man said, "That is rain."

"This never happens!" wailed a waitress. She looked anxious, but I couldn't understand why. Mine was the only tent in Eagle Plains.

The rain came down harder. I gave up hope. I'd picked the best view, but the most exposed site. I imagined my things, everything, soaked, and a grim fatalism stole over me. I ordered dessert.

The rain slackened. I drank black coffee. In the long run (the long, long run) how did it matter? The rain stopped. I went out. There was a campervan in the campground. It was the father and son from Inuvik. They'd sat out the storm in their van and were now coming in for dinner.

"Spot of rain!" I called, the black mood still on me.

"*Spot!*" the son said. He looked shaken.

I waited till they were out of sight, then approached my tent. It was still standing. I circled it, afraid to unzip the door. Then I took courage and did it quickly.

41

There was not a drop of water in there.

I did a dance, shook my fist at the sky. I stood and gazed at the tent as a man might at the wife he finds heroic as well as beautiful. I wanted to sing the Korean national anthem.

There was a bonus: the mosquitoes were gone, blitzed away. I sat in the tent door, pale sunlight on my book, firewood at my feet, reading and looking out across the sweep of yellow plain. The mountains beyond were a succession of ever-paler blues.

The hotel is built along the saddle. Every truck peels off the highway and calls in; in the heart of the wilderness, garage and hotel are Western Civilization. Downhill a little (it's downhill in every direction) is the dump: broken pipes, old batteries, tyres. I picked my way through the scrap to a rocky bank.

Not ten feet below was another world. I dropped in. It cushioned my fall, folding me in strange primordial growths that huddled under the runty spruce in a witching, glow-worm light. A little further and I stood in a coral sea, pliant white coral that sprang back into shape underfoot. There had been a rockslide, but the rocks were now cradled in a webbing of pale lichen, tiny silver shocks of it. The grey stone was host to fungus: a speckling of verdigris, concentric bands of milky green, white runes, mustard patches riddled with cheese-holes. Ferns uncoiled from dark recesses. It was an entire microclimate just below the dry ridge.

A bird called in alarm, like the warning call of a partridge, and I stalked it downhill for a bit but saw nothing. I felt a pair of eyes on me. Something black at the edge of my vision moved when I looked down and was still when I looked back up again. I looked up sharply and caught the scowl of a raven. It had been stalking me.

Ravens are the Yukon's territorial bird. In the North one was never far from their mocking gaze. They pillaged the garbage cans, they pilfered from picnic tables, they stole like professionals, and always they flew to a perch just out of reach, to eat and gloat. Ravens are the cynics of the natural world, drawn to man, but without the vapidity of the sparrow, independent of him, but without the aloofness of the eagle. They need an object for their scorn, and man fits the bill. They have little use for one another's company; they will tolerate a rival on the same tree but not on the same branch.

42

It's human company they crave — and despise, as if humans alone can appreciate their guile. There's something stagey about their villainy. They lurk like malcontents who wish to be caught, the hunchback cousin with a grudge in some music-hall melodrama, envious and unforgiving of the featherless biped who branched off successfully aeons ago and inherited the earth. A favoured raven posture is leaning forward with the head lifted so the ruffled crop juts out and the beak strains open. If you turned quickly in passing you often found ravens in this attitude of leering. They were the gargoyles of the forest cathedral. I learnt to look for them in the most silent trees.

I needed my woollen cap that night. The wind whipped over the crest of the hill and the tent trembled, but sleep came quickly.

The next day was 15 August, India's Independence Day, and Toby Thompson's wife's birthday. I slept in to mark the occasion, my tentcloth snapping madly in the wind, like a flag.

I breakfasted; then, because lunch would be essentially the same as breakfast, I felt I should eat it somewhere else. I rearranged the ingredients and walked in the opposite direction, down the west side of the saddle, the windy side. There I found the colour that was lacking in the undersea grotto of the previous day. It was the tundra I'd missed north of the Arctic Circle. Or rather, it was that tweed of tundra and boreal forest and alpine cover that clothes much of the northern Yukon. There was still the strongly resinous spruce — I plucked some needles to sniff at on the way down — but under the well-spaced trees there grew to knee-height a tawny mesh of shrubs that stretched endlessly down the slope and across the immense flat, giving the plains their colour. The colour was changing with autumn; the berry bushes, the wild mint, the ivy, even certain needles, were turning red. On the ground itself were stranger growths, velvet brooches and buttons of dark green, mushroom cudgels, fungal lettuces, and an assortment of desktop ornaments of a bygone age: the huge moss pincushions I'd seen from the plane, succulent snowstorm globes, and spangled paperweights with red and green explosions caught in the glass. A whole boot could disappear into one of these spongy mounds and emerge wet and glistening.

Back up on the crest, I sat on a rock and sunned my boots.

There was more drying in the wind than in the sun. On the wind came a liquid call like a bellbird's: three or four distinct notes like water plip-plopping in a pool. A raucous raven call – from behind, of course – and then again the delicate bellbird.

In the afternoon I sat at my table and wrote. Father and son had gone; I had the campground to myself. The wind, which had been shipping white bales of cloud up from the west, stacked them in the east and left the sky blue overhead. It grew still. One could now work without holding down the page. The air took on a sharp resin of the trees roundabout; I didn't need the sprig that had somehow stayed with me throughout the walk. A pair of black flies wrestled on the table; I killed them for sport. There was an Olympian intoxication about these heights. Here was the high clean place I'd dreamed of in those months of preparation, in those years when the spirit felt swamped by books, when one longed to trade distance and irony for immediacy and directness. From here I could look out across the high plateau to mountains at every compass-point. The wind brought and took away clouds. I watched their violet shadows drift across the immense yellow plains. The sky changed from minute to minute. Directly overhead, where it had been blue a moment ago, there appeared white shavings that the wind swept up and snuffed out. At the horizon lay fuller fleece, white and rainless. The spirit of Eagle Plains was not on the dark east side of the saddle or on the bright west, or even on the plains themselves. It was in the sky. Up there was Eagle Plains.

I heard the liquid birdcall again and looked up at the nearest spruce. A raven sat there, watching me. I turned away but kept an eye on him, and – *plip-plop* – he let fall his bellbird call. Ravens, I learnt, are fine mimics; they steal not only man's food but other birds' songs. To rub it in he made a new gargling sound, like a magpie. He ended with his own derisive laugh and flew off well pleased.

Immediately there came a harsher chatter. A helicopter flew up out of the east trailing a load of oil drums. A pickup truck raced down to meet it at the dump; a man jumped out and unhooked the net. He stacked the empty drums and the helicopter flew off the way it came. Half an hour later it returned with another load. It was the only outdoor work at Eagle Plains.

The water at dinner was yellow in the glass, sulphur. The fish

44

and chips were a mistake. I felt distance and irony return. There was an Englishwoman across the room whose voice carried in a way that would have distressed Norma Scobie and amused Jack Morris. "How would you fill in two days at Norman Wells?" she wanted to know, and Norman Wells grew suddenly precious.

Friday, bus day, the rain returned. In the bar were truckers. Fabio, I recalled, hated them with a passion; bus drivers and truck drivers were cats and dogs. On the walls, arranged chronologically, were photos that told the story of the Mad Trapper.

Albert Johnson, trapper, was a man people let be. He trapped and hunted alone and brought his kill home to a cabin where he lived alone. He walked the whole distance between British Columbia and the Arctic; there were even stories that he came from further south, across the US border. Stories circulated about him. He was thought to have been responsible for certain disappearances, but nothing was ever proven, and people left him alone. Until one day a team of RCMP constables knocked at his door. Someone had complained that he was springing traps in the area. Johnson told the cops to go away. They did but they came back. Johnson shot one of them dead; the other escaped. For the next forty-eight days, during the winter of 1931–32, with temperatures at 40° below, a posse of policemen chased Johnson across the white country. A wire story got out: the whole world knew about it. There were four shoot-outs, and each time he got away. It took a plane to track him down finally, and twelve armed men. He was surrounded and shot dead on the frozen Eagle River. His grave is in Aklavik on unconsecrated ground – in his own back yard. Johnson sleeps as he lived, alone.

At one o'clock my bus arrived. On it was Norma Scobie, full of her holiday weekend. The North, she said, had taught her to make do. And there was another lesson.

"With native people," she said, "especially up North, you learn to sit quietly. Otherwise," (she smiled and leaned forward) "I'm so *gabby*!"

Our drivers had finished their lunch. We shook hands and went our way, north and south.

4

Yellow Fever

I was the only passenger so I sat up front with the driver, Chuck Terry. It was a newer bus than Fabio's, the seats covered in fabric, not vinyl. And the outside was smarter too, because the road south of Eagle Plains is better than the road north.

At our back the Richardson Range, the mountains God put there, lay between us and Inuvik. Ahead were the higher Ogilvie Mountains. To right and left the rivers flowed in opposite directions, into different seas.

"Anytime you want to stop, you want to take a picture, just sing out," Chuck said.

I sang out. He stopped. I sang out again, we stopped again.

"I got nowhere to go in a hurry," he said. "Let's take a walk."

We parked the bus and ambled down a slope. The ground we crossed was covered in painted tundra bush. In the valley ahead the Ogilvie River meandered through the colours. Chuck knelt down and picked something blue.

"You try that," he said. It was a blueberry, mildly sweet, with a freshness like rainwater. When I looked down the ground was covered in blueberries; we'd been walking over them. He knelt again and came up with a cranberry. We hadn't moved, but when I looked down it was cranberries I saw. Then there were bunchberries and soapberries. "The bears like that one," he said.

We drove on. "Them're seismic lines," he pointed. Cutting clean across the tundra were tracks, sharply ruled, that oil and gas prospectors had made in mapping the underground with depth charges. Then oil was discovered offshore in the Beaufort Sea and

46

interest shifted further north. The Dempster Highway, finished in 1979, was a result of that shift.

"You know what the god of the Dempster is?"

"What?"

"Shale. You got to sacrifice rubber to it. It's soft and it breaks easily with sharp edges that eat up your tyres."

He waved at a pickup truck. "That was Icecream Jerry. He owns a lot of claims. Couple of summers back it was real hot and he felt like an icecream, but he'd left his wallet behind. So he turns to the guy next to him and says 'Trade you a gold claim for an icecream.' And he did. That guy found gold on the claim. He's like that, Jerry. The other day he was cleaning out his camper and he found a scratch-and-win ticket with ten thousand dollars on it. But it had expired in 1988."

The Yukon is the land of the lucky strike, and for every strike there are ten hard-luck stories. There are big-spender stories, penny-pincher stories, sunshine stories, stories to break your heart. It was tempting every time you heard one to imagine its pedigree, how it hung around like a virus, mutating, adapting, going dormant, waking up to plague another generation. It started with gold a hundred years ago, a nugget that brought cheechakos, or tenderfeet, in droves. But the land is so forbidding for so much of the year that it is possible to see even the Indians who came here before as having been pushed, defeated on their preferred ground, their luck run out elsewhere.

Chuck was a thick-knit man of middling height with grey in his Yukon beard. He spoke of his youth as if it was a long way off but he was just middle-aged.

"I always had a li'l bit of a wandering soul," he said. "I travelled across Canada in my teens. As a young lad I travelled with thoroughbred racehorses, which took me to New England, Maryland, Mexico. I started out as a hotwalker. I'd walk the horses after the race. Then I became a groom, then an exercise boy. I kind of had a romantic thing about horses. But I had no money in them days. I married a gypsy too, my first wife, the girl I went to school with.

"Our house burned down one night," he said, and went quiet.

Later he worked the tugboats that sailed out of Vancouver. "I toured all over the Gulf Islands, Rupert, Kitimat, Graham

47

Islands, Masset." The names he spoke so casually were magical to me in my childhood. "In eight years I went from deckhand to mate to captain. I got a temporary master's certificate for forty gross ton. That's a tricky coastline, the west coast, all broken up, hidden rocks and reefs. The handbooks advise you to engage the services of a Canadian pilot. There was one run where I'd have to shoot this railway bridge. That really got me. I'd come in with a gravel barge loaded, fifty foot wide, drawing twelve foot of water, forty-five-foot tug, three hundred and twenty-five horsepower. And there'd be three inches clearance on each side!"

"What else did you tow?"

"Chip barges, gravel barges, paper, lumber, landing barges."

After that Chuck was a fabricator welder in BC, Alberta, and the Yukon, in heavy construction, mainly sawmills and mining equipment. The sawmills had their heyday in the 70s, he said. Then the automatic timber sorters came along. He helped install the new machines and spoke of them with a mixture of regret and awe. "The bin lowers itself onto running chains that take it to the drying kilns, and there's an automatic stacker putting a quarter inch of wood between each layer! Two men can do what it used to take forty."

Unemployment led to talk of politics, but politics was a thing of phrases. "We've got big business governments. Lyin' Brian [Mulroney] is a quasi-American trying to give our country away on a silver platter. He smiles when he lies."

"Would you go along with Western separation?"

"Yes I would. I reckon Quebec is a spoilt child."

"Wouldn't the West be swallowed up by America?"

"They like to flex their muscles sometimes, like they did when they went through the Northwest Passage. They're a bit of a bully in the schoolyard. But if you look at their education system you see they learn very little about other countries. It's all about how beautiful America is, like they created it. Canadians don't take credit for what Nature's done. On the other hand, they're not complacent like we are. They get the job done. They're not afraid to invest their time and money in doing something. We may complain about them a little, but we're a bit protective of them too. They're like our southern cousins, they're family. But I'd go to war before I'd be an American. I'm proud we don't go shooting our presidents. We many be a bit complacent but it's better than being trigger-happy."

I asked him about immigration.

"I'd like to see the colour tone change," he said. "We're all going to be one in a thousand years. I grew up on the wrong side of the tracks in Barkersville. It was old army housing turned over to the public. We had every race under the sun so there was no room for racial prejudice. It was us versus them – the rich.

"We had a Sikh at work. The guys used to give him a hard time, but he just smiled. I got to know him, and one day he said to me: 'You whites don't even *know* what racism is. My own people hate me because I'm trying to bring up my children as Canadians. They come into the restaurant where my wife works and loosen the lids on the pepperpots and sugarpots. They threaten me with petrol bombs.' So I told the guys how he was getting shit from both sides. They quit.

"My wife now, she's Scottish. She's a bit of a racist. She hates the English."

We stopped at Engineer Creek, where the water ran red. Terry filled a cup – it looked like tea – and took a pill for his blood pressure.

"Stress," he said. "But I'm on top of it."

The lower Dempster crosses an area left untouched by the Wisconsin ice sheet, so the tundra cover roundabout is of an older vintage than that of the rest of Canada. Here the colour climbed into the mountains but the cloud damped it down. We stopped to look down on an ice-ringed pond, the edges kept iced in summer by the permafrost.

It was the only ice I would see. My Arctic was a mild place of berries and flowers. Rain, not snow, had caused my anxieties; dust, not frost, my discomfort. But I was content. Three Michigan winters had dulled my appetite for snow. Bred to tropic heat, I liked my ice in a glass. I could only marvel in an abstract way at the deeds of W.J.D. Dempster commemorated on a plaque by the roadside. Like many early travellers, he would have used the passes we used; the highway that bears his name must often run, raised up on its gravel berm, where his dogs ran.

In time the shale top will be paved (where will the god of the

49

Dempster go?) and the journey made smooth, less disgusting, for campervans. Until then the limits of the frontier are watched over by Tombstone Mountain. The mountain lifts a bony finger and the road ducks down into the Klondike River valley. From here on the rivers drain into the Bering Sea. It was this valley and the next, the Yukon, that gave the territory its mythic and its common name, and for decades both signified one thing: gold.

Gold was not always a disease of the mind. The Indians valued it, along with other rare and glancing things, and further south they worked it and used it for adornment and trade. The pathology of gold in the Americas dates from the Spanish. With the conquistadores it became a ruling passion, one that sank into fevered misrule. Accounts of the Gold King, of the Seven Cities of Cibola, cities of gold, faded with the Spanish. They were almost forgotten when, at the end of a more practical century, a prospector in the Klondike valley found a nugget that set it all going again. What it represented was quite simple: something for nothing. The labours of conquistador and cheechako were heroic, but their goal was always out of proportion.

Today's cheechakos are content with regular jobs, in government offices, with bus companies; they take on and discharge responsibilities. For their ancestors the frontier often meant an escape from responsibility. For others it was the romance of a simple life; their dream cabins rot on hillsides, and new ones are coming up. For still others there was the belief that here was a life closer to the source of life, a source, as many discovered, that can also kill.

The frontier ends where the Dempster joins Yukon Route 5. From there to Dawson City you drive on tarmac. At the junction we came on Jo Lily, studying the route map posted there. She was bound for Inuvik. Her bicycle leaned up against the zero milestone. I chatted with her; Chuck stayed at the wheel. When I got back on he looked slyly at me.

"She's ridden her bicycle across Canada," I said, "alone."

He raised his eyebrows and leaned out for a parting glimpse. I couldn't tell which part of the picture impressed him most. (I was not sure which part impressed me.) Jo Lily was English, with a china doll's compact features, tanned from four months on the road.

"A man's allowed to look," Chuck said, but he turned away, remembering perhaps his wife's Scottish racism.

All the way down the valley we skirted a series of pointless embankments that snaked along the road or up a creek or simply filled a clearing with an ugly heap of rocks.

"Gravel tailings," Chuck said, and I was none the wiser. Just short of Dawson was a settlement, Guggieville, set in a maze of gravel tailings. "We'll set you up here," Chuck said. The Trail of '98 campground was unfinished, but their sign said HOME COOKING. I left my bags there and Chuck drove me into town.

Guggieville, bought and named for a Guggenheim, is a clapboard encampment at the head of the original Dawson trail. Up the track are fabled creeks, once home to nuggets as big as racehorses. Tucked away in there is the world's longest (or largest, or oldest) wooden-hull dredge. Other memorials of Dawson's past stand at people's gates: old dredger buckets planted with geraniums, as dairywomen might use old milkcans, or vintners leaky barrels. Latterly the gold has come out of tourist pockets – a return to placer mining of a sort – and that trail leads into town.

After Guggieville the highway crosses the Klondike River by a new iron bridge, winds past a helicopter pad, past newer claims and more tailings. Mining was in progress by the roadside: a rotating cylinder, tilted and punched with holes, like a giant kitchen grater, was sieving out the finer gravels at the top and letting the bigger rocks roll down and out at the bottom end – the tailings.

You enter Dawson City side-on, at the prim government end. The road takes a bend – the bend is the river's but you don't see that – and then you're on Front Street. With just two thousand residents, it's a city only in name, but a hundred years ago there were 30,000 men here, living under canvas. Even today there are two hundred more males than females in Dawson, but in gold-rush days that proportion would have been a miner's wet dream, and a nightmare for ladies like Diamond-Tooth Gertie.

"Take you up to the Midnight Dome tomorrow," Chuck offered. "But don't say nothin. Boss might get the wrong idea."

The reception centre had women in period costume at the counters – long black skirts, white blouses, tiny boots – and sheaves of fliers for distribution. On a rack were glossy brochures, and in a nook by the door, complimentary coffee. The walls were hung with old bromide photographs of morose panners kneeling by a creek, and butchers glancing up from butchering hogs, a world of work staring out mistrustfully at a world of play. Not that the old Dawson was all work: there were gaming tables for all comers. But few miners would have had cause to celebrate or much to celebrate with. The saloons would have been busier, and the eateries and stores opened by the more prudent cheechako. A replica store had shelves dressed with old labels: Bear brand apricots, Reindeer condensed milk, Little Chief canned corn.

It began to rain. I sat down with my Dawson map. A man of thirty sat there, studying his Dawson map. The skin on his face was stretched tight, drawing the lips apart and narrowing the eyes like a man about to sneeze. He spoke first yet he disdained speech.

Mike had just canoed down the Yukon from Whitehorse, a six-day journey. He'd done it alone, camping in the wilds by the river. He was from Yellowknife, a surveyor and geologist. He spoke of Jack London and there was something of London in him: not the man but his men. He'd needed help with his canoe just now, he said, carrying it up from the river, and had approached a group of Indians. He offered to pay, but they just laughed. Finally one of them agreed, but with a lot of "White Man this" and "White Man that". He didn't mind. It was like that in Yellowknife.

He talked of Indians and mining and Western writers, then abruptly he got up and stretched a brief smile and was gone. He looked – and left – like Clint Eastwood.

I walked back up Front Street. The reason you don't see the river when you come into town is that there is now a dyke. The dyke protects the town from floods such as that of 1979, but it has severed Dawson from its historic lifeline. Stranded on the town-side of the dyke is a painful reminder, the paddle-wheel steamer *Keno*, another relic for pilgrims to pore over in a town where the past has become the official religion. I clambered up the grassed walls of the dyke and got my first view of the Yukon River. It had a gravity and presence that struck fear, and it moved with the dignity of a neglected god.

After that, whenever I walked into or out of town I used the dyke. Its top is in fact a promenade along the Yukon, but the Klondike end is not much used. Poppies nod on the bank and the scent of balsam poplar is everywhere.

I walked back to Guggieville in the twilight. Night fell earlier down here. It was too late for the home cooking so I had a Swedish ribbon sandwich, long and colourful and cold, and went to pitch my tent. The field was an abomination, clods of earth and stones and weeds. On four sides were gravel tailings and an untenanted caravan was parked at one end. I pitched in its lee for protection, or perhaps company. The ground was so wet I imagined the tent sinking without a trace while I slept.

Next day was Discovery Day, 17 August. It was why all the campgrounds, except my Judas field, were full. There were beads of rain on the silver tentcloth. In town I bought a black and red notebook from the People's Republic of China. Its plain cover stuck out among the glossy diaries like a gold-rush pigtail. I was waiting for my burger when a girl with an icecream cone sat down opposite me.

"What are you doing here?" I said. It was Jo Lily. I'd imagined her halfway up the Dempster.

"I broke a spoke." She'd ridden forty kilometres back that morning. As it turned out, she'd have missed Discovery Day.

On 17 August 1896 George Carmack was up a creek beyond the Judas field when he and Skookum Jim and Tagish Charlie struck gold. The creek became Bonanza Creek and the hill above it King Solomon's Dome. I tried to imagine what Dawson was like the day before, on 16 August 1896, and then again on 18 August, but in fact there would not have been much of a difference. It took two years for the crowds to arrive, and the mobsters and priests and madames whose houses and stories are being renovated today.

At noon there was a parade: the Mounties in red coats, on foot; the old men of the Pioneer Order; an antique fire engine and firemen; a new 59,999-kg hauling truck; and a float with can-can girls. Afterwards I had to go with Chuck; Jo Lily and I agreed to meet at the brass-band concert.

The short cut to the Midnight Dome is straight up the hill behind town. Chuck was driving his own car, with gas at Yukon prices. The road goes up King Street and into the trees, past the town cemetery. The dead lie there in a green gloom, Catholics to one side, Chinese apart, Jews in a plot with blue-and-white palings. At the top we looked down on the Trail of '98, my tent a silver point in an empty field. Dawson City was the other way, spread out on the flat where the Klondike sent a blue spear into the side of the yellow Yukon. There were wooded islands in the bigger river. A hundred miles downstream the Yukon enters Alaska. When Chuck said they were thinking of crossing the border to get a new car, that was the border he meant,

"We'd be crazy to get one here. A new car would be fifty per cent cheaper there, so even after duty we'd come out ahead."

I'd heard it said that Yukoners have more in common with Alaskans than they do with other Canadians. Their river too, to make a point, flows north and west, away from Canada.

The brass band were from Alaska. They were the US Air Force Pacific sector brass quintet and they played Bach against a painted pioneer set, Bach's mathematical manner squaring happily with the plain brass and still plainer carpentry.

Afterwards there was a salmon Bar-B-Q, but Jo Lily was a vegetarian. I bought some smoked salmon for myself from a metis pickup and we sat on a bench by the river. I wondered what her countryman Toby Thompson would make of an Indian carnivore consorting with an English vegetarian.

"We used to give the beggars tins of our bully beef," he had said remembering India, "but do you think they'd touch it?"

"That's religion," Kevin Joyce had put in in his conciliatory way, "that's religion."

Thompson would have none of it. "Now *me*," he said, staring at me and pointing, "if I were hungry, I'd eat *you!*"

I could well believe him. I felt safer with Jo Lily. Lily had been on the road since April. She started on the east coast and made her way to Ontario, where she had a friend whose father was in the police. There they'd worked out a toll-free method by which she could call once a week and report safe. People were helpful, as a rule. There was a trucker who showered her with gravel three times and bought her a meal the fourth. She allowed herself one book at a time, and carried no mosquito repellant. Mostly, she said, you longed for a bath.

*

54

We crossed the river by the free ferry and the town looked happier shipping water. The highway on the other side is a gravel road like the Dempster which crosses the Alaskan border at Little Gold Camp and turns south at Chicken.

On the ferry back was Edmund from Germany. He had round blue eyes framed by round blue-rimmed glasses and a pale head of hair cut square and crimped at the top like instant noodles; New Wave had come to the frontier. We had tea at Klondike Kate's.

"Are you going to the Pancake Breakfast?" he asked.

"When is it?"

"Ten till noon at the Curling Club," he said as we reached for our programmes.

I said I wouldn't mind going to the Robert Service reading.

"*Two* readings, ten a.m. and three p.m."

With his bright unblinking eyes and glasses he was the cartoonist's wunderkind. It gave him such transparent pleasure we began to test him with questions: the Jack London Reading, the Tug-of-War, the Log-Sawing, the Raft Race. It was tempting to invent competitions, to widen the field, to include all knowledge.

The next day I saw London's cabin, or half-cabin (the other half was in San Francisco), brought into town and set up in Jack London Square. It was a Sunday and raining. The streets became mud puddles and people kept to the wooden sidewalks.

"*Got to keep our famous boardwalks clean!*" some drunks taunted a passing cop car. Everyone had muddied cuffs all the same.

"*Alice!*" a woman with a camera called across the street. "*Go stay-and in the do-or of the Sourdough Saloon!*" Her voice must have carried as far as Inuvik and Norma Scobie.

At dinner Germany, Britain, and India carved up a Mexican pizza and the Gipsy Kings sang flamenco. I should have known the old Yukon was dead. I'd seen its ghost that morning when a white-bearded wraith in a floppy prospector's hat waved to me on the road from his old pickup. There are still prospectors in the hills, but there are also videos to while away the winter.

"There are itinerant prospectors too," Al Fisk told me. Fisk was the man in charge of Parks Canada's renovations. The migrants arrive typically in April and work until September and then move on to Australia, to New Guinea, to Indochina. Like resident miners,

55

they've staked their claims: 500 feet along a creek longitudinally, 1000 feet on either side, measured from the centre of the stream. And they do find gold, still. The family operations – Mum, Dad, the eldest – get by too. Mining is the least controlled of Canadian sectors.

"When gold appreciated in the early 1980s," Fisk said, "Dawson was inundated with entrepreneurs of every sort. Miners are an independent lot. It's not uncommon for a miner to build a vibratory plant here instead of having it brought in. It's not uncommon for a miner to build a trommel, to change the pitch of a box, to experiment with riffle depth and water velocity, to load the rocks differently, to build a de-rocker."

But gold mining had to come to an end. It was tourism that would keep Dawson going.

"Is there a danger of Dawson becoming a theme park?"

"Not as long as people continue to live here. There's a legacy of people staying on. There are still miners living on the creeks. There's a school population of two hundred, though they do have to leave town to get jobs."

I said I'd passed the Dawson Golden Age Social Club and Drop In Centre and found it boarded up.

"Well, that's another story," he said, but didn't tell it. We talked on a wet morning in the kitchen of his restored house at the quality end of town. The house had been built for the Guggenheims and once lived in by the Commissioner of the Yukon. Fisk sat at the kitchen table, a mild-mannered man without airs. He had sleepy eyes – it was Monday – and leaned his head on his hand.

"Will you stay on here?"

"I'll retire here, but I can't stay. I couldn't afford to. The utilities on this house alone come to a thousand dollars. Electricity is thirty-eight cents a kilowatt here; down south it's four cents. I might become a summer visitor."

"What's it like in winter?"

"Winter's a different experience. The community slows down. Any day now it'll start to get cold. I'd say there'll be a frost tonight. By October we'll start to have temperatures of minus twenty, by November minus forty. In January, February, March, it gets down to minus fifty and sixty. It's a season of anonymity. Outside you'll see a shape in a parka: it could be anybody. Then in spring people come out, renew old acquaintances."

Fisk didn't see any crisis looming in Canada. He was born a Maritimer. "On a relative basis the *East* is hard done by, not Quebec or the West. When I grew up on the farm we had to kill our pigs and put our crops in the gully to rot, the prices were so low. But there's always cross-pollination. Lots of families have Eastern ties. Used to be the harvest in the West was done by Easterners."

The phone rang. His week was beginning. It had been a slow year for tourism, he said at the door. "We try and capture some of the rubber-tyre traffic," he said, "but mostly we're a stopover, not a destination."

I walked back along the dyke for the last time. At lunch the 98's home cooking was lasagna, but there was Yukon sourdough bread. I did a load of washing at the trailer park next door, where a coachload of tourists was in the shop buying gold dust. My purchase was more urgent – half a cup of yellow detergent powder – but I had to wait my turn. I was running late for my bus and took my clothes out of the dryer damp. As I sprinted to the Judas field I heard my name called. It was Chuck and his wife, Gwen.

"Vairy pleased to meet you," she said. I was pleased too – I'd wanted to tell her about the English bicyclist – but now I was very late. I asked how long it had taken Chuck to understand her broad Scotch. "Foraiver," she said, tossing her head. She wore a black headscarf over bouffant hair and black sunglasses that she did not remove. Just above the wrist of the hand she extended me was an exquisite red and green tattoo.

In the Judas field my tent pegs, which had slipped in so easily, were now set in concrete. I gambled and called a cab; the pegs came out first. The cabbie was Dene Indian. He got me to the depot just as the bus driver was locking the luggage bays. Then the bus rolled out of town and back over the Klondike River and right past the Judas field and Guggieville, where the tour group were boarding their coach clutching little phials of gold.

5

The Chilkoot

The Whitehorse bus was a proper bus, with an aisle, and other passengers. It tore up the Klondike valley, past mile after mile of exhausted tailings and hopeful markers: Bear Creek, Rock Creek, Sulphur Creek. Then we began to climb high above the Tintina Trench, hemmed in by poplar and birch, taller and stouter-trunked now, and always, on either side, a strip of purple fireweed.

At Stewart Crossing we stopped for the hamburger of the journey. It was served plain in the lodge by a woman of preternatural calm. She was sixty and loose-fleshed, with a level grey gaze. She took orders for a busload of customers, gave change, rubbed a credit card, wrote out kitchen slips, carried them to the Indian woman at the grill, and picked her way back to the till through the crowd. She had the diligence of an ant, without the ant's frenzy. It was too much for one person, yet in the middle of taking orders she found time to seat a blind man. She told him the day's menu, said the soup was chowder, that there were no tuna sandwiches but would he like egg? The passengers looked on. Yes, egg. Small unhurried steps to the refrigerator, small unhurried steps back. He might have been the only customer in the room.

My order was a long time coming. The bus driver was finishing his soup when she appeared with my plate. She set it before me, arranged my knife and fork. "Don't worry," she said, "the driver always lets the passengers finish." I ate, calmed. The driver left the room, the passengers followed. I ate on. Now she glided up and drooped her fingers over my plate. "I'll put it on a tray for you." She padded away to the kitchen, reached for hidden tools. Then she came back with a tray sealed in foil. I felt drawn to the source of her serenity. The bus was waiting. "Here, take these along!" She reached into a bin and came up with two ketchup sachets. "One should do," I smiled, returning the other. The words sounded lame. I meant to carry the transaction beyond commerce. I said goodbye and felt a pang. "Goodbye," she said evenly.

From the bus I looked back at the lodge. It was the only building in Stewart Crossing; it *was* Stewart Crossing. A sign on the front said FOR SALE.

In front of me was a Canadian and across the aisle from him a Teutonic American whose pale gold hair gave him the look of Nietzsche's Overman. They got talking. The Canadian looked like Christopher Reeve and sounded like Clark Kent. "Right," he said, "right. Sure, sure."

Up front two little English girls were playing a sign-spotting game. Their voices rode up high above the men's.

"Deer Crossing is ten points!"

"Right."

"No, it's not!"

"Sure, sure."

The road hung over the notorious Five Finger Rapids, where many a gold-rush craft came to grief. To get to Dawson, prospectors who came by sea had to land at Skagway in the Gulf of Alaska and carry a year's rations over the steep Chilkoot Trail; from there they rafted by a combination of lake and river to reach this perilous point, and then they were halfway there.

Carmacks was our own halfway point. At the store I bought a green New Zealand apple; Chinese gooseberries had reached there too. Then we were rolling through sugarloaf hills, and a new kind of tussock on the flats, yellow and shaggy at the edge of dark ponds. Marsh appeared, and wide stretches of calm water reflecting the evening sky. It was hard to tell the colours outside from the varied windows on the bus; the glass replacements, tinted pink, yellow, green, a reminder of bad roads. At ten o'clock the sun set in a blaze of red. The Japanese boy in the row behind me made a frame with his fingers and squinted through it.

"Getting dark early," the blind man said to the driver.

"Ya, pretty early now. It's a quarter after ten."

It was after dark and raining in Whitehorse. I looked under

59

Hotels in the Yellow Pages, and my last quarter got me into the Chilkoot Inn.

The son did the talking at first; the old man stood aside, blinking. When I said I had a load of damp washing it was the old man who led me downstairs to the laundry. He opened the big dryer door, the motel dryer, not the small pay one. I said I was from Dehra Dun.

"Dehra Dun!" He took my hand and bowed his head. "My brother went to the military academy there. We are an army family. My father was an officer, and his father, and before that, going right back. We weren't in business until we came to Canada."

In baggy pants and canvas shoes, he didn't look like army material. His bald head and courteous manner gave him the look of a timid genie. He spoke in a whisper and when he smiled his eyes lit up with a sweet sorrow. He folded a hotel towel as if it were an heirloom. I realized that the boy upstairs with the narrow tie and McGill education was his grandson. There was a generation in between, of my own age.

The Manns had come to Canada from Punjab in 1972 and lived in Vancouver. Four years later they bought the Chilkoot. They had remained in the Yukon ever since, pioneers twice over: not one per cent of Canadians choose to live in the Yukon. The grandson ("he was called Tommy before we came to Canada") spoke no Hindi. "He speaks Canadian," the old man said.

I was disoriented all next morning. Walking down Main Street, Whitehorse, with its traffic lights and big stores, I realized I'd come out of the wilderness. Then there was my encounter with the Manns. I looked at a pale face and wondered: What country is this? The first shop I entered was a chimera, half bookstore, half post office. The river was the wrong colour and it was flowing the wrong way. I'd got used to a yellow Yukon, and this was green. In Dawson it flows from left to right, as reliable as prose; here it ran the other way.

The information centre gave me a city map. In the basement I switched off the tourist video. "Thank you," said the girl who worked there, "but don't tell anyone I said so." Her boyfriend came in. I asked them about local history.

"You should talk to Irwin Armstrong," they said. Armstrong

was a local figure who used to run a mining camp. He lived alone, they thought, in a shack on Copper Road, but was once an advocate of communal living. He was anti-drinking but pro-poker ("cards, not bars") but most of all he wanted to move Whitehorse up to the highway because some day the dam was going to burst. It was the sort of sinister thing I expected of the river myself. When I asked how I could meet him they said Don Branigan would know.

"The one thing in life that really disheartens me," said the boyfriend, "is that Don Branigan is going to be re-elected mayor."

I went straight to City Hall and made an appointment. Then I looked around town, at the postmodern buildings coming up, at the scarlet-coated, pillbox-hatted students paid to tell stories to visitors. On every street flowed a stream of pickup trucks, as vital to a frontiersman's esteem as a horse once was. All at once their wipers came on. I took shelter in a SupaValu where there were bunches of fresh dill. I'd thought it peculiar to India and nipped a piece to sniff.

Back in the Chilkoot there was a knock on the door. It was the father, the missing generation of the Manns, with a TV set. Their sign did say CA8LE TV. I said no to it and he backed out, a big bearded man.

City Hall was furnished in turn-of-the-century pinks and greys – the turn of this century. Like much else in Whitehorse it looked brand new, state-of-the-art, a reminder of the city's capital status. But Whitehorse was not always the capital of the Yukon. Dawson was, at the turn of the last century. The Yukon was in fact declared a territory in recognition of the discovery of gold there. But Yukon gold ran out anyway, and Dawson's importance began to wane. Oil would eventually outweigh gold, but there was a third element with a still greater specific gravity: government.

Whitehorse is a government town. Dawson is too, and so is Inuvik, but those are outposts, and Whitehorse is, or means to be, a centre. That would explain the extraordinary building I saw coming up on Main Street, a government building, a whole city block clad in pink granite with green-tinted windows through which civil servants yet unborn will stare out over their domain. The whole town exudes this air of preparing itself for bigger things, of a territorial capital bent on becoming a provincial capital. In terms of its municipal area it is the second largest city in Canada, but progress has yet to fill in the blanks, for while most expanding towns generate their own wealth, Whitehorse depends on a handout, one that comes from a long way off, from Ottawa, with strings attached. The Yukon territorial building, a handsome wooden building with an abstract totem pole in front, houses those who decide how to spend the money. Down the street from it is City Hall, and spreading on both sides of the river are the acres that await development. In the Qwanlin Mall SupaValu, amongst the exquisite hot-house peppers and flawless grapes, the cantaloupe and camembert, one might imagine full provincehood had already come. The frontier looks a long way back.

Presiding over this city was Mayor Don Branigan. His office was done out in expensive wood at the very back of City Hall. I waited in an antechamber that owed its pictures to China, its furniture to Sweden, and its plants to the Congo; the panelling may have been Canadian. The other person waiting was, by some coincidence, the bearded owner of the Chilkoot. He gave me a small preoccupied smile. He was in there some time and I heard his voice raised in near-hysterical complaint. The secretary offered coffee, but then Mr Mann came out. He had recovered his composure and we nodded again.

Mayor Branigan had pallid Irish skin tinged with coral at the ears and a handsome head of curling, kelp-like hair. He looked steadily at me while I explained my errand, nodding and taking it in. He was in private practice a holistic physician. "When I came to Whitehorse in the 1970s," he said, "this *was* the frontier. In those days you were *posted* here; then people just started to come. Today only a third of the population of twenty thousand were actually born in Whitehorse."

I asked if it was true that Yukoners had more in common with Alaskans than with other Canadians.

He said, "Northerners experience the same weather. They tend to share the same qualities: they're pioneering types, they're more entrepreneurial, less conservative. We in Whitehorse twin with Juneau, their capital. We have a joint marketing board with the panhandle. We interlock in a hockey league. There's a dogsled race. As neighbours we come and go: they drop a few bucks here. We have only thirty thousand people in the Yukon, but we get half a million tourists, and most of them are American."

But he drew a distinction between commerce and politics. "I don't think you'll see Canadians willing to change their form of government for the American. Canadians are very unpatriotic – until you move them out of Canada."

In the Yukon, Branigan said, the population was one-third native. He named the tribes, described their traditional occupations. Alcohol, he said, was a measure of the distance between trapping and regular modern jobs. "The older ones are past it; the young will have to change things."

The secretary called. There were people waiting. Branigan laid his hands face-down on the glass top. I asked quickly about Irwin Armstrong.

"He lives with me, on my ranch," he said, and suddenly I had to adjust my picture of the alternative physician to accommodate Branigan on horseback under a wide-brim hat drumming up dust on the Circle-B. "You have to remember he's eighty-four and . . . mildly schizophrenic. Outside of that he's a brilliant man."

But I never did get to meet Armstrong. Branigan said he had a man going out to the ranch, but when he checked the man had already left.

I returned to the information centre. The woman at the desk stared. "You're staying at the *Chil*koot!" The whole frozen North was in that *Chil*. "We've had so many complaints about them we took them off of our list." I felt I'd stumbled on a local intrigue and caught a glimpse of what it was the Manns faced.

"What's it *like*?" she wanted to know, and I felt obliged to take the Chilkoot side.

"Well, the building's seen better days. But the linen is clean, the towels are fresh."

"We've had *so* many complaints about the noise."

"They have some tenants who get drunk."

"*Get* drunk!" Stay drunk, she would have said.

That evening I heard the middle Mann scolding the people next door. "All of you, *out*! I didn't rent the room to all of you."

A slurred voice said, "All right, all right," and there was quiet. Then a quarrel flared up. Someone fell against the wall. A shout. A woman began to wail. A scream: "*Don't!*" A smack.

The woman began to howl like a dog. "*You fuckin' leave me alone or I'll leave you!*" It went on like that till I fell asleep.

The next day I moved to the Fourth Avenue hostel. A shared room, but the walls were concrete. They were also freshly painted and the room was bright and airy. The window looked towards the Yukon River and another marooned ark, the paddlewheel steamer SS *Klondike*.

The morning paper had a story on a local author. Jane Gaffin was an American settled in Whitehorse. When I rang she was going out for lunch and suggested I join her.

"This has become a government town," she complained, as we sat in a Chinese café. "And I've watched it happen over twenty-five years. Whitehorse has lost the old feeling, and it's the work of people who've come North with their regulations. 'You got no laws? We'll fix that!' And they did, real heavy-duty stuff. Environment Act, Heritage Act, We Can Come Into Your House And Put Out Your Cigarette Act. And these are people who use the place as a stepping-stone. Three years and they're gone."

"Do people still see you as an American?"

"The other day somebody asked me, 'Where are you from?' He would have to be a government person. Old-timers – *long*-timers – would remember my column *Kane Tuck*."

Gaffin comes from Kentucky. "They used to call me Kane Tuck when my accent was broader. I grew up in Cynthiana, Harrison County. My parents are still there. They still call me Home, but this is home now. Do you mind if I smoke?"

"I'm an incorrigible passive smoker."

"When we were kids in Kentucky we were active smokers. We smoked the pods from the Indian cigar tree. We smoked ropes – that's cigars. Tobacco was everywhere. We smoked it rolled up in brown paper." She had tobacco-coloured hair.

I asked her about *Missing in Life*, her account of the disappearance of a local pilot, Edward Hodgkiss.

"I used to date him," she said. "He was a good pilot, but he was flying a British plane, you know, a big concrete Harvard, built to crash – and it crashed very well. He did a forced landing on an island where you need a machete to get through the undergrowth. There's this salal, a beautiful bush, just beautiful floral display, leathery leaf, black berry, but you get stuck in that . . . the loggers will tell you about it. Hodgkiss and his girlfriend Kathy went down in 1969 and just disappeared. The plane turned turtle, they got out, left the log, a note, a sleeping-bag, and that was it.

"It was bad terrain. Even the trained parachutists wearing cork-soled boots could only go so far. It was a long search and they used everything: two Albatrosses from the Comox base, a Labrador helicopter – they're huge, double-bladed, and they take twenty-five people – RCMP boats, three tracking dogs. But it became too expensive. It was only three months later that they found the plane. The case is still open."

I asked her about *Cashing In*, her history of mining in the Yukon.

"I like big equipment," she said, "noise, dust, crawlers, earth-movers. But now they're shutting down the mines. I predicted placer would finish in two years. There's still some future in hard rock, but now it's tourism. We're hurting. Nobody's got any money. But you look at Alaska. Mining's coming back there, but the companies are dealing directly with the Indian bands and it's working. The Indians get a percentage, it's an option agreement. We can't shut our resources down, but that's what's happening – timber, trucks, trains. Oh, my Mum" (she said *Mum*, not *Mom*) "thinks I'm on the other side, I club harp seals for kicks. But it's all closing down. I don't know if I would vote again. Our politicians just sit there and giggle. I've seen it: they pass each other notes and *giggle*."

"I wondered what went on in that building. Do you think you'll stay?"

"Yukoners retire outside."

"Do Canadians need protecting from Americans?"

"Ugh! Canadian Content. There was a ten per cent tax on US books, but the booksellers hollered and it only lasted six months. You can't legislate that sort of thing. They tried to ban blue jeans in Russia. That's where the barbed wire starts to go up. Canadian Movies, Canadian TV, Books . . . The US will come and rip the barbed wire down."

That evening I went for a walk upriver to see the fish-ladder on the dam Irwin Armstrong fears. Drawn by the scent of balsam poplar I left the road to follow a track that led into the trees.

There were birches too, their small leaves clapping in a breeze that skimmed the treetops. The path was damp, the black earth showed up startling yellow leaves. Whenever it grew springy underfoot I looked up to find pine and spruce. The day's cloud broke up into cream and gold fragments and the last of the sunlight streamed across the river. It became brighter than it had been out in the open. The cottonweed glowed, and lower down, tufts of white mustard. The water ran a clear green above smooth stones and moss cushions worked in needlepoint. Somewhere in there were salmon. "They're running now," everyone in town said, and the newspaper called it "one of the heaviest runs this century". At the rapids that give Whitehorse its name, there were canoeists arm-wrestling with the river, going through fixed manoeuvres over and over again.

The fish-ladder was empty. Not one salmon stared out through the glass the fisheries people had installed there. On the opposite wall hung consoling photographs and text. The Chum salmon's life story is so tumultuous and glittering I wondered that no Canadian novelist had turned it to account. Seagulls and rabbits make good money-spinners, but there is the ultimate beast fable, matter for a saga or at the very least a picaresque tale entitled *Chum*.

The Chum starts life (*Chum started life . . .*) in the shallows of a placid stream, but leaves home to travel many thousands of miles, from fresh water to salt, through currents warm and cold, over riverbed and seabed, past fixed corals and flashing sharks, over the deepest trenches and undersea mountains – and then all the way back again, to die. It homes with a sensor the tern might envy, for it returns unerringly – choosing from hundreds of possible streams – to its native river, often to the very shoal where it started life. It's a heroic life, fittingly concluded. The beaver builds, the spider spins, but the salmon's life is its art.

The Kutchin Indians of the upper Yukon built elaborate weirs across the river with catwalks and cantilevers and basket traps to catch their prized salmon. Above the present ladder is the dam. I climbed past the spillway to the top of the bank just as a seaplane was coming in, and there – still undisturbed – was the calm face of catastrophe. It mirrored boatsheds, a jetty, and a pink turban of cloud. There were booms laid to guide the salmon but slim pickings for a pair of white kingfishers on patrol.

Back in town I strolled up Second Ave, windowshopping. Kama

Sutra massage oil had come to the frontier. Venhoff's Chimney Sweep went by in a van. The swimming baths stank of chlorine. In the hostel kitchen a woman was cooking frozen salmon. I decided to leave the next day.

Sharing my room was a radiant American who was going to kayak down to Dawson. He had to be up early, he said, turning out the light.

"Have a good trip," I said.

"It's not a trip," he replied. "It's a quest."

"Well, have a nice quest," I thought and watched the moon rise over the SS *Klondike*. Next morning he was gone, after his grail. His bed was neatly made, the sheets so eerily smoothed down he might never have been there at all.

6

The Alaskan Highway

The Alaskan Highway was built as a strategic road to contain
Japan. Today Japan is a friend and trading partner, but not the
United States' No. 1 trading partner, as two American presidents,
Reagan and Nixon, publicly stated in their time. That partner is
the country through which the Alaskan Highway happens to pass,
Canada.

The oversight is characteristic, and it is resented. "A brother,"
says James Joyce of Stanislaus, "is as easily forgotten as an
umbrella." Canadians are apt to view the slight not as acci-
dental but as systemic, less a lapse than a disorder: the man who
mistook his wife for a hat. Hat or umbrella, Canada is regularly
mislaid in Washington. The matter doesn't end there. Driven to
pan-continentalism by their destiny, Americans have frequently
seen all North America as theirs. Cartoonists who draw Uncle Sam
with Florida for his chin (and the Yucatan for his beard) will borrow
all Canada for, again, his hat. And as recently as Harry Truman,
the presidential memoirs show that the United States was ready
to annex Canada if its political evolution went astray. (There's a
secondary consequence: deprived of real power, Canadian leaders
are condemned either to nonentity or to flamboyance.)

The highway began as America's string on the Alaskan kite.
American soldiers built the road after Pearl Harbor, starting at
the small town of Dawson Creek and ending at Fairbanks, 1500
miles away. Whitehorse, then a town of two hundred people, was
the last Canadian stop. By starting there I was working backwards
to the zero milestone.

On the bus was Mike, the canoeist from Dawson City. He told

me he'd met a geologist there who said those endless tailings by the road were full of gold. The miners had used 1½-inch sieves and anything bigger than that had got away.

"Moose!" the driver called and pointed at a glittering lake. An antlered silhouette rose, dripping sparks of water.

Mike had studied the *Bhagavad Gita* with a man whose PhD was in Hinduism. "But he wasn't an Indian, he was Canadian," he said. I liked the way he said *Indian* and not *East Indian*, unafraid of confusion; no other Canadian did. I asked him about Americans. He said, "They're there."

At Johnson's Crossing we entered cinnamon bun territory. Cinnamon buns are to the frontierswoman what pickup trucks are to the frontiersman. A woman at the Crossing was said to make the best buns in the Yukon, but we shot through. At Swift River I shook Mike's hand and got off at the next stop, Rancheria. It was my last night in the Yukon, and it was the middle of nowhere. The hotel staff, a boy and girl, were waiting.

He: Are you the hired help?

I: No.

She: Did you miss your stop?

I: No. This *is* Rancheria?

Both: It sure is. (*Exeunt, shaking heads.*)

I picked a site under a clump of young pines: frost was forecast. From the river came a great cackling of geese, but when I got there it was just a placid stream, the Rancheria.

The area was first surveyed long before the highway. George Mercer Dawson, he of Dawson City and Dawson Creek, came this way in 1887 with his team and surveyed 60,000 square miles of the northwest, *taking the work*, said a plaque, in evangelical tones, *of the Geological Survey of Canada above the Arctic Circle for the first time*. It was a feat. Dawson was made Director of the Geological Survey. He had been a cripple from childhood.

There were raspberry canes on the sandbanks, the fruit quite sweet. The river flowed quietly past stands of skeleton pines, dead and bleached on their feet. Windows opened in the cloud cover and the whole mass moved together, blue clouds sailing in a white sky. On a pebbled bank were oily duck-droppings; on the forest floor a silvery fungus sent up suckers with vermilion lips. A cat's cradle of fallen trees trapped me in a meadow lit with fireweed. The ducks –

not geese — I heard before flew over; just three had made all that racket. A line of unstrung fenceposts led me home.

At dinner there was a couple from Florida and a cop with a pistol on his hip.

"You get people goin' crazy up here?" the Floridans asked.

"Naah," the cop said, but he didn't sound sure. He put down his spare ribs and told the waitress he would give the strawberry delight a try. I felt relief when he wiped his weapon hand.

The waitress said to the boy in the kitchen, "I'll clear the tables, you wash up. Next year they'll have to work it out better."

Night fell slowly, the darkness drifting down. I sat on a bleached log by the river listening to the water run over a stony patch downstream. Master Basho would have built his hut by such a stream, quietly becoming the picture, erasing the picture. My breath steamed, a yellow moon rose at my back. The trees and hills turned black, sky and water lingered silver and gold. A lone duck sped overhead, more sound than sight.

I woke to a fleet of five yellow school buses, their engines idling together. Rancheria was garage and hotel. At breakfast — a cinnamon bun — the truckie at the next table said there was snow on the Dempster. I wondered how Jo Lily was getting on.

"I was in Inuvik in *July*," another man said, "and we got snow. I don't think I took my jacket off once."

I tackled the bun. The shortest way with cinnamon buns, I found, was to unroll the spiral, picking your way through the vile syrup to the nothing at the centre. But this bun, sweet to nausea, defeated me.

"Enjoy your bun?" the waiter said. He made it sound like a vacation.

"Yup." But the tell-tale heart lay untouched on the plate. Afterwards I climbed a hill.

Lunch was perogies and bacon, Slavic Canada approaching. A mother and son, the son middle-aged, came in with flasks for coffee. They looked around the place with loud approval.

"Nice aquarium," she said.

"Nice fish, too," he said.

"Now look at those pictures! Aren't they the cutest?"

The pictures were of animals and Eskimos, photos mounted on glazed wood carved and laminated. Facing me was a flock of

70

Dall sheep with their spiral horns on a mountainside, trapped in laminate. Above was a real Dall head, its eyes turned to heaven.

"I knew somebody who used a harness to frame a picture."

"Oh yeah? Let me pay, I want to get rid of some of this money. Look at that! PLEASE DON'T SHOOT ANYTHING THAT'S NOT MOVING IT'S PROBABLY THE HIRED HELP."

The driver was the same man as the day before. An Indian in a leather hat kept up a running conversation with him. The hat came off when his head needed airing. I began to notice hats.

"That's Steve Painter's daughter," the Indian said as we passed a group of roadworkers. She wore a hard hat and was holding a SLOW sign. Across the aisle the metis's straw hat didn't come off once; he wore a hunting knife in his belt.

SOUTH TO ALASKA bragged the Cassair Highway sign. When you start with the Yukon, Alaska seems tame. At Watson Lake the new bus driver had no hat, but his uniform was immaculate. He was young and tall, with high arched eyebrows that left a narrow, supercilious forehead. A girl in every garage, I thought. He wore tight grey trousers and his uniform jacket was more a waistcoat with sleeves: its high cut back gave him the look of a matador. The small owlish boy beside me, his nose in a book, wore a bright pink baseball cap that commemorated the 50th anniversary of our own highway.

The matador drove holding the crossbar of the steering wheel, his little finger curled around the rim. The bus climbed high into the mountains. At dusk a woman rose out of the mist and the matador stopped in the middle of the road. She handed him a peach and they whispered nothings as the bus looked on. Then the matador remembered we were running late. He popped the peach into the speedometer socket and suddenly we were flying. Once as we bottomed out of a rollercoaster dip we were actually airborne. Everyone in the bus felt that lightness; the owl smiled uneasily. The matador came to his senses: the North was his bull, but life mattered too.

The highway ran across a high open plateau then climbed still higher. A full moon rose behind a skeleton forest just as the sun went down red on the opposite side. The two orbs (*orb* for sun is a Jack London failing) hung suspended; then the balance tipped. The owl switched on his reading light at once: he was reading *Berenger's Last Case*. The matador did a lunatic overtake on a double yellow line, and then we were alone on the highway, the moon going before us like a presence.

When we got to Liard the owl was fast asleep. "The kitchen is closed," the cook announced gleefully. I pitched the tent, opened my last can of salmon, and ate under a moon that gathered lustre as it rose.

At breakfast there were more staff than guests. A wholly one-way conversation was in progress at their table, a young mechanic talking, an old man sitting like a stone idol. "A mixture of diesel and oil coming out . . . gonna be something wrong . . . kind of a knocking . . . boy, a wrist sure takes a long time to heal . . ."

"Yeah," the old man sighed. It was only breath escaping, but the mechanic pounced.

"How's your son, then? He get a job?"

Cornered, the old man growled. The mechanic got up. "Bring some life into this place," he said fretfully. I thought he might be going for the juke box, but he simply disappeared.

"Fuel truck tipped over back there," a man said, coming in.

"This what you call work?" said a plump metis girl, joining them.

"Yup," said the old man. "Working on the coffee pot."

The Liard lodge overlooks the Liard River and a fine suspension bridge. The bridge, taut and serene as a kitestring, presides over the landscape, imposing a discipline on cloud and hill. At mealtimes I returned to the same window and looked out on it until it became a shape in the mind. It was there when I closed my eyes.

I went down to it, then down the bank to the river. The rock it sat on was good black rock, not treacherous and sandy like the rock at Rancheria. I walked back up the highway into rain. To get warm I ran to Trapper Ray's, a roadside café. Ray brought me some furry spiders on a plate and a newspaper clipping on the spider invasion. They were for sale, toys; he had orders from Japan and Korea where they used spiders as sex medicine.

A party of Germans came in. Trapper Ray produced more spiders. Orders from Japan and Korea, he said, sex medicine. The Germans laughed politely. A couple entered; Ray showed them the medicine. "Australia?" he said, and read them Australian graffiti from the ceiling: BIG RED KANGAROOS SWALLOW BLACK BEARS WHOLE.

There was no escape. The rain was pouring down. On the cabin wall hung skins (Ray had used one as letter paper), pelts, T-shirts, old snowshoes, a kind of divining rod with a can of 7-Up speared on one tine. I looked away from the rod in case it produced a story.

"These work better," Ray said. "They're penis bones." He came to our table. "Penis bones," he said to the German girl opposite me. Her mother blinked. The men giggled. Trapper Ray pointed to his penis by way of translation. The girl stuck the bone under her nose like a cannibal, and he let it go at that.

Trapper Ray's brother burst on the scene, to music. He did accents for us: Italian, Chinese. He told jokes. I began to long for Mexico. The mother across the table sighed and stood up, rubbed her rump and sat down again. The party, full of food and drink, were subdued. All but two went out into the slackening rain.

"You get many big parties?" I asked the waitress.

"Not too many, thank God."

"Bunch of Germans in here the other day —" Ray began. The two remaining Germans began to talk loudly in German. Trapper Ray looked around, lost his thread. He got up, began to wipe off placemats. Then he went to the kitchen. "Damn waitress," he said, coming back. "Just puts the cups down and clears out." His good humour was gone; no more jokes. The rain was gone too. I ran with a sense of deliverance all the way back to the lodge.

The next day I crossed the bridge and scrambled down the far bank, singing and knocking the rocks with a stick to scare off bears. Hikers, I was told, wore bells so as not to surprise a grizzly. From the river's edge the lodge was hidden. There was only the bridge in the wilderness. It seemed to levitate, a thing of supernal intelligence. On the way back I stood a moment at its dizzy centre high above the green river and felt the tug of that immense cycle of waters that began in the shallows of the Rancheria, passed under my feet, and ended at the mouth of the Mackenzie.

Back in my tent I slipped into foreign dreams: tropical heat, rain. Down the slope from me the hotel generator kept up its monotonous tom-tom beat, fading in and out of the hotel's consciousness.

73

That night a storm came up. The wind drowned out the generator and raged over the campground and hotel. It came roaring through the poplars with the sound of a train on a bridge. My tent trembled and I hung onto the fibreglass pole, expecting every time to be flattened. Again and again it struck: *I'll blow your house down* . . . I'LL BLOW YOUR HOUSE DOWN . . .

I woke to a strange tapping on the tent. Not the pointed stroke of raindrops but something lighter and more diffuse. I looked out.

Snow! After ten years. I drew out the tent pegs with numb fingers. I hadn't noticed the cold until I took a waking sip of canteen water: it burnt the tongue and jangled teeth. At breakfast I took my window seat and saluted the bridge. In the heart of the storm it wore a haughty, unyielding look. The balsam poplars blanched and shook, the young birches bent right over, the snowflakes ran like a panicked populace. The bridge merely closed its eyes. I imagined the wind playing its Aeolian harp: the main cables were 12-ply steel, but the vertical rods might twang. I recalled the night's fears and the nursery-tale line I fell asleep to. Why would a wolf *blow* a house down? No: the wires had got crossed somewhere. The wolf belonged in another tale; this tale belonged to the wind. It registered an ancient fear of people huddled in their huts as the beast of the air swooped down on them.

The bus was not till late. On an impulse I loped through the snow to the hot springs. At the Alpha pool were a few pink bathers cooking like stunned lobsters. There was a Beta pool deeper in, where the forest came down to the water's edge. It was deserted. I hesitated – a hot pool was something new – then slipped in.

Heaven is a solitude where snowflakes settle on the skin as hot water bubbles up from below.

Then it was Trapper Ray's or a cold. Ray, looking like Rasputin, was wrestling with three blondes. They chorused as he chalked up: "Ha . . . m, Fri . . . es, Gr . . . een Bea . . . ns, Pine . . . app . . . ple!"

"Grizzly up by the top pool this morning," Trapper Ray let fall. "Good size, with a sandy hump." That was why I'd had the pool to myself.

That evening I watched TV with a little boy and girl who

74

were playing by the fire, apparently parentless. The movie showed a naked woman being strangled; the little girl looked on as if it were a fairy tale.

Muncho Lake, Toad River, Summit Lake, Pink Mountain: I'd picked them for their names. Now I saw they were night stops. I tore a strip off my ticket as far as Dawson Creek and settled in. Snow fell thickly, hushing the tyres.

At eight I woke to a terrible dream: the car I was driving went out of control and rammed several other cars. I felt sure I'd cried out in my sleep. The sense of shame was worse than the dream. The man beside me coughed and looked out of the window. I shut my eyes and feigned dignified sleep.

I opened them on another world. Canada had gone from blue-green to yellow, mountains had given way to rolling hills covered in wheat. The trees grew in clumps, islands in a yellow sea. Signs of habitation returned: red barns, farm machinery, wooden silos. The silos, a prairie trademark, were part of the Alberta Wheat Pool, but we were still in British Columbia. Dawson Creek is a prairie town governed from across the mountains, and even a stretch of sea. Somewhere down the line politics misprised geography, but the people ignore politics and deal with Alberta anyway.

Dawson Creek is small-town Canada, in its shops, its main street, its art gallery where wedding-cake Rockies run with caramel streams under skies crammed with macaroons. I was still in pickup country. (Whenever I left the pickup trucks behind on the journey I knew I was going astray.) But there were complications: Chrysler New Yorkers parked beside Trans-Ams on Main Street, and fluffy pink teddy bears nextdoor to cowboy gear (no contradiction there perhaps). Bloated women with cigarettes and prams shared the sidewalk with Save the Rainforest ladies; the Whole Earth health foodstore rubbed shoulders with Black Art tattooists.

I heard my name called. It was Chris, the cabbie who'd taken me out to the campground. He waved as he went by, small-town warmth. Once again I was on the edge of town – bad policy in wet weather – but my tent looked out on yellow fields and low blue hills. Wet birch leaves stuck to my tent wall. Chris had turned off his meter and helped me pick a site.

The waitress at lunch was Egyptian and looked like the hiero-glyph for waitress. Side-on, she served stir-fry vegetables worthy of Shanghai. Snowpeas and mushrooms on the frontier! When I slept cheap I could eat dear. MAKE SOUTHERLY, I wrote on the placemat, looking out at driving rain. Museum weather, still.

The Dawson Creek Museum is housed in the old railway station on Alaska Avenue, one block from the zero milestone. The curator was Ellen Corea, a portly woman in jeans, her hair cut short. She was born in Edmonton and got her Fine Arts degree in Calgary.

"The week we graduated," she said, "we got in our truck, a '49 Ford pickup, and headed North. I was seven months pregnant, and we thought we'd go someplace no one else wanted to go. The minute we drove into town my husband fell in love with the place. It took me a little longer. I was raised a prairie girl and I thought the houses were painted funny colours. Now I belong. There's something about living in the North that sets you apart from people who don't. My husband won't go south of Pouce Coupé — that's on the edge of town. We have everything we need here: we have the North's largest library."

Whitehorse will see about that, I thought. "Where do you holiday?" I said.

"My idea of a holiday is to go to a big city. I go there and I can't stand standing in line, the crowds, the traffic. 'The hicks from the Crick', my aunt in Ontario calls us."

"How long have you been here?"

"Thirteen years. Ours is a young community — this railway station was built in 1931 — so you never feel like a newcomer."

I asked her about the United States.

"I've been to Alaska more than the States," she said. "Sure there's a fear of being swallowed up, but I think there are regional ties." She made a series of downward cuts in the air, separating off the coasts from her prairies. "I go to Montana, Colorado, and I see people who could be my grandmother or my father: old, traditional, farming people. Just like BC ties up with California, and Ontario with the eastern states. But I'd be very upset if we lost our sovereignty. Our culture is different. We don't get cable TV at home. I listen to CBC radio. American news is scary. We don't have the dirt, the violence, the race problems."

76

An assistant came in. "Use my car," Corea said, and handed over the keys.

"Canadians are diplomatic," she said. "We're a less aggressive people. We're apathetic, but it keeps us out of trouble. Our present PM is so American, he's their Joe Boy. I always liked Trudeau, but I never voted for him once. I voted prairie conservative."

The price of flamboyance, perhaps: people admire you without supporting you. I recalled an occasion when, towards the end of the Trudeau years, a woman in the crowd coming up suddenly against the man (after having lived with the myth) said, famously, "My God! You're *old*!" All Canada aged in those few seconds, and the mask fell apart. Real power was always elsewhere anyway, and after Trudeau it was the turn of nonentity: Joe Who, Joy Boy.

I asked about the American soldiers who built the highway. "I suppose many of them married local girls?"

"No, not many. Some did." (She was clarifying, not making a political point.) "Some just left babies – but don't write that down!"

She had to go, to Edmonton. "Talk to Gary Oker," she said, and got me his number. There was no answer when I called. I went to the public library. "You should meet Gary Oker," the librarian said.

"Who's your pre-eminent local author?" I asked her.

"She's dead." To make amends she got me out a copy of *Toleration Point Zero*, by a retired local RCMP officer, D.S. Halliday. Halliday's foreword said: "We Canadians are the most difficult people on earth to anger."

The punk withered as gasoline poured onto his crotch area.
"Got a match, Peter?"
"You bet!"
"Now get this, you two maggots, how many girls you raped and killed?"
"I don't know. Maybe eight or nine."

I tried Oker again. He answered. "I'll pick you up at the zero milestone," he said.

A black space shuttle – not a pickup truck – hove up and I got in. Gary Oker was going to pick up a fax at the institute where he taught design. "Is that one of your creations?" I said; nodding at the jacket he was wearing. It was part leather, part cloth, with tassels and trimmings; my half-price London Fog looked sad beside it.

"Yes, I try to design clothes with some individuality. Otherwise you get" (with a nod at the Fog) "standard stuff."

In the room where he taught were dummies dressed in halfmade jackets. He took up a beaver pelt and wrapped it around a dummy; instantly it took on the look of a finished collar. On a rack hung bright shirts, hand-dyed, and a black jacket with white loon spots. Posters of Indian scenes lined the walls. Oker was a Beaver Indian, and his students were mostly Indian. He was also a dancer and had taken many young Indians off the streets into his dance company; the Northern Shadows had just returned from a tour of Germany. Also on the wall was a Canadian flag Oker had designed: a stylized tipi superimposed on the maple leaf.

"I'll take you home," he said, fishing the expected fax out of the machine.

Home was a house on the edge of town, looking out across a swell of yellow rapeseed. I took a photo of Oker against the field. He faced the camera casually, a man of perhaps thirty with hair down to his shoulders and glasses on a model's face. Inside, sitting at the kitchen table, was a woman of striking beauty. She was Connie, a Cree from Prophet River.

"Cree and Beaver are traditionally enemies," Oker smiled. "They used to steal women and horses from each other."

On the table was Hugh Brody's *Maps and Dreams: Indians and the British Columbia Frontier*. I was on that frontier now. "In Beaver culture," Oker said, "there's a lot of dreamers. Like prophets, yeah?"

Oker was born at Doig River near Fort St John, not a hundred miles up the highway. Connie came from further north, Mile 232, she said, where there's a church by the road and one store. He left home at sixteen, planning to be a rock star; she ran away from an alcoholic home where her white father discouraged the use of her mother's language. "They put a lot of shame into you," she said. Oker studied design in Montreal and New York. But over there, "how they looked was all that mattered." He came home, wanting to be with his grandparents, to record their songs and words before

78

they died. Connie trained in counselling at the Nietzsche Institute in Edmonton. Now she worked with street children in Dawson; that was how she and Gary met.

All evening Oker's grandfather hovered as a voice on the stereo. He sang, he spoke, he chanted, and constantly he drummed. The drumming filled the house like a heartbeat. It forms a grave, dark frieze on the tape I made in the kitchen – a tape of a tape. Oker's grandmother had just died and his grandfather had officiated at the last rites. He brought out photos of the ceremony.

"This is her funeral tipi. Traditionally the dead were placed in a tree. There's still singing and dancing and a big feast."

"You get buried with fresh moccasins," Connie said.

"So your spirit can dance to the spirit world."

It was a happy thought: Alice Morgason, aged sixty-nine, dancing her way to heaven, in fresh moccasins.

"Elders are like the tribe's books. They know the songs and stories. They get first cut when a moose is killed. They hold the family together – look what happened to the Tanners when Sally died."

Oker lit some sweetgrass. The incense filled the room.

"When you die," he said, "you should know at least one prayer song to guide you to the spirit world. You learn it from nature. In the olden days they had a puberty quest where you got power from an animal. You purify yourself for four days and four nights and then the animal will choose you. It talks to you, shows you special things."

"We have a boy in our village who walks with animals," Connie said.

"To become a good medicine man, a herbalist, to become a music-keeper like my grandfather, takes a lifetime."

Oker brought out a drum he had made. "There are kids' songs, animal songs, courting songs. Each one has a different beat. Here –" He demonstrated a courting beat, a kind of flutter. "See? The heart is pumping! With this beat geese will land. There are dancing songs, war songs."

"You can send a spirit a long ways," Connie said, "hundreds of miles to kill an enemy if you have the right medicine."

"You can also send warnings," Oker said, "through I guess good medicine. Bad medicine backfires. People used to use bears to kill an enemy, but the bear could turn on you. There's love medicine too. There was this nineteen-year-old professional model from Edmonton who gave up modelling, a gorgeous blonde, and went with this ugly guy. But he got drunk one day and lost his pouch and she was gone the next day. She couldn't remember where she'd been."

"What does it take?" I asked, interested.

"Pieces of hair," Connie said, "or a cigarette butt, or even saliva – something personal. You make up a potion. They can't walk away from it. It's weird.

"We saw a spirit together, Gary and me. I seen an image of an Indian with long hair on Gary, and on me, on top of me, Gary seen an Indian woman. And when we woke up our hands were joined together across the table and we were *screaming*."

"When I was twenty," Oker said, "I went to the top of a hill at sunrise and made some prayers, burnt sweetgrass, and was singing songs to the Great Spirit. This robin comes flying out of nowhere. It kept calling me, he'd go in front of me. Afterwards I'd see it in dreams, in between sleeping and waking, and I've always followed it. In music I try to write native songs for today."

"You sing?"

"We got a group. Traditional drum, shaker, bass, guitar." He fetched out his guitar. "You want a drink? A beer?" He went to the fridge. Connie drifted out of the room. We opened a bottle each. He took a swig and sang a song of his own, "Hear the Ghost on the Open Plain". He had a full voice and did the chorus of hunting cries with gusto. Next he sang a song dedicated to his grandmother, "Things to Remember to Make Us Strong", and another, "Just Like a Wild Horse Running Free". Then he put on a tape of his grandfather chanting and disappeared the way Connie had gone. I heard her voice raised. In a little while she came out and said goodbye.

"She doesn't like me drinking," Oker explained. "She grew up in a drinking home. I don't drink all that much. Once in a while it's good. I can handle it. When you're in my position it's easy to be attacked. People will say, 'I told you so, he's an Indian.' "

I saw what he meant. Two prominent townspeople had spoken highly of him – remarkably, neither had said he was an Indian – but the feeling could easily run the other way.

80

We opened another bottle. "It'll pass over," he said. "We're well matched." He sang some more, then was quiet. "I have good students," he said. "I make them do research, say, the history of costume, or beading techniques, types of beads, whatever. Then from there they have to go make some garment, out of that research."

We listened to his grandfather's drumming.

"The rhythm gets you," he said finally. "You go all night long, for days sometimes."

I told him of tabla players who played till they dropped.

"This last song's the best my grandfather done, because it was for my grandmother's funeral. He was breaking down on us. But I really encouraged him. All his emotions were coming out. He broke down when her body came out. I put the drum in his hands. It was pretty tough for everybody. When he was singing it was OK."

He went and got a tin box. "Here are some herbs that I have. This here is bear grease."

"How come it's liquid?"

"It's screened, eh. It's good for your skin, to soften dry skin. I use it for sores and stuff like that."

I examined a leaf. "This stuff was growing right by my tent in Inuvik."

"Is that right? You could have made yourself tea with that. It'll knock you out just like that, relax you. If you're in pain, like if you get hurt somewhere down in the bush, or after a long day you're overtired, you drink that and you're out for the night. This here is moss. It's good for absorbing things. Women used it for their menstrual period. This stuff we call Old Man's Fart! This here is a kind of mushroom. You cut yourself, you put that in there and it stops the bleeding and cleans it out. It's very pure. You get no scars. It grows everywhere in the fields. This is Old Man's Beard, good for starting fires in the bush. It's raining and you can go under those big trees and it's all dry. This is the gum from spruce. They used that for sealing canoes, you know, waterproofing. And it's good for toothaches. This a white fungus, grows on trees."

"It's like a seashell."

"Ya. I burn it when I want to purify the place, kill the germs. This is sage. You can burn this also but also you can make tea. It

81

purifies the blood, makes it nice and thin. Nice smell to it, eh?"

"When you were a kid your elders would have shown you what to pick and what to avoid?"

"Oh ya, there's poison mushrooms and stuff. Just like the white man's got a drugstore and they have poisons too in their cabinets. It's like when you learn to read."

"The Book's out there?"

"All this stuff, the whole of nature. And it takes a life-time to go through it."

He went to the fridge. "One more! Might as well."

"Last one!"

"Ya," he poured. "I still got a wild streak in me. Empty the fridge, then 'Let's go have a game of pool,' then 'Let's have a one,' then 'One more,' then 'Closing time, where's the bootlegger!' "

"What – moonshine?"

"Oh no, just the regular stuff. Triple the price."

"Where are most of your friends?"

"On the reserve. Lots of people live there. It's a good life there. Out in the bush way up in the mountains. Only way you can get there is flyin' in and with horses, that's all."

It was raining again. When he heard I was camping Oker offered me a bed. I said I'd grown fond of my tent. He drove me back to the campground and flashed his lights as he drove off. I stepped straight into a mud pool, crawled out, and went to bed.

I woke to a bird-cry very like our red-wattled lapwing. *Pity to do it!* The morning was chill and grey and beautiful, with wet yellow leaves on the dead grass. I wiped off my boots with the leaves.

Breakfast at the Dawson Grill was called the Alaskan Kickoff, for those starting from zero. My waitress was a sprightly woman of fifty with yellow hair bound in stooks. She was very honoured to meet me, a gentleman from India, and very pleased to serve me. I must have a good trip now and take care of myself and *enjoy* Grand Prairie. Was I going to Drumheller? Wonderful! Was I going to Medicine Hat? *Gorgeous!* She sprang across to the bar where Lee sat drinking coffee under his hat. She danced around him, punching the air while he sat motionless in the eye of her storm. In a black comedy he would have drained his cup, got up, felled her with one blow, and stalked out. But she had already danced away to the kitchen, where she was sparring with the cook.

7

Mozart and the

Duckbill Dinosaur

In the *Golden Stamp Book of Birds* someone had left among the magazines at the Dawson Creek Greyhound Station, I saw for the first time a picture of the Mexican quetzal. It was a good omen, that exquisite emerald-green bird sacred to the Aztecs: I felt I was leaving the rain and snow behind, entering a new phase of the journey. That was how the first Americans must have felt as they struck out across the prairie, making southerly, free at last of the mountains and the fickle mountain weather.

I had a wet tent in my luggage, but the sun was climbing over the prairie as we rolled out of Dawson Creek and past Pouce Coupé, south of which Ellen Corea's husband will not go. The fields were brilliant yellow and green and, where the earth had been turned, black. Tractors, horses, white fences, windmills, red barns, silver grain silos, orange railway wagons: all spoke of heat, though in fact the summer was over. The wheat stood ripe in the fields. My one regret in leaving the North was that I'd missed the Northern Lights.

At Beaver Lodge I lost my second seat to an old lady. She got on at the local store, where the old Coke thermometer was still working. The needle pointed to 50°, so it wasn't hot. *Coke 5¢* said the weathered sign.

"The dark yellow is wheat," the old lady said, "the bright yellow is canola. The rain's come at a bad time for the farmers. They've just cut crops and hay."

I told her of the snow on the Alaskan Highway.

"Some years," she said, "there's just a skiff of snow on the ground about now, but it doesn't last."

I remarked on *skiff*. She gave a little laugh.

"I guess that ages me!"

I pointed to a bird in the fields and she said, yes, that was a magpie. As a girl growing up on the farm she knew all the plants, the birds, but she'd lived in cities so long now she'd forgotten most.

By Dawson Creek the magpie has replaced the raven. (More likely the raven has yielded unwanted ground.) *All populations must have a jester*, the raven seems to say, and gravely plays the fool. The magpie, the prairie jester, is more buffoon than fool. He has the pied uniform, he struts and tumbles, but he is a mischief-monger, given to antics no raven would stoop to. He doesn't steal, he scrounges; and he laughs at his own jokes — a long burbling yodel — before the joke is told.

The map of Alberta shows very little in its upper half. Grand Prairie, no southerly town, almost slips below the fold. But those empty spaces up north are of consuming interest to Alberta's No.1 trading partner. Those tracts, adjoining the Northwest Territory, are Alberta's Arabia Deserta, her Rub Al-Khali or Empty Quarter; in plain Australian, her Great Bugger-All. And as in those distant worlds, the quarter proves not so empty after all. Timber, not oil, is the treasure here.

At White Court (Knights of Columbus Welcome You) on the McLeod River, the bus stopped across the track from the big pulp mill. The mill bulks white and blue over river and town. A giant yellow crane straddles the neatly stacked logs the trucks have brought in. In the vast forecourt stand polythene-wrapped cubes of product awaiting the trucks that will take them away. The old CN railway track goes nowhere in particular.

Three roads strike like the prongs of a pitchfork deep into the province's timbered north. They are frontier roads; dirt roads like those opened up the West. It was the approach of such a road that sparked Western Canada's most memorable revolt.

A hundred and twenty years ago Louis Riel led the Red River metis against encroaching settlers in a short-lived rebellion that took the army to put down. Riel was a kind of Northern Toussaint L'Ouverture, one of those happenchance soldiers who have greatness thrust upon them. A Catholic Franco-Indian, he formed a provisional metis government with its own flag. Defeated, he dodged across the border to the US. In 1885 he was persuaded to return and promptly declared another rebel government. He was captured and, a year later, executed, thus passing into legend, into a modern opera, and into a short story I read on the bus.

The road to Edmonton joins the west prong of the pitchfork. Where the prongs meet is Edmonton and then the highway becomes freeway, running due south down the shaft of the pitchfork in a bold yellow line on the map that connects all the major towns and cities of Alberta. The forest ends at White Court, at the mill. After that you look down onto lakes of yellow wheat among the trees. The prospect would have delighted Master Basho, but the Japanese have little use for wheat – and Japan, not the United States, is Alberta's chief trading partner.

In Edmonton I took a room at the (whilom) Grand Hotel and called the author of the Riel story. I got an answering machine. I then called a publisher whose small empire had been hurt by Free Trade. His dog answered the phone. *Hello, this is Oliver. My master and Valentine are out for a walk . . .* I had maligned the poor magpie: the prairie fool was the answering machine.

With the sun came real heat. I bought a cotton shirt at Hudson's Bay and jettisoned my frontier flannel. The snow on the Alaskan Highway was a distant dream. It seemed unlikely that a legislator sitting in Edmonton could remember his constituents at the end of one of those northern roads; a single day's journey was a world away.

After lunch I walked up Jasper into a poster:

THE ATHABASCA FUR-TRADING ADVENTURE
OF WOLFGANG AMADEUS MOZART
(World Premiere)

It was a small audience, but then it was chamber opera, and new. Mozart is brought out to the Canada of his day, the fur-trade Canada of men like Mackenzie, who offers the composer a fat purse for a frontier opera that will attract European investors to the North, and worthy Sam Hearne of the Hudson's Bay Company, who swears that the new fur traders are the ruination of the land. Embodying the land is the distinguished Chipewyan chief Matonabbe. Canada is more than a beaver pasture, he sings. Caught between developers and greens, Matonabbe offers a solution: let us bring the furs to you. This cuts no ice with the vicious trapper Peter Pond; to him Canada is all beaver. Mozart, a soprano in pants, makes peace, and Mackenzie sings a soothing aria: Canada is an ice maiden asleep. (A few acres of snow, was Voltaire's verdict.) A new bird here is winging, says Mackenzie. At dawn the bird calls. Mozart, who has sat up all night, stirs to the music and springs offstage pen in hand.

It works beautifully, moralizing and all, but Canada wasn't listening. Awaken Athabasca, sang the chorus of camp-followers, but even as they filed offstage Edmontonians were queuing for tickets to a sell-out Andrew Lloyd Webber musical.

Mozart's frontier librettist was Paul Conway, his music a pastiche of eight early operas. In the green room Conway, who played Matonabbe, consulted his diary and agreed to meet me after breakfast the next day.

Breakfast was Transylvanian; the paprika lay on my fried potatoes like proof. The paper had a story about one Raghubir Singh, who'd been asked to remove his turban in a Canada Legion hall. He was going to sue. Conway picked me up in a four-wheel drive. Even seated he towered over me. On stage he made a magnificent Matonabbe, his shaven head gleaming in the spotlight, his bulk wrapped in a red Hudson's Bay blanket. We drove across the river to Strathcona, Edmonton's twice-born suburb of brick terraces and cafés. A table was freed at the Old Strathcona Coffee Factory and we sat down.

"There *is* an audience for opera," Conway said. He had a tenor's speaking voice, with an edge of earnestness. "*Figaro* filled eight thousand seats last spring – three times what we need – but the established companies won't hire locally."

That was why he formed the Edmonton Chautauqua Society, whose logo, a chautauqua tent, recalls the itinerant troupes – Shakespeare-wallahs – that once brought culture to the West.

"Our financial position is gruesome to behold. So it helps if I can produce and direct *and* play Matonabbe: we can write off ten thousand dollars' worth of functions."

Conway lived for opera but not by it. He was a professional researcher who'd travelled the North for two decades working on projects for native communities and municipalities. All those miles – "hundreds of thousands" – had given him that feeling for the North that was the opera's strength.

"Mackenzie came out as Pond's assistant," he said. "And I suspect Hearne of Hudson's Bay and Peter Pond knew each other. Hudson's Bay simply wouldn't come inland – they collected furs at the coast. The Chipewyans and the Cree were the great middlemen."

"Who was this Pond?"

"He was a shady character who travelled all the way up to the Arctic. He could trap like an Indian but he wanted more. He was accused of several murders and was actually tried in Montreal. He came from Missouri, an American."

Another Mad Trapper, another goblin from south of the border. "Canadian in those days," Conway said, "meant French Canadian. It didn't acquire its present sense till after Confederation. Around the First World War we began to suspect that the British were not all sterling. There's a story about a Canadian general, Curry, who heard out his commander, Field Marshal Haig, at a war conference in France. 'Any comments, gentlemen?' And Curry says, 'The Goddamnest pile of horseshit I ever heard!' That sort of feeling was pretty strong by the Second War, and yet in the 1950s it was still The Empire.

"In Canada we're uncomfortable with responsibility. It was very comforting to Canadians that Britain took responsibility for the colony. Britain fought off the Americans. After the Second World War the Americans stepped into that role. The thing is Americans were prepared to take *risks*. What they did a hundred and fifty years ago was to borrow the money they needed. We've sold the equity."

"Do you foresee political absorption?"

"I don't see how we could help it. We don't know who we are. I would like to see people have a sense of identity based on a knowledge of history, of survival. That was the common ground between the peasant in Quebec and the peasant in Alberta – a knowledge that the countryside could kill them. Our school system could *tell* this story. Our history has been too orderly, our Charter of Rights was too politicized, not emotive enough. You compare the United States' case. The Declaration of Independence put everything on the line."

88

"You could manufacture a crisis."

"We have one, but the quality of it is pretty low. This country came together under two pressures: one, a belief that British institutions best served people's interests, and two, military fear of the United States. Now neither is working: we take the first for granted, and as for the second, they could walk in any time. There's nothing sacred about nineteenth-century political boundaries, but I personally would grieve to see Canada absorbed.

"I'm in some ways more American than Canadian. I don't expect the government to take my risks. That's why I do stupid things like putting on operas!"

Conway dropped me at Fort Edmonton Park. I might run into his son there, he said: one of the student guides. The fort is a reconstruction, and there are mock-ups too of later Edmontons, all staffed by workers in period costume. In the Hudson's Bay store were pelts and blankets, red blankets like the one Matonabbe wore, which the traders and Indians exchanged. Two black lines at the end of a blanket indicated its pelt value; heavier blankets carried more lines. In the cellar were barrels helpfully stencilled RUM and SALT. Outside the fort was a mock tipi with Indian chairs around the campfire. I sat on one, a skin spread on the ground with a backrest of woven twigs, and did a sketch.

A teenage boy came up to watch my tipi develop. A sketchbook makes friends, a camera enemies. (Master Basho say.) I looked up at him. He was in costume. "You were at the opera yesterday," he said.

"You must be Adam."

He was Conway's son. He showed me around his domain. He had something of his father's gentleness. Then I turned a corner and gained a century. In Rutherford House, house of the first premier, there was an old refrigerator in the kitchen. A woman in a 1905 skirt told me the lock on the fridge door was to keep teenagers out. But fridges in India still have locks: against servants. There'd been servants in Rutherford House two generations ago – the woman was in a maid's costume herself – but democracy had worked so well their lives had been forgotten, even by their actors. The only thing that smelt real at Fort Edmonton was the horse dung in the stables: it was sharp and strong and sweet.

Next day was Sunday. The downtown streets were empty, the

89

sky even emptier. Prairie skies are vast and comfortless. Even in the city they looked wide open: the glass mountains multiplied the blankness and cropped passing clouds. At 97th St all the glittering towers ended abruptly, making a sheer crystal cliff. The dwarfed Chinatown gateway opened onto nothing, just a wide parking lot, the land under the cracked tarseal appreciating slowly. This was the end of town I'd been told to watch out in. On Sunday there was nothing to watch out for. Winos shambled past, one man rubbing his eyes as if amazed at the wreck of his life.

On Labor Day I overslept and missed my telephone interview with the hurt publisher. When I called I got Oliver in his master's voice. I put the phone down and bought a ticket to Drumheller. Outside, nothing moved; even the bus was not till later. The museum was airless, my legs grew rubbery. I leaned on a cabinet of Brazilian butterflies, the homeliest one a fluorescent purple; after that the ash-coloured prairie butterfly came as a relief.

"It's one hundred per cent Canadian," said the waiter at the Café Praha, serving Clamato, a clam-flavoured tomato juice. He'd been in London when the product was launched at Alberta House. A fellow colonial, I recognized the national, the provincial pride, and the overstatement: "It's just about wiped out the Bloody Mary." I took a sip and remained a loyalist.

The south face of Edmonton gives the city its grace. Here the glass cliff is flush with the coulee: the towers rise out of the river, gold and gorget green and blue, a matchless cabinet of alien butterflies abandoned on the prairie as the bus pulls away.

There was a covered wagon in the museum, a Studebaker, with iron tyres. As prairie schooner the Greyhound was much better, but our driver's name sent mixed signals:

Your Operator: GARY WILD SAFE RELIABLE COURTEOUS

The small town signs were like milestones in a man's life: Lucky Dollar Foods, Husky Gas, Hacienda Car-Wash, Mt Pleasant Funeral Chapel. You could speed by it all in a minute.

The farmers were harvesting wheat and dust. Evening light glowed in the fields, flared in the tall grass, stroked the flanks of cows. It made soft corduroy of the furrows, warmed old wooden sheds, spun gold from straw. In one paddock a signalling station of six delicate towers made a giant birdcage open to the sky. I

90

imagined flocks of twittering radio waves swooping in and out. At sunset the harvest continued on farm after farm. The road ran ruler-straight, and Gary Wild steered with one hand, the other cradling his chin. I never saw a more melancholy face in a rear-view mirror. At nine the sky was still a luminous blue. The harvest continued by tractor light. In the west the horizon was an old typewriter ribbon: a band of red above a band of black.

Night fell. Oilpatch chimneys hung out burnoff flares that skipped like orange windsocks. Towns shrank into anonymity; one was no more than a store that doubled as the bus depot. A man stood in the doorway casting a long shadow on the grass; in the tubelit window dangled two huge plastic icecream cones. We dropped a mailsack at his feet and swung back into the dark, steering by the stars.

At Drumheller I lugged my bags to the nearest hotel, a seedy Waldorf. The boy who led me upstairs plucked a price out of the air. It was absurd for a plywood cubicle entirely filled by a double bed. There was no register: he took the money and ran. I stripped the sheets off the bed and went after him. After that it became routine to demand new sheets whenever I checked into a dive. I was never refused. The next day I pitched my tent among willows by the river.

In the spring of 1987 Wendy Sloboda of Drumheller, a grade 12 student given to solitary rambles, chanced on a nest of eggs on Devil's Coulee. They were not ordinary eggs, and they were not freshly laid. They had been there for 70 million years. Sloboda took a specimen to an archaeologist at school, and some weeks later returned from another walk to find a note on the kitchen table: *Found dinosaur babies.* She had stumbled on one of the richest known dinosaur breeding grounds, dozens of nests with embryonic remains of the duckbill dinosaur.

The duckbill or *Hadrosaurus* had more teeth than any other dinosaur, but was a strict vegetarian. Its eggs were smaller than an ostrich's and its thighbone was barely a metre long. The reconstruction at the Tyrell Museum in Drumheller had a jolly camel's head and looked altogether friendlier than the *Triceratops horridus* of Montana, or the *Tyrannosaurus rex* which found its way onto the Drumheller coat of arms.

91

Half a century ago Drumheller was a coal town. Today there are 3000 oil wells in the vicinity, and if you clamber up the coulee you see spread out a golden tableland of wheat. The village of Cereal is not far away to the east, and to the west the town of Carbon produces mostly grain. But it's bones that bring the visitors.

When the hadrosaurus eggs were fresh, Drumheller was a coastal resort (for dinosaurs) and the sea stretched all the way to Texas. There's a Well of Ages in the museum where you can watch the continents take shape. I kept my eye on North America but was constantly distracted by India, whose journey is surely the more spectacular. When all the other continents are in place, India leaves its neighbours South Africa and Australia to travel to the northern hemisphere, where it crashes into the Asiatic mass to form the Himalayas. Meanwhile the Rocky Mountains, a mere compost heap in the duckbill garden, begin to swell. Then the inland sea dries up, ice sheets move in and out, and Wendy Sloboda makes her find.

Back in town I met Marilyn Laframboise, who headed a team of palaeontologists putting together a dinosaur exhibit. The project was a joint Chinese–Canadian venture; when I looked in at the Ex-Terra office it was a Chinese technician who greeted me. I'd seen the latest exchange pair working on a plaster cast at the museum. Laframboise trained in the Tyrell herself. She had the specialist's cautlibraryion and put me onto a generalist.

"Local people have been collecting fossils and sharing their knowledge for years. Talk to Leo Pluto. He's ninety."

I asked her about the West.

"I've been out here ten years," she said, "long enough to get the feel of the place. We have a sort of disgruntled conservatism here, but not enough to pull us apart from the east. There's seasonal migration, marriage ties. The cultural divide is with the United States. The differences are subtle but they're there, whether you're looking at foreign policy or folk music. Down there it's a uniform thing: a common enemy or standard country music. Here we don't think you have to arm yourself against your neighbour. And we have a wider range of music: jigs and reels in the Maritimes, the Quebec fiddle, Arctic folksongs. The only regional music they have is Cajun. The rest is the same four chords."

And the North, logging?

"In fact we need never cut down another tree. There's this new superwood which is made of shredded plastic, bonded and glued. They use it for fenceposts. It's a Canadian product, from Edmonton."

"Where would you go from here?"

"The Yukon maybe, or the Northwest Territories. Right now I'm getting ready to canoe down the Red Deer River."

I went to the library to read the papers. The Raghubir Singh turban saga continued. His lawyer pointed out that the Canadian Legion allowed country and western singers to wear hats on stage in a legion hall. The management said rules were bent on special occasions.

Dinner was a sandwich by the river. I lit a fire and stayed up. Laframboise told me she'd seen the Northern Lights recently. This far south it was hard to credit, and that night there was nothing.

In the morning I returned to the Ex-Terra office. Laframboise had a pickup truck going to the museum and had said I could get a ride. I'd seen the museum; now I wanted to walk the badlands tracks. The pickup was driving off when I arrived. Laframboise gave chase. Two Lo's stopped and took me on: Lorraine from Nova Scotia was driving; Lo from Beijing moved over to crowd the gearshift. A coyote stood over a carcass by the side of the road.

The badlands are not as bad as they sound – in the morning, in fall, in small doses. Farmers and horsemen gave them their bad name, but for the small creatures that live there, life seems quite satisfactory. The land is deeply fissured, the soil friable and for the most part barren, but it makes burrowing easier for the burrowers, and where purchase can be had, tough plants spring up and thrive. Spiny grasses and cacti, but also broad-leaved shrubs do well; on the sheltered side of gullies there are green macracarpa and wild rose, even mosses in damp crevices. Prairie dogs sun themselves, ready to dart back to their holes; hoppers fiddle until dun-coloured birds make a meal of them. The landscape takes on a hummocked look from steady erosion, a succession of flat-topped mounds called benches stretching into the distance. The weathered rock strata show up in distinct bands: white sandstone, yellow mudstone, red sandstone flecked with black coal, volcanic ash turned clay, and in amongst the exposed layers, the precious fossils.

*

In an empty restaurant on empty Centre Street I sat reading the Drumheller Community Resource Booklet. It was mid-afternoon and hot. The Greek lady who served me wore slippers. She sat in a corner sighing and swallowing her lunch. The booklet went from the Alberta Alcohol and Drug Abuse Commission to the Zion Baptist Church, by way of the Big Country Swingers (the local square dancing club) and the Child Abuse Hotline. Among some two hundred listings were:

Dinosaur Valley Heritage Society
Employment Standards Branch
Farm Credit Corporation
Hi Neighbour!
Imperial Order Daughters of the Empire IODE
Junior Forest Wardens
Kaleidoscope Theatre
La Leche League (Breastfeeding)
Meals on Wheels
Native Counselling Service of Alberta
Order of the Eastern Star
Potters Guild
Royal Canadian Legion (Turbans under consideration)
Salvation Army
Twin and Triplet Club
United Church Women
Valley Figure Skating Club
Weight Watchers

I was toying with the Baha'i number when Leo Pluto's name surfaced. I called him from the museum – his museum downtown, not the Tyrell.

"I'll come pick you up," he said. Ten minutes later a long blue Vectra pulled up.

Pluto was a puckish man just a head taller than his Vectra and twice as spirited. He left the museum in a shower of gravel and we were on the highway before I had properly shut my door. A young man came roaring up the fast lane. Pluto put his foot down. The Vectra leapt forward and powered away. Pluto narrowed his eyes and went *Heh, heh!* He was not reckless, he was ninety.

There was a 1950s blue and white Impala parked in the drive with ray-gun brake lights mounted on the tail fins; the

Vectra was just his runabout car. Pluto looked over both cars, a small, shrewd man in a grey suit with wide lapels and a straw hat with a multi-coloured hatband. He wore no tie, a concession to the heat. Inside, he introduced me to June, a handsome middle-aged woman with a voice like mulled wine. June looked after him and helped mind the museum. She marshalled his souvenirs as he spoke.

"We started in a small place the size of this room," he said. The room we were in looked like the beginnings of another museum, the parlour of a man who throws nothing away. On the table beside his armchair were a large globe, ebony bookends, a china clock, a cut-glass vase designed to fit in a 1932 Duesenberg, and the preliminary drawings for a fountain he intended for Drumheller. In a cage were two budgies, and on the floor, in troubled sleep, an ancient terrier. "Then we moved to the swimming-pool building. Then finally we got the present place."

The Tyrell is a newcomer; the first dinosaur bones were exhibited in Pluto's hotel – in Pluto's Window – in 1950. When Leo Pluto came down from Edmonton to make his million ("I'm still trying") Drumheller was a coal town.

"There was bones laying about all over. First thing I see a big leg laying there. I wanted the Chamber of Commerce to put glass over it and keep it there."

"In those days," June said, though she would have been a young girl, "when he went to a café they would call him the Dinosaur Man. They made fun of him, called him crazy. If anybody had a dinosaur bone chances are they'd use it as a doorstop."

"They never thought anything of bones – of anything that died before them!"

"Now you have to have a permit and be a caretaker of them. You can maybe pick up little bits and pieces, but you can't dig."

"I'd go out at five o'clock on a Sunday –"

"– take half a yard of garlic sausage –"

"– and beer. Fifty, sixty mile away sometimes. I went to where they'd crush rocks. When they'd see a dinosaur bone they'd throw it aside. But some got into the crusher. So you see a lot of your roads are made from bone."

"What was Drumheller like in those days?"

June answered for him. "It was a rough, tough place," she

said in her smooth voice. "All the coalminers — there were so many different nationalities, foreign people here. Where Leo's hotel was located was called the Western Front. I can remember people saying 'He's Ukrainian!' and 'Hungarians carry knives!' They had names for every nationality under the sun and they'd call you that to your face."

"Couple got killed around there," Pluto put in.

"Oh, I wouldn't doubt it. There were fights every night."

"Throwing glasses around."

"Years ago if you went to Calgary you wouldn't say you were from Drumheller."

"I sat in a barber's chair once and listened to them talking about Drumheller. Said I was from Edmonton."

Pluto's father was a blacksmith. "He'd fight horses so he had to be tough. Every Sunday he'd race to church in one of them big buggies, four horses, big lights on the sides. He raced sulkies. He owned racehorses. There was about eleven of us. I'm the only boy left, and two girls in Vancouver. I left home when I was a kid. I was going to be a printer but it took too long to learn. I used to feed the press like this —' He slipped a page gingerly into the air and I wanted to snatch his hand away.

June got coffee and cookies and some photo albums.

"That's him when he was young. Is it 1932, that car? This was the first car with the automatic gearshift."

"It had the gearshift right on top, nine hundred and six dollars."

"In this one he had a big wad of money in his pocket. Can you tell by the look on his face?"

A dark-haired elf stood smiling more for himself than for the camera.

"I just sold a car."

"He owned this place that was a chop suey house and the workers and him went out on this picnic. Here he's boxing. He got him down by the look of it. This is *Mr Leo J. Pluto, Prop. Acme Taxi Company, Edmonton*."

"I had a flock of limousines. It was a crooked business, taxis. Bootleg. After I sold out one day I went back to pick up my safe and there was detectives there already. I told them, 'Don't worry about me, I'm *out*!' "

"And he had to clean up the hotel here. There was prostitution."

"More people at the *back* door! Had to put up a fence."

"This is him with the Premier. This was when Leo gave Newcastle to Drumheller. It was like a village or a hamlet where his hotel was and it joined Drumheller."

"I got a golden shovel."

"Once when he had his taxi business this gentleman pulled a gun on him. Leo still has the gun."

"Had to drop him off at the police station. Heh, heh!"

"In 1959 Leo took a group of geologists out. They were from all over the world. They had six big Greyhound buses and they went out into the hills and he showed them how you find dinosaur bones. They would be standing right on a dinosaur and they'd say, 'Well, where are the bones?' "

Pluto took my arm. "See, what you do is you walk in a dry creek, or even a wet creek, and when it rains the soft earth comes down, see, and bares the bones gradually. That bone'll come down. So if you find it here, you look up there – and you'll find the rest of it."

"What do they feel like to touch?"

"I'll take you downstairs and show you."

"Here's one," June said. "See, some of them you can see the cell structure on the inside of them."

"That's all cleaned up. It could be covered in mud, so you gotta know what you're looking for. You've got to have the shape in your mind."

I wondered if Pluto had the shape of Drumheller in his mind all along. He'd come on it when it was a coal town in decline. In 1930 it had a population of 10,000; in 1948 when he arrived there were only 8000. Today there were 600. He'd given Newcastle to the city and moved to a modest house. He'd been one of those responsible for the federal penitentiary's coming to Drumheller. And his museum – and before that his Window – had paved the way for the renowned Tyrell. Not many men shaped a town so completely.

We went down to his basement and there in the gloom was every object Pluto had ever owned: clocks, tools, lamps, paintings that had hung in the hotel, old designs (including, invariably, a Canadian flag – his had a beaver), every *National Geographic* since Creation, books, rugs, china, keys, door-knobs, whistles, hats, walking-sticks.

97

And bones, dinosaur bones.

He gave me three as souvenirs (small ones, at my request) and then I wished June goodbye. Pluto dropped me at the bus depot and we shook hands in the twilight. I felt a twinge as the long blue Vectra leapt away.

8

Head Smashed-In

or Medicine Hat?

On the Calgary bus was Tina. It was after dark and she was the only passenger reading so I took the seat beside her. She had both lights on. She wore red-rimmed glasses and long red nails. After twenty minutes I asked if I could turn my light out. It had been a long day in the badlands.

"You can turn mine out too," she said.

I protested: she was welcome to read on. But she said she'd read enough, and put away her book, *Not Yet, My Love*. I turned off both lights with a sense of having trespassed, but she said it was a silly book; she didn't always read trash.

Tina was a hairdresser of thirty, with watery grey eyes and a frizzy poodlish hairstyle. She was returning from a visit to her family in Elrose, Saskatchewan. She had just broken up with her husband and was going back to Calgary to move her things out into a flat. She liked Calgary and would continue to work there. There was a woman who cut hair in Elrose, so she didn't want to go back and compete. Whenever she went home she gave the family haircuts; invariably cousins turned up at haircutting time. "I go prepared," she said, "in case the sewing scissors come out. It has been known to happen." This time she'd decided to leave her shears behind and just have a break, but at the last minute she slipped them in. Sure enough, everyone's hair had grown.

I slept at the youth hostel. In the morning I went to the Glenbow Museum. It had more Emily Carrs and a renowned collection of native art. Carr's trees were portraiture in wood and leaf; the same seriousness informed the Indians' animal paintings. Probably the last Europeans to treat animals with matching gravity were the Dutch, in someone like Melchior de Hondecoeter. The disappearance of animals in western art, and an ever-sharpening focus on man to the point of total abstraction, would surely puzzle an alien. In the Glenbow it was tempting to plan a theft to restock the earth with Kenojuak Ashevak's *Enchanted Owl*, Ipeelee Osuitok's *Four Musk Oxen*, Lucy Qiunuayuak's *Man Wanting a Seal*, and Alexander Jackson's *Muskeg*. The thief, an honorary member of the Ojibwa False Face Society, might wear a pair of metis beadwork mittens, and a Kwakiutl salmon mask with movable wooden pieces (for the Kwakiutl, salmon were fish people dwelling under the sea).

The next day I went to Banff. Tina said I shouldn't miss it, and Paul Conway said it was so clichéd it went past absurdity and became worth seeing.

It was bus No. 854. I wrote the number down for the retired brewer beside me who wanted to get out for a smoke and was afraid he'd lose track of the bus. He'd been in the Ordnance Corps during the War. When he got on the Holland-America Lines vessel they handed him a bedding roll. "What's this?" he asked. "It's your death blanket," the quartermaster said. That shook him.

After forty minutes the mountains closed in. The old man grew fidgety. "I need a smoke," he said, and added, "It's solid rock around Banff." He made it sound like good steady smoking ground. "You sketch good," he decided. The Fine Arts students across the aisle didn't think so. They began to talk about amateur art and didn't once look out of the window.

Stravinsky hated mountains, and with cause: they demand silence. Our town of Dehra Dun lies in the foothills of the Himalayas. The bus from Delhi takes six hours. For the first five one is speeding over flat land; conversation is a help. By the sixth hour the mountains appear, a band of blue in the distance across the mustard fields. They impose their silence. Then the forest swallows up the bus and a sigh escapes the passengers. There are still the Shiwalik Hills to cross, hills far older than the Himalayas, but a boundary has been crossed. The Rockies around Dead Man's Flats are younger than the Himalayas – they have a jagged, punkish look – but their silence is ageless.

It was hot in Banff. I slipped my jacket behind a bureau in the museum and walked upriver with an escort of yellow poplars.

Unlikely peaks crowded the sky; the top of one whole ridge was a giant rasp that had worked well on the underside of passing clouds. On the ice-green river there slid, around a sudden bend, a red canoe. The forest came up close. Here of all places I imagined grizzlies, but Canada had been exporting them to Romania, to Ceausescu's celebrated hunting grounds – before the hunter became the hunted. It was the unsociable skunk cabbage that startled me, burning like a votive candle on the black mirror of a marsh. On the way back I folded weeds into my book. The Indian Paintbrush kept its red for months but it was the unreachable skunk cabbage that lasted best.

At dinner my seafood was a long time coming; crustaceans will not be hurried. The couples at the table beside me were young and Japanese, the couple behind me old and English: master races future and past. There was hilarity at the Japanese table. Behind me the white-haired man said to his wife, "No, it's not sore, but it feels like it's coming up. I saw stars."

We rode back in total darkness. The Rockies were simply not there; thus Berkeley might refute Dr Johnson. I switched on my light and read in the Calgary *Herald* this letter:

> As one of the veterans for whom the president of No. 1 Branch of the Royal Canadian Legion professes to be showing "respect", may I say that I feel nothing but shame at the exclusion of turbanned Sikhs from certain of their premises? Are there no senior members of the legion to remind the peacetime executive of the mutual support Sikh and Canadian soldiers gave each other during the arduous Italian campaign? Does no one remember the crossing of the Moro or the Rapido?
>
> In those days it was my privilege, as a member of the Eighth Indian Division, to fight alongside and, on occasion, under the command of, Sikh officers. When our division was out of line, and we established a "pukka" officers' mess . . . protocol permitted the Sikh officers to wear their turbans at all times and in all places.
>
> Sikhs of all ranks decorated for bravery by King George VI wore their turbans in the state rooms of Buckingham Palace. It would seem to me that what is good enough for the home of our monarch and the officers' mess of a fighting unit should be good enough for the bar of a peacetime club.
>
> Peter Fitzgerald Moore, *Calgary*

I read and reread the letter. The whole argument proceeded like a model campaign, every element supporting the forward line, nothing superfluous, nothing out of place. I hoped the present Canadian army could do as well.

Back at the youth hostel there was a team of travelling tapers in my room: two Canadians and a Cockney.

"Tapers?" I asked.

Their job, the bigger and louder of the Canadians explained, was to finish a room with putty and Polyfilla so all the cracks were smoothed over: tapers came between the carpenters and the painters.

"You walk into a fuckun' room and the first thing you notice is they've got the fuckun' edges all wrong. I mean you look at that fuckun' wall right there. The whole fuckun' thing is wrong. See they've covered it over with angle wood, but they didn't fuckun' do it right in the first place."

The Cockney, Tim, said very little. He was their mascot, handsome to the point of feminine beauty. While the others talked, he groomed himself carefully and then borrowed the big man's after-shave, the more expensive of two bottles.

"See, he goes for the fuckun' Brazilian one!" the big man said indulgently. Tim grinned. It was his job, he knew, to attract the girls they were going out to find. They were all slightly drunk already and threatened to bring the girls back to the room. But late that night they crept back in without turning the light on, and tiptoed to their bunks like choirboys.

The next day I had a surprise. I'd been wavering between two opposite destinations: the town of Medicine Hat and the buffalo jump called Head Smashed-In. I wanted to take the train to Medicine Hat to get a taste of the Canadian Pacific Railway. In our school geography that railway was legendary. It didn't just bind together Canada's far-flung provinces: it *was* Canada.

"There is no train," the boy at the desk said.

"No *train*!"

"No."

And that was it, another boyhood myth dismantled. The endless track, and the river jammed with logs: that was Canada. And now neither image mattered. Al Fisk's rubber-tyre traffic had taken over both functions.

So Head Smashed-In it was.

In her salon Tina gave me a professional cut — too professional for my liking. *Whatever currents may have passed between us on the bus*, her look said, *I hereby switch off*. She held up the mirror — a clean slate — this way and that, money changed hands (enough for thirty haircuts in India) and we said goodbye.

Down the road was a bar with live music, Johnny V and the Houserockers. The waitress shouted in my ear, "The hot wings are on special!" and left half my money on the table. The wings, fresh from the pan and red with chilli sauce, were so hot I wept real tears and burned my lips as never in India. Johnny V sang, but the crowd turned to the windows. V could make his guitar sing, but he was up against a prairie cloudburst.

"Is it Vee?" I asked him as the hail rattled on the plate glass. He gave me his card. It said:

JOHNNY V

AND

THE HOUSEROCKERS

NOTHIN' BUT THE BLUES

1294 Ranchlands Road, NW Calgary, Alberta (403) 239-4864

V was born in Toronto. His father played guitar too. "He did some real heavy bluegrass, but he had to raise a family so he drove truck. I grew up listening to Ronny Hawkins, Roy Buchannan, but Otis Rush was my big guy."

"Do you do much touring?"

"Oh yeah. We're going to be heading down to the Carolinas, then we go to Europe. I'm waiting on my friend King Biscuit Boy. We go back a long way. He's played with some of the big names, and he plays like you wouldn't believe."

"Do you have a tape out I can buy?"

"I got an album out, but I done it myself and it's selling. That record has sold some copies, I'll tell you. But I do it myself. I don't fuck with distributors."

I knew how he felt. I had two books out and they had sold some copies. We were both trying to change our luck. When I complimented him he said, "Hey, I'm just a white guy playin' the blues."

The shuttle bus to the Greyhound was late. A well-heeled

103

couple stood waiting with me. When she learnt I was bound for the United States, tenting, the woman said, dispensing cheer, "What about loonies?" I said you took your chances. "Not that we don't have them up here," she added, but implied that Canadian loonies were not as loony. "You never know who's coming," she warned, mine jolly hostess. When the shuttle arrived the driver said, "Lethbridge? Holy Mackerel!" and drove at high speed to the terminal. As we swung in he called, "One for Lethbridge!" To me he said, "You go get your ticket," and grabbed my bags. I sprinted the length of the terminal and back and sprang onto the bus. It was a leap of faith: the hatches were down on the luggage bays.

The bags were there in Lethbridge. There was a hamburger war on in town so dinner was cheap. At breakfast three retired farmers' wives were catching up.

"Well, we sold our farm. But Bill gave his to his son. And every time he went up there they had a new car."

"We seen that happen too, but now Kyle he reckons Jim Tobin's a better farmer than his father."

I rented a car and drove along the Crow's Nest Highway through the country they had farmed. It was even yellower than up the pitchfork. Yellow, I decided, forsaking Arctic blue, was Canada's colour. It paled and ran when the wind rippled the wheat. There were few trees. From further south, Willa Cather recalls that prairie trees were so rare and beleaguered that "we used to feel anxious for them and visit them as if they were persons". I drove edgily — I hadn't driven on the right for years, and I'd had three dreams of crashing — but the car handled well. It was good to be able to stop when you pleased, Henry Ford's talking point. It gave you the illusion of control: once or twice I pulled over for no other reason. It must have amused Napi.

According to the Blackfoot, Napi is the creator of the world. This news would, in turn, amuse the raven Nekilstlas: he thought *he* created the world. For the coastal Indians Nekilstlas started with the clam; for the prairie Indians Napi created the nodding onion and the blue canna, balsam and silverweed, plants with edible roots and bulbs. But something was lacking, so he gave them the buffalo. There is another link between the two givers: both are tricksters. It's a sobering thought, the universe created by a joker, so the Blackfoot perfected a hoax of their own.

They chose a stage as wide as the prairie, and built an elaborate set. Next they dressed up as coyotes and wolves and crept up on the grazing buffalo, urging them gently towards two curious rows of rocks and makeshift thickets. The herd ambled along unsuspectingly till it was past the point of no return. At a signal a pair of braves leapt up on either side of the herd and began to whoop. The buffalo panicked and began to gallop down the improvised corral. One by one the rock piles showed screaming men. The herd thundered past, looking for a way out, but the lane was narrowing and where it ended was a cliff.

The buffalo went over in a mass and broke their necks. Down below, the squaws finished them off.

Head Smashed-In is an ancient buffalo jump, one of many on the prairie. The earth at the foot of the cliffs has yielded bones dating back many millennia. After the killing, the women removed the tongues and organs first, delicacies reserved for notables. There followed days of feasting. But there were also preparations to be made for winter, the meat dried on racks, the skin cured, a bladder turned into a bag, a splinter of bone into an awl. The hunt was not without its risk for humans. One local story tells of a young man who, not yet old enough for the hunt, concealed himself in a niche at the cliff face. He was found crushed to death when the mound of buffalos was cleared away. His head was smashed in.

There is a museum at the site. I talked to its director, Cliff Williams, a former Londoner, at closing time. The late afternoon sun came from behind us – the way the buffalo would have – and poured into the Oldman River valley at our feet. Swallows nesting in the cliff made loops in the golden air – dust from distant harvesters.

After the Spaniards introduced the horse, Williams said, buffalo-hunting techniques changed, but it was not the increased mobility of the hunters that wiped out the buffalo. That was part progress and part policy. As long as the buffalo roamed free, the Indians did too. Men like General Sherman ("the only good Indian is a dead Indian") saw the link and persuaded the US government that the only good buffalo was a dead buffalo. The buffalo count went from sixty million to a few thousand by 1900.

"Today," Williams said, "the pure plains buffalo does not exist. It merged into the coast buffalo. There are maybe 50,000 now."

The Head Smashed-In re-creation has helped put an end to the belief that Indians were socially disorganized. It took planning and cooperation to mount a buffalo hunt. The museum has bridged the gulf between Indians and whites at nearby Fort McLeod. The town earns some $3 million a year from visitors to the buffalo jump. As a rule, Williams said, Indians and whites went to school together but lost touch afterwards. Now they were on the same board and talking.

"Is there much intermarriage?" I asked.

"Not that much. Usually an Indian male to a white female. That way she gets native status, which a white man married to an Indian woman wouldn't get. Isn't that so, Doreen?"

Doreen, the Blackfoot shuttle-bus driver, came over. "Yes," she said, "the white woman and the children get status with the government, but not with the reserve."

"Where are the reserves?"

She pointed to a fence in the valley. "Beyond that is the Peigan reserve."

"Our staff are all Blackfoot," Williams said. "Peigan are part of the Blackfoot nation. For many of them it's their first contact with white people."

Next day I talked to one of them, Murray Small-Legs. Small-Legs, a big man, was born in the township of Pincher Creek west of the Peigan reserve. He had done two years of college.

"I understand Blackfoot," he said. "I picked it up through my folks, but my father said 'Teach them English,' and that's what I speak. In the 1940s when my parents were at school they'd be horsewhipped if they spoke Blackfoot. Now there are several young people on the reserve who can speak it, not just the elders."

I asked him about his religion.

"I would practise a native religion," he said, picking his words. "It's a matter of levels. At the highest stage there are sacred bundles, medicine bundles, but I'm at a much lower stage."

"Do you pray?"

"I choose not to speak of prayers."

"But would those prayers be addressed to Napi?"

"No, not to Napi. He is mythological. But legends are useful. They pass on morals."

I sat a while at the foot of the cliff till the shadow line passed my bench. The museum was closed and everyone had gone home. 6000 years ago the cliff was twice as high. I was sitting on generations of buffalo skeletons piled thirty foot deep. Earlier in the century the bone meal was sold as fertilizer. It was impossible on that serene evening to conjure up thundering hooves and falling bodies. The swallows flickered silently overhead and ground-squirrels popped in and out of their holes in a grass called needle-and-thread.

At the parking lot were a father and son from Pocatello, Idaho. John Kunicki, retired from an aluminium smelter out east, said his grandfather had been Polish, groom to an Austrian baron. He'd left a wife and child and come out to work in a steel mill. Later, they came out from Germany, travelling steerage. Dan Kunicki was a scientist at a nuclear testing facility near Pocatello. It sounded like an American progression: from steel to aluminium to atoms.

On the way back to Fort McLeod I picked up the Holy Family. Calvin and Malvina looked like children, but when I pulled over to his thumb I saw she was carrying an infant, their child. They'd been visiting her father at his farm on the Peigan reserve. Calvin came from a reserve up towards Calgary and worked in a family restaurant at Fort McLeod. He was hard to draw out; his wife said nothing the whole way, but smiled beatifically in the mirror. At the very end he said, "Where are you from?" and nodded silently when I told him. "What's the child's name?" I asked as they bundled out. Malvina spoke for the first time, proudly: "Bethany!"

At the free campground were the Kunickis, brewing coffee. Dan gave me his map of the West. At bedtime I saw a green beam light up the sky above the highway. It looked like a truck beam but it didn't pass by, and it was green. I stood up for a closer look. There was a tree in the way so I walked to the edge of the campground. Could it be?

It was the Northern Lights.

What I'd seen from my tent was the eastern extremity of a wide arc, the frayed end of a great billowing curtain of light. It furled and unfurled slowly, breaking up and forming again. Directly overhead was a second band of light, more diffuse, like

107

the Milky Way but running across it. Both bands appeared to be rising, the one overhead fading away as it rose. In a little while there was only the curtain with its fringe. The passing trucks made no difference, nor did the glow from a gas station in the distance. The fringe formed tassels that stirred as in a cosmic breeze.

A figure loomed up in the darkness, Dan Kunicki come to make sure I didn't miss the display. I asked him what caused the lights.

"There are gases up in the stratosphere," he said, "that get charged with energy. Those are your electrons flying through the gas and it just stimulates the gas, you know, excites it, and in order to get back to its rest state, its unexcited state, it emits light."

I said, "Ah hah," and he saw I needed more help.

"See, there's an energy exchange between particles. These energetic electrons run into the old gases and the energy from the particles goes into the gas and the gas in order to get rid of its energy emits the light."

"Ah *hah*." On my last night in Canada Napi was not only treating me to a display of the Northern Lights, he had a nuclear physicist on hand to explain them to me. "And the rippling effect?"

"I'm not sure what causes that. If you get one of those popular astronomy books it'll tell you."

"It's become two bands again."

"Yeah. This is a good display."

"I've never seen anything like it."

"There must be some real solar activity, like a big solar flare. Jeez, it might even start to ripple over *there*! You try watching it by yourself and it gives you the willies."

It was eerie even with the trucks going by and the glow of the town lights. Dan said goodnight and disappeared into the dark. Then a little yellow came into the fringe to warm the ghostly green and white. I leaned back against the Peigan barbed wire to get a better view. It was impossible to sleep. I kept the fire going and boiled up some water in the sooty saucepan. Half an hour later it started up again, the light sweeping across the sky and doubling back with sprays that reached directly overhead.

In the morning I bought the first loaf of bread at Fort McLeod. It was so hot and fresh I ate it plain and threw the old loaf into the middle of a vast flock of seagulls. At that hour it was a serious breach of the peace, and I left town at once. Back in Lethbridge I found the bus to the United States had gone. There was only one a day and it left early. I was put out, but there was some cheer at the local library: they had my first novel on display. The odds against it were so staggering I warmed at once to Lethbridge, Alexandria of the West.

At dinner I heard one waitress tell another, "Customer in that booth goes, 'My daughter was conceived thirty years ago to the day upstairs.' Guess it was some kind of bordello." I fell asleep working out a story where that would be the last line.

9

Cowboy Pictures

I was worried about the border crossing; citizens of India usually
are. At every border in the world there is the special twitch, the
stiffening, the treatment. The officer who has been relaxed and
affable now remembers his job, his country. The queue which
has been moving along briskly comes to a stop; those in it begin
to chafe. The businessman with briefcase peeps at his watch, the
blue-rinse granny sighs, backpackers with the right passports, eager
for adventure, slump where they stand. I have sometimes contemplated a small book, *Travels on an Indian Passport*, dedicate to my
stubborn Modestine.

In fact the neurosis begins earlier, when you are applying
for a visa. Ordinary post will not do: it must be a courier, the
more expensive the better. (Funeral parlours since ancient Egypt
have traded on this anxiety.) You demand a letter from your bank
manager; when it comes you mark it like a fanatic schoolteacher.
You begin to hate invisible men, harmless consular officials who
have not yet refused you entry. You stage border confrontations
in which you are by turns suave, ironic, tight-lipped, irate – and
your form is still in the travel agent's drawer.

The ten o'clock bus to Great Falls left at a quarter past.
Our driver was a brooding orang-utan, with a jungle of red-gold
hair on his forearms. The bus was his big car. He listened in
silence to the man behind him tell me about the Mormons.
When we passed Cardstone he pointed across the wheatfields
and said, "That's where the temple sits. There's still a lot
of bad feeling about that right now. The whole town sits on
native land. The way the Indians were treated in this country is

110

sickening. If you were white you got a hundred and sixty acres for the asking."

The man across the aisle from me nodded, a little embarrassed. He was a young building contractor. Two white-haired ladies behind him pricked up their ears. The orang-utan was letting down the side.

"Do you know," he went on, turning his head towards me but keeping his eyes on the road, "the status Indian could not vote until 1962?"

The contractor nodded helplessly and glanced at me.

"Oh yes," the orang-utan said, "they put them on reserves, they gave them the worst land." He seemed to speak of legendary peoples. "The conditions on those reserves were sickening. In the twenties and thirties when TB was around they were dying like nobody's business. The government dumped them in mass graves."

The contractor looked like he might say something. The old ladies were scandalized. For a red-haired man to talk so.

"And do you know," he turned his head a little further, "the government couldn't spend *five cents* to send their folks a letter to tell them what had happened. Oh yes. Canada doesn't have to point a finger at South Africa or any other country. Hardly a day goes by that you don't hear about some new atrocity they've uncovered." I pictured him scanning the paper greedily.

The old ladies weren't going to listen to any more of this. They went back to talking, loudly. The contractor came to the rescue.

"Do you know what Snowbirds are?"

"What?"

"Canadians who winter in Arizona." The joke was that the Canadian Air Force aerobatics team was called that too.

I asked him about the sect I'd seen in town: the men wore black outfits, including black cowboy hats, and the women wore long dresses and polka-dot head scarves. They were Hutterites, he said.

"In fact I'm building a church for them right now."

"I thought they'd do that themselves?"

"There was talk of a conflict of interest so they contracted it out. The men are called Black Crows 'cause they're always buying up stuff. They'll often do other people's harvesting. They have better machinery. Good people. We talk about Polka-Dot Thursday — that's when they come shopping."

We talked about Drumheller and the dinosaurs. There was a town up ahead, he said, where they'd dug up some specimens. They had a big plaster dinosaur by the side of the road.

"You want a picture?" the driver said when we got there. And he stopped the whole Greyhound across the road from the dinosaur. "It's a good museum," he said of the Tyrell, "but they don't give Creation equal billing. They talk about the millions of years the earth has been around but their theories are not consistent. There were seven days of Creation."

The contractor gulped. I looked out at the created world. There was the odd derrick pecking away at the prairie; the odd grain elevator kept watch. But neither the derrick nor the elevator, nor even the dinosaur, is Alberta's symbol. That, sentimentally, is the wild rose. The sentimentality is apt: Alberta is Canada's Texas, and no doubt the cowboys of Calgary, where many a Dallas oil man migrated, have matched the Texans with a song to their own rose. It's a charming flower (it tugged at Parkman's heartstrings as he followed the Oregon Trail far from home, and it has rambled as far north as Inuvik) but it is pink. I would have chosen the more piquant — and prairie-yellow — Black-eyed Susan that flourishes along every highway.

As we approached the border it was curious to reflect that nine out of every ten Canadians lived within a couple of hundred miles of it. I'd travelled 2000 miles so far with the tenth man. A satellite photo of the Canada–US border needs no dot-and-dash to mark the international boundary. Nowhere in the world is there a longer, sharper, straighter — or more notional — edge between two countries. The false colour shows the difference in land use on either side of the 49th parallel. North of that clean line stretch vast rectangles of open land; to the south, jammed up against the border is a crazy quilt of grainfields, hundreds of smaller holdings, the land parcelled out among many more sons. There are ten Americans for every Canadian, and it shows, not least from the sky.

Prairie painters dwell in a world of horizontals, but there is a painting by Claude Breeze in *Contemporary Canadian Art* that draws the line another way: vertically. The painting is called "Great Divide" and is part of his Canadian Atlas series. It's in two halves, with the divide down the centre. In a predominantly green painting, the left or western half is greener than the right. At the bottom of the eastern half, man's half, is a black lake, perhaps Lake Erie, which at the time of the painting was declared dead. A kind of black pall rises from this industrial corner and drifts across the painting to overhang nature's half. Man's half has all the engaging colours, and there is even at top right a suggestion in mauve of the Northern Lights, but there are malignant clots of black there too. At the far left of the painting is one of those tiny thunderstorms that flicker at the corner of Italian Renaissance paintings and Mughal miniatures alike, only this storm is apocalyptic: brimstone, comets, thunderbolts rain from the sky; the sky itself is falling. I took the whole painting as an allegory of acid rain. No doubt another reading would occur to the painting's owners, the Imperial Oil Company.

The Eskimo's cancer comes over the pole, the orang-utan said; to the south acid rain drifts over border and divide. Boundaries have ceased to have simple, classical meanings. Ever since the Fluted Point People spread southwards, nature has yielded to the boundary maker. The old ice-free corridor ran from north to south, leading Asiatics to America. The next wave of arrivals, from Europe, cut across it as wagon train and railroad ran from east to west. So deep did that thrust go into their being that a hundred years after the frontier closed Americans continue to think in terms of east and west. But the fact is the continent has undergone another geopolitical shift: for the first time since the land bridge the axis runs north-south again; the new stresses are vertical, not horizontal. The Free Trade pact reflects that shift, one that occurred with very little grinding while most Americans slept. It began when rail gave way to road – our Highway 4, which joined US I–15, was the concrete proof – but today the real field is in the air. The houses in that long Canadian huddle against the border face south for good climatic reasons, but their satellite dishes are not aimed to catch the sun. American TV has spared the US Army the marching.

"Why blur the map?" Keath Fraser asked with some anguish in Vancouver. "We've sold the equity," mourned Paul Conway in Edmonton. It's too late: the dream world of Canadians has been infiltrated. The silver sold, the pictures are the next to go.

"We're the blacks of North America," Fraser said, and I saw what he meant. Mexico, a far poorer country than Canada, is culturally – pictorially – far more secure. Its dreams are still its own. "Blacks," Fraser said, "know more than whites because they have to. Not only have they grown up with white TV, white films, white books, they've grown up invisible in the dominant culture. We have too. We know more than Americans do – we have to – and yet we've written less well of ourselves. Possibly because we know American culture better than our own."

One aspect of this competence is that often the best American economist or literary critic or biographer turns out to be Canadian, in the way the finest English novelist or poet or dramatist once turned out to be Irish. John Kenneth Galbraith, Northrop Frye, Leon Edel: Canadian *éminences grises*, but it's the same with actors, sportsmen, supermodels. Rambo, Canadians are quick to point out, is a Canadian creation: a necessary one perhaps.

I wanted Rambo on my side as we approached the border. At Coutts, Alberta, Canada, we left the orang-utan and transferred to an American Greyhound. "Blast from the past!" Joe the contractor said as we boarded the American bus, an early 1960s model.

A man with a badge got on and took a look at my passport. How long would I be in the United States? How much money did I have? Did I have a ticket out?

And that was it. I felt cheated. Three Englishmen had to leave the bus for further examination. We waited a long time for them, then drove to the diner across the way – in Sweetgrass, Montana, USA – to wait some more.

"In another ten years," Joe said as we sat at the bar and ate beef barley soup and crackers, "there won't be a border."

"You mean politically?"

"Oh no. Canadians and Americans think too differently. No economic border. You'll just drive through."

Joe was going down to Great Falls to meet his wife's plane. "She's an American from Nashville. We met on a blind date. It's cheaper for her to take a domestic flight and drive across the border." He seemed conscious of being on foreign soil. "We in Canada don't have anything like the race problems the US has. Down in Nashville they hate the blacks. My father-in-law hates them. My brother-in-law has to deal with them in the force, and he hates them."

114

US Interstate 15 ran across a bald plain. Then came dry dun swells dotted with cattle. Marlboro country. The tough cigarette, Joe said, had been a low-selling brand aimed at women until the admen changed its image. Cowboy pictures still worked. The land lay so drear it would have taken a brave artist, among the early Europeans, to copy it out. No wonder Frenchmen painted Arcadie with Indian nymphs and swains and bison that looked like sheep. Not till the age of Cook and his botanist painters does the North American landscape begin to yield to the European eye.

"Conrad!" the driver called. All the shops in Conrad had black stars in the windows. "That's support for the Gulf War," Joe explained. A pickup truck wore a yellow seal painted on the door: THE GREAT SEAL OF THE STATE OF MONTANA. The licence plates said: BIG SKY COUNTRY.

Big. Great. Black stars. Already the rhetoric was piling up. Our own bus and driver looked harder worked, less innocent than their Canadian counterparts. I felt we'd entered a more punishing country. MIDWAY BAR said a giant sign at Vaughn. The only other moisture was a high spray of cloud like foam on an invisible beach.

At Great Falls I stood in the door of my motel room and stared. I counted twelve towels in the immaculate bathroom. There was even (to tempt the tent-dweller from his ways) a writing table. I tested the massage-jet showerhead scrupulously and watched day-time TV – surely a greater sin than daytime sleep (St Benedict) or daytime lovemaking (D.H. Lawrence) – from the Montana-sized bed. Halfway through a black-and-white movie with the Mexican spitfire Lupe Velez I spirited Velez away (the remote device said "Assembled in Mexico") and unpacked. The room compelled order and instilled a sense of belonging. It even sparked the wild thought that one need travel no further.

Darkness had fallen when I stepped out. I walked past familiar houses along a street I knew in my bones. The trees were familiar, the very sidewalk was familiar, and yet I had not been in Great Falls before. And then it struck me. That air of quiet inconsequence, the tranquil ordinariness of the moment, had wrenched me back to a Kalamazoo evening. Walking through the twilight I was overcome by the sweetness of it, by a painful nostalgia for the town that had almost become my own. The windows I passed were yellow pictures of domestic life. In one a ceiling fan

115

turned above invisible presences. Dishwashing noises came from the kitchen window. The fan was something new – more India than America – but the house could have held the family I came to love. Perhaps the sense of recognizable life went deeper, to the small towns of my childhood. Underneath the difference in the shape of the houses and trees was a spirit I knew intimately, bred in the enduring patience of unchanging things.

With the lightness of being came a sense of the solidity of place, a sense that grew with daylight. The city looked generations older than those I'd been passing through. It showed in the trees, but also in the buildings. Most of the remarkable buildings in the Canadian West are new, of concrete. In Great Falls I struck brick, brick of a hard clean edge. The post office used it like stone, the Masonic Lodge with stone. It gave the public buildings an Egyptian severity. A milder, wetter climate might have softened those edges; in Montana they kept their sharpness and that air of slightly remote incongruity, like Pharaohs among cowboys. A truer solidity was in the houses – good wood cunningly joined – and in the sidewalks. The best of the sidewalks were laid by the Miracle Concrete Construction Company in 1912. (The name and date were impressed along with the street name at corners, a detail later abandoned.) It was the newer, paler sections that showed cracks, so a recipe, or something, had been lost along the way.

They were still boardwalks when Great Falls' most illustrious citizen came to town. Charles Marion Russell was born to money in 1864 in St Louis, the jumping-off point for journeys west. He came to Montana in his teens. He worked as a night-wrangler on a ranch, spent a winter with the Blood Indians in Canada, painted the last of the West, and ended up in bronze on the lawns of the C.M. Russell Museum. "You can paint a horse and a cow and a cowboy and Indian better than any man who ever lived," said Will Rogers in 1926, the year Russell died, and that has remained the popular feeling. Russell's work was avowedly illustrative; he is a kind of Rockwell in boots. But the paintings have an energy and seriousness that carries them past sentimental evocations of a vanished past. Singly and together, they have a filmic sweep, and in a sense all cowboy movies are animated versions of Russell's work. He was an eyewitness, the bridge between the real thing and the movie camera, which came along a quarter-century too late.

116

I lunched in the shade of a spreading tree outside his log-cabin studio, an all-American lunch: beef jerky, cheese stick, V-8, and a Hershey bar, once ten cents, now fifty. The heat bent the Hershey bar into a barber's strop. Inside the modern gallery next door is a lifetime's work, from early pen and ink sketches like *The Horse Wrangler* to the late *Spearing a Buffalo* of the year before his death.

"This is a famous painting," said a lady in front of *Sitting Bull*. And in fact the memorable works of the Cowboy Artist are of Indians. One of the finest, *Attack on the Red River Carts*, is seen not from the perspective of the defending whites but from that of their attackers. Eleven years after the winter he spent with the Blood he could produce a haughty bust of their celebrated Chief Crowfoot, a man who ignored Riel's risky appeal and steered an independent course for the Blackfoot confederacy.

Cowboy or Indian, Russell's was a man's world. Even in *The Beauty Parlour*, it's the warrior who's being made up by his squaw. And only in *Indian Maiden Braiding her Hair* is there a glimpse of anything approaching sexuality. The same woman appears in the Kiowa series and in *Indian Maiden at her Toilet*, properly clad, her features not Europeanized after the fashion of calendar Indians.

Russell married a woman half his age who was in many ways the making of the CMR legend. Nancy Cooper became his manager, asked prices that made her homebody husband wince, and by the last decade of his life had made him the highest-paid artist in the world. Big money, bad art: it must have haunted the man, if not the wife.

"This is the one the Elks donated to the museum," a man told his wife, "because they couldn't afford the insurance."

We were standing before *The Elk*, a big romantic canvas worth over a million dollars at the time the bills were deemed too high. Such was the popularity of his paintings that Russell began to introduce beside his signature (and his trademark buffalo skull) his copyright, a fortuitous circle C.

My favourite was *Brother Van Hunting Buffalo*, which shows a black-cassocked cleric in a flat black hat (the only flat hat in the West) galloping alongside his prey, as he fires a pistol. The painting is inscribed "To Brother Van Orsdel from his friend C.M. Russell" and it typifies Russell's tendency to paint for his friends.

117

He described himself as "a good mixer" and has remained in lore one of the boys, a bluff yarner always willing to put on the pan for a mate in his log cabin. "Simple cowboy fare of beans," said my catalogue, "maybe some bacon and real, Honest to God, cowboy biscuits." In between these simplicities he travelled the world with his wife, yearning for home while she saw to his exposure. Among his foreign pieces are two waxworks, *Elephant with Rider* and *East Indian Cart*, accurate renditions as ever, and there was also a vein of European medievalism with fools and knights. Later he turned out coaches and highwaymen. Friends kept his illustrated letters. From New York ("the big camp") Russell sketches the city's progress from Dutch to English to "Mose Kauffman's cousins"; from Florida he tells of pirates, and in England ("this is shure a cold bread country") he reports on the instruments in the Tower. The picturesque was never far, and the Russells were never short of Christmas cards. Towards the end these began to feature a familiar figure on horseback: CMR himself.

"Was he a good painter?" I asked the museum's director, Lorne Render, the next day.

"He was a good painter of the West," he said. "He had his strong suits. He was a keen observer. His oils are good and faithful depictions of the land. There are a lot of sketches that show his spontaneity, his speed and fluency. He's a good storyteller. There's often a bit of a surprise in the paintings, a wolf waiting around the corner, an automobile about to run over a fallen rider.

"He's out to tell the viewer something about the West, to convey his feeling for the subject, his love of the country. He's very much a man of the West, even though he was born in St Louis."

"What is it that brings people here?"

"I don't know. They're looking for opportunities. Russell was. It's probably the job."

It was the job that brought Render to Great Falls from Toronto. He'd spent fourteen years in Canada, but was raised in Oregon. A slim man with a light tread, he appeared beside me at precisely ten o'clock and led me to a conference room where a deal table shimmered between us. When thinking he folded his hands and leaned a cheek on them, a man of gentle and diffident charm.

"I don't know," he said. "The people were, and are, fiercely
. . . proud. They have a real love of the land. They're . . ." (he
flinched at the impending cliché but decided there was no other
word) "independent, hard workers, honest. Russell was like that
too."

"Do you see a development in his work? I found the first
and the last pictures much the same."

"There *is* a development." He got up and fetched down a
catalogue for me. "In some of his very early pieces – there's
The Wrangler for instance from 1890 – you don't see the
later sophistication in the use of the paint, in the shaping and
modelling. At a certain point in his career he started to get very
prolific. We have a few pieces in our vault that are not up to his
own standards."

"What's left of the West?"

"There's a little bit of the romance left. What's left is up here.
Colorado is now an extension of the West Coast. Robert Redford
has a ranch hereabouts."

"I understand the Japanese have too."

"They have indeed!"

"What keeps you here?"

"I've only just arrived. I like the land, the people. There's
a sense of personal freedom here, of intellectual freedom, from
fashions, say – being just back from the East. A sense of emotional
release that's refreshing and . . . *good*, if I can use the word."

"Do you find the United States changed? Do you think Americans are different creatures from Canadians?"

He blinked and smiled and spoke slowly. "I think there are
enormous differences. Americans are very much more independent.
Canadians are more socialistic. I don't use that in a pejorative sense
– parts of that are very good, their health care for example. But there
are serious drawbacks. Their government tends not to control its
expenditure. Provincial governments run deficits regularly. State
– and municipal – governments here don't. I think also Canadians
are more insecure. I can give you a simple example – it may sound
silly, but on their letters they'll put *Toronto, Canada*. Down here
we'd write *Great Falls, Montana*. There's a much stronger sense of
patriotism here, of country – this country."

"Is that a good thing?"

"I think it's a good thing, though it made me uncomfortable when I first came back. It holds people together. They have a common understanding of their purpose. Part of it is a greater sense of . . ." (he rested his cheek on folded hands) ". . . pride!"

He heaved me a weary administrator's sigh and handed over the catalogue as a souvenir. I was already in the museum so I wandered back among the paintings for a free round. There was more to it than Russell. There was O.C. Seltzer's Montana century, scores of tiny paintings that fit a single wall. It was a Western peepshow, the titles alone a potted history: *Sitting Bull Making Medicine* (he looks like a Shiva mendicant); *Sir Alexander Mackenzie on the Peace River, 1793*; *Lewis and Clark at the Great Falls of the Missouri*.

Nearby were two bronzes by the actor and sculptor (and painter, and cabinet-maker) George Montgomery. One of the sculptures was *Custer's Final Moments*; the other, *The Legend*, a bronze John Wayne, had been presented to the Reagans. Beside it was a letter from the former president:

> *Dear George,*
> *Nancy and I found your truly magnificent sculpture awaiting us at the ranch . . . There are no words to express our gratitude.*
> *We are both lovers of Western art . . .*
> *Thanks again from the bottom of our hearts and our warmest regards.*
> > *Sincerely,*
> > > > > *Ron.*

Cowboy to cowboy, with thanks for a cowboy, the letter works. Anywhere else "the bottom of our hearts" would look corny, an oversize stetson; here it fits snugly.

I returned to the motel keeping to the residential streets. Midtown Great Falls had a dreariness about it, with cheek-by-jowl beauticians and funeral parlours; death, a confidant in Asia, is a lover in America. At dinner the taco salad was a titanic deep-fried shell fatally loaded with cheeses that would have baffled a Mexican. But it came with a sauce to ravish his heart. I recalled Tina the hairdresser speaking of *her* salsa recipe as if every Canadian had one. In one respect the three countries were already integrated.

I took a night walk along Central Avenue. It was wide and brightly lit and deserted: the width of a Western street shrivels the pedestrian, the way skyscrapers shrink him out East. The cars that cruised by were sleek black Buicks or blunt black Bronco wagons with a black star in the window. They were doing 20 mph. According to my map there was no daytime speed limit in Montana. Motorists, the law elegantly stated, might do "whatever is reasonable and proper". I decided to rent a car. The Freedom Isuzu dealer I'd asked about buying a cheap car said he wouldn't advise it.

"Rent one," he said. "Anything under fifteen hundred dollars has been rode hard and put away wet."

The Chevy Celebrity had Utah plates. I was returning a Salt Lake City car to headquarters. To cut costs I turned down the insurance and drove carefully south.

Ten miles out of Great Falls I left the freeway to follow a gravel road that ran along a winding stream. It was the Missouri, much reduced from the wide river that ran through town. For the next 200 miles it would get narrower and narrower: I was following it to its source. It was an appealing notion. I slowed right down to keep an eye on the dwindling waters as they shone between stands of willow and balsam poplar. I missed writing up my bus journal so I began a tape addressed to Master Basho and drove lazily with the windows down to let in the warm air and the crickets' drone.

At Cascade I realized it was Friday. I had letters to pick up in Helena and it was mid-afternoon. I got back on the freeway and drove blinkered by purplish bluffs of granite. The Chevy got me to Helena at a quarter to five. At ten to I found the American Express had moved. I asked for directions. "You can't miss it," a woman said and pointed. I missed it. At five past I found the office and stumbled in like the lone survivor of a notable massacre. The staff looked up and blinked. They didn't close till 5.30.

The mail was a fat wad, worth the race. The girl who served me wanted the stamps. I would have given her whole countries. I stocked the car with a week's groceries and went looking for a campground. It was dark when I found Black Sandy by Lake Helena. "All yours," the keeper said, and recommended the last pine. Across the lake was York, the town named for Captain Clark's black servant. There was a painting by Russell called *York* that I wanted to see in town. It shows the man standing bare-chested

121

at the centre of an Indian lodge, facing the chief, who is seated on his painted buffalo skin with Lewis and Clark on either side. He is surrounded by a circle of squatting villagers, old and young, braves and squaws. An old crone leans on a staff by the fire, goggle-eyed, a young boy shins up a lodge pole to get a better look. Behind York stands an Indian who has laid a hand on him and is inspecting his own fingers to see if the black comes off. The smoke from the open fire fills the lodge and rises to a hole in the centre of the roof.

I pitched under the pine and supped on Turkish apricots and pistachio nuts so highly salted they stung the lips. Then I read Basho till book and flashlight slipped from my hands.

Next morning I dumped a wet tent in the trunk and named the Chevy Sora after Basho's companion, that invisible who travels with his master and sometimes carries his load while the master speaks only of *I*. I was getting lazy and liking it. Breakfast was Mexican: fajitas had arrived at McDonalds (when all seemed lost), shredded chicken wrapped in flour envelopes, soft like the finest chapatis.

The State Historical Society was closed, so that was it for *York*, but there was another museum hard by on a hill. It was in fact more shrine than museum, dedicated to the piety that nationhood inspires. I wandered at will in a state capitol that was – like a church – virtually empty. In the Senate chamber I sat on rich yellow leather and examined Russell's *When the Land Belonged to God*, a copy. Next door in the House of Representatives was an original, *Lewis and Clark Meeting the Flathead Indians at Ross' Hole*. Again the perspective is that of the Indians, with the explorers lost in a giant canvas, a small intrusion to the extreme right. As a statement it is historically accurate and morally pointed; the work was commissioned by the House and one can imagine Russell composing it with especial thought. As a painting it answered the first question I put to Lorne Render. "Is he a good painter?" He is, here. In the midst of blustery frescoes that celebrate the taming of the West – the driving in of yet another Last Spike; the ratification of another constitution that left the Indians out – Russell keeps his head, chooses dignity and proportion.

The rest of Helena was downhill from there. I strayed into Last Chance Gulch, the original mining camp now turned into quaint shops, then drove on out in search of the Missouri.

10

The Game Department

The Missouri rises at Three Forks and flows due north as far as Great Falls before turning around and flowing back down. In my school atlas it was always a mystery when a river flowed upwards, as did the Nile or the Mackenzie, instead of down, as the Ganges or the Mississippi. Even the Amazon, flowing sideways, seemed in perpetual danger of rolling back and flooding its many tributaries. A consequence of this top-northerly fixation is that a journey from the Yukon to the Yucatan looks much simpler running down the map, from top left to bottom right. The slope must have been at the back of my mind as I planned the trip. With the upside-down map of New Zealand cartographers I might have had second thoughts.

The Chevy, Sora, once blue, was now yellow from the slush it took on at Black Sandy. It was still a showery sort of day with ragged black clouds scudding the opposite way fast enough to make me doubt my speedometer. The traffic was pickups with men in stetsons. The car set up a judder at 60 so I began to dawdle. I stopped at Prickly Pear Creek for its name and watched the light cast violet shadows on indigo hills. The whole range was a bolt of shot silk. The road crossed and recrossed the Missouri, which got younger and lovelier at every turn. A flock of starlings sitting on the blacktop rose in a cloud as I drove through and settled in the rear-view mirror. Dairy cattle, black, red, white, and mottled brown, shone like salad beans. The sun was low at six; a month ago it had set at midnight.

Three Forks sounded like a good place to eat. I needed a hot meal for a cold night. Jonathan's on Main Street sounded wrong. The Headwaters Café looked better but was up for sale,

123

and the Longhorn Café, best of all – I salivated and sped up – was closed. So Jonathan's it was, where the salad bar offered American motley: coleslaw with peanuts and raisins and bacon bits, cold beans, and grated carrot and marshmallows in green Jello. When I was a boy American missionaries brought the gospel and the Jello salad to our small community and it was hard to say which was more popular.

There were deer at the Lewis and Clark Campground, brown shapes in a brown night. A high wind came up and blew the clouds away but then kept blowing. The water pipes had been torn up. I brushed my teeth from a trickle at a tap that dripped all night onto a stone and into my dreams. Once I awoke to the sound of coyotes howling and took a leak under a sky hung with blue stars.

The morning was quiet and still. The flannel weed by the roadside stood rigid and the sagebrush kept its counsel. A sign at the park gates said they opened at 8.30. I strolled up and down the empty road and soaked up the pale morning sun. At 8.29 the ranger's jeep appeared. Punctuality in the wilderness! From the top of the track I saw the Jefferson River, the most westerly of the three forks. It flowed just below the shrunken campground; I might have heard it during the night. The rock face swept up at my shoulder, antlered with dead juniper and the delicate fringed shrub that the Sioux and Cheyenne called women's sage and used for tea.

I took the road south, down the Madison valley. In Harrison the general store wore festive bunting, but there was nobody about to celebrate. The loose end of the bunting cord tapped a random code on its aluminium pole. It was the only sound that noon in Harrison. I bought the only roll of slide film in the store and took a photo of the Tobacco Root Mountains fringed by the colourful string of plastic flags; on the post office roof next door the Stars and Stripes made the last in the series.

Ennis had a turfed tentsite, green and springy, washing machines, and the Wildlife Museum of the West. It also had at the head of Main Street a shop selling fudge, so I braced my self for fellow tourists. They were there, in galleries and curio shops, and up and down Main Street. I passed one family going up one way, then crossed the street and met them again going the other way; we smiled uncomfortably, like people caught trespassing.

In the Wildlife Museum were all the dread beasts of the Rockies, safely dead. The exhibits were the work of Larry and Stephanie Altimus, professional taxidermists, whose workshop was behind the museum. The Altimus team were hunters who had shot, with bow and gun, most of the animals on display. The grizzly, of course, greets you: a large black 500-lb male, five years old, beside a blonde female of twenty-two, "quite old", the plaque says, for a grizzly. You wind past a mountain lion preying on a mule deer buck; pronghorn antelope in rut; a whitetail buck also in season, his head lowered and his neck stretched out; a massive buffalo bull "harvested" by Stephanie Altimus; the wapiti or Rocky Mountain elk that also breed in September, the male bugling threats and endearments as he gathers his harem; the Shiras moose; the black bear, the Dall sheep, the bighorn, the mountain goat. And looking on, from up a tree or halfway out of a hole, the lesser creatures of the forest, the owls and martins, ptarmigans and badgers, squirrels, porcupines, racoons. The Altimuses were down in Utah, hunting, but were expected back that night.

Outside the Ennis Café was a pickup truck with one of those therapeutic wooden-bead seat spreads. Had the West come to this? I must look out for wooden-bead saddles. Beside the pickup was a cop car; the sheriff was in the café on a barstool.

"Anything exciting goin' on, Billy?" the waitress said. "Did you ever ketch the guy as stabbed Neil?"

The sheriff said something I missed.

"I don't know," the waitress went on. "There's some real weirdos. I hope it's a cold cold winter. That'll get rid of a lot of them. I gotta go home and make cookies for my boyfriend for his birthday."

Behind her the owner was talking on the phone. "Don't go to hospital, Jake. You *know* you get sick when you go there."

"Goes to Soddy Arabia at 5.30 in the morning, comes to see me at four."

After dark I had dinner at Betty's Café, a set menu.

"*I*-talian bean soup," said the cowboy at the next table to his wife, reading from the menu. He held the card up and read as if reciting a pledge. *I, Talian Bean Soup, do solemnly swear . . .*

*

125

In the morning I returned to the Wildlife Museum. The Altimuses were back from their hunt.

"It was ninety-four degrees in southern Utah and hot, just terrible hot," Larry Altimus said. He sat on a stool at a workbench, a man of maybe forty. "I called the girl who was runnin' the museum yesterday and she says: 'Oh, the mountains are white and it's forty-five degrees!'"

I asked him how he got started.

"We've been workin' at it for nineteen years, collecting the animals. They're pretty much all taken by my wife and I. In Montana you have to draw special permits to hunt most of the species, and so it's tough to draw the tag. We had to wait till we had enough tags to build the diorama. And then trying to acquire the small animals like the little bighorn lamb and the buffalo calf is difficult."

"The calf died naturally?"

"Yes, and almost all the small ones have. Or for some we buy 'em at confiscation sales from the game department. Maybe a mother bear might be hit on the highway and the little bear dies. They take that small animal and they present it back to the public at a sale. They might be confiscated for whatever reason – poached, illegal kills, over-limit, whatever. That little bighorn lamb took us fifteen years to get. That was hit on the highway and it was mangled just terrible but we put it back together. It was quite a job. Most all of the small animals are. I got way more hours in the little buffalo calf than I do in the large bull standing next to him."

"What's inside them?"

"They all have a urethane foam mannequin under 'em and there's a lot of foam alteration to get it to fit, not so much in a standard pose like this deer – this is for a customer in Texas – but for a lot of things in the museum."

"Like the deer leaping over the log that has its hind leg raised up?"

"M-hm, yeah, it's only on one foot that deer."

"Where do you get the mannequins?"

"All over the United States. Like here's a catalogue and it's full of hundreds of different kinds of mannequins."

"They look strange without their antlers on!"

126

"Or anything, yeah! Here . . . ostrich, penguin, nyalas, ocelot, oribis, lizards, monkeys, lions, cougars, every animal there is."

"What would one of these cost — that hippo for example?"

"I would guess probably three or four hundred dollars."

"Would some of these be for do-it-yourself types?"

"There are a few amateur-type folks but most everyone brings it to a professional. People think it's a kind of dying art but it's really going the other way. Years ago head mounts used to be pretty poor-looking. They used the original skull and they sewed up the neck a little bit and then just stuffed it full of anything they could find. I've torn old mounts apart with rags, newspapers, straw, just anything. I'll show you."

He took me to a room further in.

"These are the old mounts. They were neck mounts, they never had the full shoulder. Now they're all sculpted out, and they all have turns in 'em where the old ones were always straight ahead. This one you can see I've split open, and there's the original jawbone inside there. This one's stuffed full of excelsior. And they didn't tan anything, they just pickled it, so the hair won't stay in, it'll crack and split apart. Everything now is commercially tanned, at a tannery in San Francisco. This is just like a fur garment, same process, only they tan it with the head on. Here's the head, this pronghorn animal, and there's the eye, eyelashes, ears, everything's intact, everything's perfect."

Perfection in death was another American link with ancient Egypt. I was handling a mummy. "They leave the eyelashes on!"

"Oh yeah, all the whiskers are left in place. And we soak this in water and that relaxes the leather and brings it back to the original size, it'll stretch out, and then we take the antlers — this is all that we keep of the original animal other than the skin — and we bolt the antlers onto the top of the mannequin there." His movements, like his descriptions, were precise and accurate. "And we'll take that skin and slip it over there and sew it up the back. The eyes are glass eyes made in Germany. They used to have an old piece of tin inside the ear to hold the shape of the ear. Now it's all plastic." He unpacked a plastic ear. "This is what a mule-deer ear looks like, or an elk ear. The jaw sets — this is for a wolf here. The teeth are plastic, the tongue's rubber, just pops

127

out there, just a piece of rubber!"

"I bet the old guys envy you this new-fangled stuff."

"Oh yeah! They had a hard time of it."

"Was your old man a taxidermist?"

"No, no. I learnt the trade from a fellow down in Billings that had been at it for forty-three years when I went to work for him. Our goal was to get this museum finished before he passed away and I didn't make it by a month. His wife has given us these birds of prey he mounted. He was the premier taxidermist of his time."

"What was his name?"

"His name was Art Spurway."

We went back to the studio. "I have some glass eyes here," he said. "These are an elk. See they paint the colour in from the back side and then bake it right in."

"That's beautiful!"

"Yeah, they're very nice, they're very accurate. We still use the German glass. After we mount the animal, then Stephanie, my wife, will go around and do all the finish work. This here has all to be cleaned up and redone to make it look wet and clean. If you look at the deer here, the eyelid looks moist and the nose is finished. The inside of the nostril is finished. It takes about a week for 'em to dry. The mannequin alteration will take a couple of days; it takes us about two days to sew the skin on; and then a couple of days to build a rock and do the finish on 'em."

"Then you go out and gather the right sort of grass to match the habitat?"

"Exactly. I got a photo album right here. Here's a life-size wolverine. And we'll put snow in the scene 'cause they're a winter-type animal. Same with mountain sheep. They're walking down a ledge, so we'll build a rock and put moss there and so forth. But most people have shoulder mounts done so there isn't a lot you can do with that. Very few go for a life-size."

"Is that because of expense?"

"Yes, but the main reason is space. They don't have room. We have one fella here in town's got several life-size African animals. He's got a shoulder mount of an African elephant in his place."

"How are the numbers keeping up?"

"Our game populations are doing far better than they have for years and years and years. We talk to the oldtimers and they say we had no pronghorn antelope in this valley. Now we have hundreds and hundreds and hundreds. We had no whitetail; we have completely unlimited permits now. When we moved here seventeen years ago they had fifty cow elk licences available. Last year they sold two thousand three hundred!"

"How do you tell the age of that twenty-two-year-old grizzly?"

"They pull a tooth and they section that tooth and they can read the layers of cement laid down each year like rings in a tree. Lots of animals like the sheep, goat, and bison, you can read their age in their horns. Like this mountain goat here, this one is: one, two, three, four, five, and then you add a year and a half when he first grew from a yearling. So he's six and a half."

Altimus meant to become a science teacher. But that year Art Spurway fell ill at the wrong time – fall. If you miss your fall season as a taxidermist you lose a year's income. Altimus went to his hospital bed with a proposition. He knew how to skin animals. He would take in the work if when Spurway got well he'd teach him the trade. Spurway wasn't sure: it took time and trouble to train someone, and then he usually set up on his own and took away your customers. But he had no choice: the harvest had begun.

"What's the best part of the job, being out hunting or . . . ?"

"Oh, I like the outdoor part, not so much for the shooting but just for the experience of seeing the wildlife. The business part, I like seeing the excitement of the people I deal with. Hunting is very very expensive, so for a lot of people it's a once-in-a-lifetime experience. Most of these hunts are costing these people several thousand dollars. In Canada and Alaska it's not uncommon for ten thousand to be spent on one animal. Our time to hunt is now."

"You get a pretty long winter."

"It is, it's pretty harsh. I like that. I like the winters because it's quiet here, it enables us to get a lot of work done. During the fall there are hunters in and out, a lot of stories, a lot of phone calls. I like to educate people that taxidermy is not boiling skulls and stuffing heads and it's not a gruesome, smelly business. And you know there's a lot of people swayed by the belief that animals

129

are in trouble. That's not the case at all. The numbers are rising and the quality is too. Like this hunt in Utah. We spent eight days, backpacked in, and saw forty-two mature mule-deer bucks. They were better deer than I've ever taken."

"You've got some fine specimens in there."

"Well, thank you. We spend a lot of time at it. We're selective. It's our life, that's what we do."

"Is this the last of the West, here?"

"To a certain extent, it's alive and well. A lot of people make their living hunting, fishing, trapping. There's a lot of ranchers, a lot of cowboys, genuine cowboys that live the life. They're not drugstore cowboys that come up from southern California, buy boots and hat and they're cowboys."

A group of men came through the museum door.

"You done most of that taxidermy in there?"

"All of it."

"You do some nice work."

"Well, thank you. We been at it a while."

"How's the fishin' in these parts?"

"I've been down in Utah huntin' deer, so if you want the latest scoop I'd get down in one of the tackle shops and ask 'em just what's goin' on and they can tell you to the last bug. Howdy, Kevin!"

" 'lo, Larry. How you been?"

"I'm good. How you been?"

"Good."

"Good."

The room was filling up. "Where do you go from here?" I asked Altimus.

"If we go anywhere we'll go North, to Canada, to the Northwest Territories. We're looking at some places up there."

So once again the West was moving North, just when the Snowbirds were flocking the other way. I drove west myself, fourteen miles to Virginia City, an old mining town. Old Main Street had been repaired but not restored. Weathered shopfronts kept their peeling signs. The boardwalks had lost their verandah cover, but a strange skeletal frame for the roof guttering was still in place. On the front of a variety store, purveyors of exotica, was a faded life-size painting of an oriental soldier, a Turk perhaps from his pantaloons and cummerbund, his sheathed scimitar, his curl-toed shoes and possibly (that part had not worn well) a fez. One or two modern souvenir shops were open, selling coffee mugs which showed picturesque Main Street with its souvenir shops full of coffee mugs. But it was plain the season was over. The county museum was closed.

I turned around at the old railway station, its narrow-gauge track still intact. Sleepers from a vanished branch line were strewn about the silverbrush, more grist for the coffee mill. Up on Boot Hill the cemetery and ball park overlooked the town. On a still higher hill civic pride had cut a large V. The game stands were daubed tribally by various supporters: the Elks, Gus Harvey Custom Welding, the Silver Dollar Bar and Steak House. Someone who was not going to play along had painted FREE NELSON MANDELA in large letters. But Mandela was free and the shock of those words, there, was like more exotica, another foreign soldier frozen in time and domed to fade and peel. The Elks had their own patch in the cemetery too, though for once their BPOE – Best People On Earth – should have read BPIE.

The city museum was empty save for the old lady on duty there. I asked her how long she'd lived in Virginia City.

"Half my life," she said. "I'm eighty."

"That's all my life. I'm forty."

"I started this job after I quit at the courthouse. I could have gone on, but that having to be there at eight o'clock in the morning . . . So I quit at seventy-five."

"At seventy-five you're entitled to sleep in!"

"That's what I thought. I thought 'Fiddlesticks! Give it away, give it away.' I'll be honest with you. These computers bothered me. I thought it's not good for an old hellion like me."

I noticed an old copper-horn gramophone and went over for a closer look.

"I've been here four years," she said, "and there are still things I haven't seen. My grandmother had a phonograph like that only it had a black horn. One record we kids used to play was 'The Preacher and the Bear'. We wore it out . . . ha! 'The Preacher and the Bear'."

"Winter must be quiet here," I said.

131

"We have fun. It fills up with snow. In the summertime some of the older people get out there and have a shootout in the middle of the street. Stupid nuts! Showin' off to beat the Dickens. Pretend they're killed and everything. Fifty-, sixty-year-old coots. They jump on their horses and away they go. Bandits. 'Oh he got away! Oh goody, goody, goody!' "

Five men who didn't get away were Haze Lyons, Clubfoot George Lane, Boone Helm, Frank Parish, and Jack Gallagher. They were hanged on 14 January (it would have been a cold day) 1864, and buried up on Boot Hill. One of O.C. Seltzer's miniatures marked the event and the museum had preserved their headboards. They stood in a grim row, just leaning up against the wall.

"Up on Boot Hill there was thirteen graves and gradually you know there was finally only five markers left, so they brought 'em down."

"Who runs this museum?"

"The Vigilance Club. That's a man's civic club here in town for business people."

A note above the headboards said the city's vigilantes had *disposed of twenty-two road agents in a two-month campaign* to clean out the camps. I began to see what the Ennis waitress meant when she told the sheriff she wanted a cold cold winter. The present-day Vigilance Club of Virginia City was *Dedicated to the Preservation of Historical Lore and Monuments*. They'd saved the headboards of the men their forefathers had disposed of. Their emblem looked at first glance like a parrot in a hoop. Close up I saw it was an old-style six-gun and a noose.

Some people came in and the old lady turned to greet them. To me she whispered, "You don't have to go." We talked a little longer, then I said I had a long way to go. She said, "Sure glad to talk to you," and cupped my hand in hers.

I drove back to Ennis, crossed the Madison River and headed south on 287. There was snow on the mountains, wheat in the fields, and corn on the radio. "God is watching us," sang a country lady. Other gods appeared: a high wind had turned all the clouds into flying saucers. A fleet of them went ahead like an escort, companions on an empty Monday road. Now and then a solitary barn told of dryland farming. Silver irrigation pipes cast

132

nets of water that the wind caught up and frayed. Glacial rocks and reed-ringed kettles stood where the retreating ice sheet had left them. At a pink canyon the highway snugged up to the river; on both sides was forest. There were more anglers in the stream than fish; the woods too would be full of guns.

Just above West Yellowstone the highway straightens out suspiciously. The trees, already Christmas straight, come coyly up to the road, making a chute that conducts you with cartoon swiftness to the park. A minute before you arrive, when it's too late to turn back, a spot of gold appears on the horizon and splits in two: McDonalds' arches are just the start. A whole dormitory town has sprung up on the edge of the park. Inside, on the park roads, rubber-tyre traffic is continuous, all day, everyday. At the village supermarket you can buy crackers with poppyseed baked on or you can buy the regular kind: I saw the agony of indecision on one man's face. I heard more languages spoken in that wilderness than anywhere else in America. The vast parking lot opened onto interpretive displays, continuous films, videos, racks of glossy wilderness brochures. It was nature as Disney intended, and it came as no surprise that every year visitors were gored by buffalo and scalped by bears that had strayed from the script.

Park roads sample a fraction of Yellowstone, the map says; there are thousands of miles of back-country trails. The news came too late. I took fright and made for the south gate. By the West Thumb of Yellowstone Lake it was plain I couldn't make the gate by nightfall. I drove instead to Old Faithful, an American image from my childhood almost as potent as the Statue of Liberty or Schwinn bikes. A hundred watchers watched in silence, seated on the wooden pew that runs around the geyser. It came on time, but the display was tinged with disappointment, the way a high mass might be. Afterwards I sat over tea by the lofty bay windows that look out on the distant geyser. Old Faithful blew again, like whale spume. The name was patronizing, and I imagined it the choice of someone like Teddy Roosevelt, who hunted Yellowstone (with a cold elk tongue tucked into his shirt) and wrote of the grizzly that its dangers were overrated.

It was dark when I got to Lewis Lake. I pitched the tent in the forest by the light of two stars. Hunger gave the cold a keener edge. I gathered firewood in the dark by tripping over the bigger bits and combing the dust for kindling. Then I heated and ate chilli in the can. There was frost on the ground in the morning. The pale morning light showed I'd found all the damp firewood there was but missed a neat pile of whittled stakes someone had stacked like beautifully sharpened pencils. I swallowed a rope of ice, jogged a bit to get it down, and quit Yellowstone.

The Grand Teton National Park is like a tail pinned on Yellowstone, a stumpy buffalo tail. The Teton Range appears across Jackson Lake the moment you enter the park, Grand Teton, a kind of American Matterhorn, towering above the rest. Early trappers called the main peaks *les trois tétons* because they thought they resembled breasts. (They don't especially, but a trapper could spend lonely months at a stretch in the wilds.) At Lizard Creek I met a Malaysian couple. Why was I travelling alone, they asked, and were not satisfied with my answer. They offered to take my picture, and so, with the Grand Teton for company, I faced my own camera for the only photo of me on the journey.

The day fined up. I parked by a drained marsh and followed an old canal. The ground was dry and flat but a day's rain would turn it back into bog. At its western limit was a bright line of water and then the bandsaw of mountains. Beavers had built lodges across the canal, turning it into a string of ponds at different levels like boat locks. The grass had grown thickly round about the pools so the original cut was all but lost. The pond bottoms were dark with slime except where they were fed by runnels of fresh water that brought a cleaner silt. A kind of willow, more shrub than tree, grew wherever water collected, its red wands giving the whole marsh a coppery cast.

On the far bank, sunning itself, was a beaver. The beaver's sight is not as sharp as his teeth: he dived into the water and paddled straight for me. Through a grass blind I watched him swim up and down, not working, simply enjoying his pond. Betweentimes he returned to his cavern, where he sat upright, nibbling or simply basking as he contemplated the stream. His hearing was keener; when I shifted he plopped instantly underwater and didn't surface for five minutes – a long way off. Then he returned to his cave mouth and sat there and took stock, a ball of fur with a glittering eye.

I returned to the car to pack a lunch and found myself hurrying back to the pond as to an appointment. But he didn't show up again. He may have gone to work; there was a dam upstream. I lunched without him, using the stalks of toothpick-coloured grass Napi had put there for spearing mussels in the can.

It was a good day to be out. A white haze had spread over the sky and that and the occasional breeze took the heat off a fierce sun. Tadpoles came up from the slime to nibble at the light. It was so quiet I could hear the peep-peep of a reversing truck at the roadworks two miles up the road. All around me dry reeds clacked and seedpods snapped open. A cricket kept up a steady rattle and the thin tweeze of a small bird stitched up the general murmur with invisible thread. With every gust the air streamed with thistledown. Once a ball of it came floating down the lock and I took it for the beaver. At four o'clock I gave up on him. I'd spent a whole afternoon within ten square yards; the day before I did a loop of a hundred miles and saw less. As I left a squadron of swallows appeared out of nowhere, skimmed the dam in formation, and sheared off as suddenly as they came.

To get a closer look at Grand Teton I followed a washboard road to a trailhead, but the trail rose so steeply I abandoned it after an hour. The sun was going down anyway. Far below, the marsh exhaled a blue vapour. From a thousand feet up the beaver was a world away.

I drove into the Hole at dusk and found a tent site by the river. Filling three spaces beside me was a juggernaut tour bus whose thirty Germans were in the middle of a lively dinner. I made for the Million Dollar Cowboy Bar. The man at the door stamped the back of my hand with invisible, or possibly brown, ink. A generation ago he would have thrown me out, but Jackson Hole (hole meaning valley) was now an international town. In 1989 the Soviet Union and the United States signed an agreement here that began the end of the Cold War. A sub-clause on the agenda reopened the old bridge between Asia and the Americans: by it Eskimos on either side of the Bering Strait could now visit one another freely.

"The bluest eyes in Texas," sang Three-Legged Willie, "are haunting me tonight," and the bar lights went a misty blue. It was tearful music, more keening than singing, gooseflesh, not meat.

The trappings were right: the bar woodwork was frontier pretzel and the cowgirls on the dance floor wore fringed leather jackets, fringed boots, and likely fringed leather underwear. I ate around the corner in a burger bar.

"There's a restaurant behind every tree," the grey-haired waitress said, "one hundred and five in this town of six thousand. Two hundred motels in a five-mile radius. That's not counting outfits that take people out to ranches, chuckwagon, the lot. It's the park that done it. Used to be it quieted down about now, but. We've had two Augusts this year and it's just getting busier. It's good for the businesses, but I can't see myself getting a day off in the next month."

"Lyin' through their teeth," the chef said, sitting down to dinner at 10.30. To the waitress he said, "I like blueberries in pancakes but not in jam."

"I eat a lot of pancakes and French toast come winter," she said. "It's cheaper."

I was the last customer. "K-nap time," she said when I paid her. She seemed tired of the cowboy game. Most workers in town probably were too. But the outfitters couldn't get enough of it and neither could the tourists. The whole world came to play: one brochure showed Japanese visitors in cowboy hats spinning toy Colt .45s. I could remember a photo of myself identically rigged out as a boy. (And getting it wrong: for years I thought the cowboy whose picture appeared on the butt of my tin gun was called Pat Pending.) Japan, India, the whole conquered world, paying homage with the sincerest form of flattery.

But Americans came half in earnest, still. Long after the frontier had gone into space, and *Star Trek* was brittle footage, they continued to come here. They came to be ritually shot in the street. They came ritually to shoot one deer. For many of them, Altimus had said, that whitetail was a once-in-a-lifetime experience, so it would matter intensely. It was a wilderness memento to carry back to that hi-tech all-American house so far removed, so sadly, irrecoverably removed, from the log cabin in the heart. It was a pact with the past, like keeping faith with a long-dead parent. This necessary West had deeper roots. Americans had simply democratized an older urge that rulers, whether feudal or socialist, once reserved for themselves. The Titos and Ceausescus, sheikhs, rajahs, and Chams, monopolized the hunt. America made it open season and then created the game department. Anyone could play, for a price, and the price depended on how serious you wanted to get.

There was a scene I'd forgotten at the Russell museum. As I was leaving I noticed a man at the donation box by the door. He was stuffing dollar bills – not just one or two – into the box with the fervour of a pilgrim in Rome or Benares. "He's waited *so* long to see this place!" his wife explained, smiling. It was partly theatre, both drawing attention to and explaining away her husband's antics. But also it was a team effort, unrehearsed. She had seen her husband – that tight-lipped man she lived with – moved. She was giving voice to his emotion, saying for him what she knew he could not bring himself to say. He had been back to his – and the nation's – boyhood, and perhaps beyond.

It was K-nap time for me too, but I took a load of laundry to the 24-hour laundromat. There was a Kennedy drama on TV there. I watched by turns the screen and the dryer with the clothes going round; the screen did marginally better. Hoover's villainy was so villainous I decided he would by some cheap trick turn out to be good, and JFK bad. Two dimensions could collapse into one. Three-Legged Willie's songs belonged to the same world. The music was an advance on the cricket's fiddle at the marsh. The lyrics were on a par. It was hard to tell whether the cricket was "glad" or "sad" or "mad", words that recurred in Willie's repertoire till they attained a mournful equivalence. The sadness in Willie's voice suggested that it all came down to the same thing. I left the laundromat convinced that it did. The cricket and Willie were philosophers. The beaver was not.

It was a frosty night and I needed all the feathers I took to the Arctic but didn't use. I woke to the Germans moving house. I lay in my bag and listened to them chortle and snort and blow their noses with Nordic fury. I envied them their good cheer. They formed a complete society: they had their jester, their wise old man, their princess, their drones. They ate a steaming breakfast and left hooting with laughter, crunching up the gravel inches from my tent.

11

Angel Voices

Some hours before Jesus Christ came to America there was a
terrible earthquake the results of which can be seen to this day
in southern Idaho. According to the book of *3 Nephi*, there were
tempests and whirlwinds and "exceedingly sharp lightnings" which
destroyed many American cities, among them Zarahemla, Moroni,
and Moronihah. But the greatest destruction occurred in the land
to the north where the face of the earth was changed and highways
were torn up.

I knew nothing of this when I crossed into Idaho or I might
have been tempted to go and see. The Craters of the Moon National
Monument is located somewhere between Sun Valley and the Snake
River, and I was following the Snake out of Jackson Hole along
a more recent highway, 26. The ice on the car roof didn't last.
By mid-morning I'd rolled my window down. Up above, stands
of aspen lined the bluffs, coming right up to the edge like nervy
divers. (The reason aspen leaves shiver is that they are wicked older
sisters of a beautiful young girl they hounded and heaped chores
on – till the handsome god of the winds turned up and huffed
and puffed at their greying hair.) Some orange shrub was spread
on the rocks like washing.

Just below the Palisades Dam the road drops into the tiny
settlement of Irwin. Another breath and you are in the tiny
settlement of Swan Valley. I wrote an Irwin postcard in Swan
Valley and drove the half mile back to the Irwin post office. The
card was for my father, another Irwin, and I asked the postmistress
to frank it legibly. She was delighted and did a few test runs.

Leaving Irwin Trading, Irwin Fireworks, the Irwin Emergency

Center, and Irwin Groceries (FOR SALE, phone Irwin Real Estate), I drove north to go south. The sun grew hot. I pulled over at a rest stop and dozed in the grass. At the edge of the gorge was a bronze plaque wreathed in goldenrod. It commemorated Vardis Fisher, a novelist I'd read of but never read, a man who, Easterners felt, hid his lamp under a bushel out West. Tom Wolfe, a friend, came out to visit and saw "little pitiful blistered towns huddled down in the most abject loneliness . . . underneath huge light and scale and weather and the astounding brightness and dimensions of everything – all given a kind of tremendousness and terror and majesty. What I've seen today," he concluded, "explains a lot about him."

It touched a nerve in me. Before I ever left India I used to dwell on this stupendous West, and whenever I read of writers and painters and musicians leaving America to cross the Atlantic it seemed to me a craven act: they had all That (all This) and they went – to Paris! The puzzlement went so deep it could survive an equal but opposite journeying, my own time in the West.

Back on the highway the afternoon sun filled the car like a hitchhiker with a gun. Until, like Batman, I found a useful button: the car had air-conditioning. It was not as instant a transformation as, peasant-like, I'd hoped for, but there was cool air, Rocky Mountain air, flowing down into the plains. The instant transformation was in me: I became an American.

A British writer has said: in Europe you're on the road; in America you're in the car. The Chevy had become a cocoon, a mobile igloo. In less than a week I found my things disposed about it in a kind of order: food here, books there, bottle within reach. It was home. To be on the road in America is to be outside the car, hitchhiking. I'd done my hitchhiking half a lifetime ago; now I was ejecting a hitchhiker. I felt adult and snug and corrupt. In India A/C cars were rarer than CD plates. And here I was living in one. I had become not only an American, I had become, as Americans become, the car. I felt for a moment what the admen at General Motors intended when they named this model of Chevy – a Celebrity.

Idaho is really half a state. In that world of ruler-straight borders out West, Idaho's eastern border is the anomaly: instead of standing

139

up straight it crumples under the weight of the Rockies and caves in to follow the Bitteroot watershed. Idaho's loss is Montana's gain. Short of Ririe the Snake and I parted company as 26 took me back south. Ahead was Idaho Falls. The city of Idaho Falls must have plans on a Moronian scale: they start numbering the streets twenty miles out of town. In the middle of the potato fields and the smudge fires you look up and, yes, you have crossed 98th Street. 97th, 96th, 95th, and still no sign of a city. Then, like a troubled dream, there's an urban snarl, and suddenly, blissfully, you're out on the other side in the potato fields, counting upwards: 96th, 97th, 98th. The Gnostics had a similar view of life.

JESUS, said a licence plate. 1 WAY, said another I tailed south. Had I stayed on 26 I'd have come to the Craters of the Moon, where, says Nephi, "behold the rocks were rent in twain; they were broken up upon the face of the whole earth." Instead I came to Blackfoot, a town blessed with a healing fount of coffee, then took the freeway and pushed Sora to his 60 mph limit.

Downtown Pocatello was drowned in gloom. I found a small motel but the toilet was so vile I asked for another room.

" 'sthe only one left," the manageress shrugged. She wore a dressing gown and smelled of sleep.

" 'sthe problem?" her man called from a curtained room behind the desk.

"Toilet don't work," she called back with the barest smirk.

"*Toi*let don't work!" he muttered. Once, long ago, he'd heard of a working toilet.

"Give you a refund," the woman said, unexpectedly. "Did you mess up the room?"

"I remade the bed."

She handed back the money. I reloaded Sora, dropping my tape recorder in the process.

"God, I love America," a bikie said to his woman as I went by. I hadn't struck that before.

I drove in circles for a bit then found a bridge across the railway track that led me to a street of bright motels. For two dollars more I checked into heaven. That night I woke to a strange high chiming of two or three stretched notes, so faint I thought at first it was a dream. It was a frail vibration, like a glass harmonica, or the ghost of one. It came in drifts, tinkling in the ear, veils of some

140

ethereal music. I went to the window and it hung there in wisps. It was too faint to record and anyway the tape recorder was dead. Across the track, down some alternate time tunnel, my other self was stuck in hell.

Next day I had to make Salt Lake City by 1.30 p.m. or the car would be considered stolen. I packed my bags and Sora looked empty and rented again. Back on the freeway I fell into place behind a white-haired old lady driving a maroon Dodge with Saskatchewan plates. She kept a sedate pace. Car after car came up behind and passed us but I kept with her. A pair of Mack trucks, one black, one white, came up. Contempt glittered on their fenders as they pulled out into the passing lane. I saw now the old lady was dawdling. I pulled out and passed her and watched her dwindle to a maroon spot in the mirror. In the outside mirror she was smaller still, a dot above the words: OBJECTS IN THE MIRROR ARE NEARER THAN THEY SEEM. It looked like a jacket for a book of surreal verse. I turned the radio up high till it blotted out the scenery. Now the next car up was dawdling. I passed it, and since the next one was a campervan I passed that too. Next I gobbled up a pickup truck and caught up with the Macks. I passed them in one go. Now I was flying. The juddering that Sora set up at 60 settled down at 70 and disappeared altogether at 80. I passed a whole slew of stragglers. I'd tasted blood. I wasn't quite living in the fast lane like the white Camaro but I was spending a good bit of time in there. Then, on a long rise, the whole field lost momentum. A maroon Dodge with Saskatchewan plates ripped past every car and topped the hill and was gone.

Even in 1831 Alexis de Tocqueville, who knew England (his wife was English), declared that American roads were the best in the world. I had never seen the like when I arrived as a young exchange student. My host family, farmers from Lawton, Michigan, drove a long black Ford LTD, and as we swung out of the airport onto the I-94 in that substantial, plush, sound-proofed interior, the strip of freeway concrete unrolling beneath us was a magic carpet. A Goth would have felt that way when he saw his first Roman road cutting across hill and fen. I had struck something utterly, radically new. I had passed from a world of sinuous interpenetrating forms into one of hard, keen edges. And yet, as I alighted from the tiny plane something happened that was new in a different way. Our captain

141

got out of his cabin and picked up my suitcase and carried it for me across the tarmac.

To this day I try to imagine a pilot in India doing that, and the very thought is laughable. So my passage was not simply from anarchy to order. There were crisp lines drawn between men in India that broke down over here. Men just didn't see them. No wonder democracy became a philosopher's stone for Tocqueville. His critics said he attributed everything under the American sun to democracy, but the most striking feature of the New World, the contrast between its efficient mechanical modes and its elastic social codes, was bound to suggest a link between the two. The link was real and it wasn't evident only to foreigners. It was part of the conscious folklore of the people and their pragmatic philosophers. An abiding faith in its efficiency would in time blind Americans to a still more formidable combination – rigid social codes *plus* efficient machinery – underway in Japan.

By stagecoach and steamer, and on horseback in the wilds, Tocqueville and his friend Beaumont travelled some seven thousand miles in nine months. Had they been driving south on the I-15 in the 1840s they would have crossed the Idaho border directly into Mexico. Driving that same road today I crossed simply into Utah. Another thousand miles separated me from a sadly shrunken Mexico. Such was the scope of the United States' Saddam-style operation on its southern neighbour, and so inordinate the gains, that Destiny alone could justify it. Iraq's was a pitiful misadventure, Kuwait a tiny morsel; the United States wolfed down a territory as large as itself. Mexico for its part lost more than half its territory: Utah, Nevada, Arizona, New Mexico, all California, and Texas.

Against the Indians the American advance was more untidy. Battlefields peppered the *National Geographic* map of the region I'd been travelling through, in stark contrast to Canada, where I passed no crossed swords. While the British treated their way West, the Americans shot through. The result was much the same: reserves to the north, reservations to the south. But the blood spilt on American soil cried out for vindication, and scripture came to the rescue, most helpfully in Utah.

The Indians of North America, scripture showed, were not from Siberia at all: they were descendants of a tribe wandered from Israel. These ancient inhabitants came in two batches, the first

142

escapees from the destruction at Babel, and the second immigrants from Jerusalem in 600 BC. The first batch came in eight wicker barges "tight like unto a dish", each with a small breathing hole at the top. For eleven months they huddled in these dishes, America's first boat people. Blown by God's winds they came to the promised land carrying seeds and animals and honey bees. In the New World, their leader Jared had four sons, and the begats began all over again. The Jaradites didn't last, brought low by civil strife after a period of righteousness. But their prophet Ether foresaw a new Jerusalem being built in America by the seed of Joseph.

Not Joseph Smith, a happy coincidence (and a happy graft of Israel onto Albion's stem), but the original Joseph sold into slavery in Egypt. The next batch came in a sailing-ship built after God's plan and victualled with fruits and meat and honey. They too reached the land called Bountiful and prospered but split into two nations: the Nephites, the chosen people, and the Lamanites, who became "a dark and loathsome and a filthy people, full of idleness" (*1 Nephi* 12:23). The "more idle part" of the Lamanites "lived in the wilderness and dwelt in tents: and they were spread through the wilderness on the west" (*Alma* 22:28). The Nephites on the other hand lived in cities under constant threat of attack from the Lamanites. At length certain of the Lamanites were converted, and the "curse was taken from them, and their skin became white like unto the Nephites" (*3 Nephi* 2:15) and they became "a delightsome people" to look at once again. And the resurrected Christ came to America and ministered to the Nephites in fulfilment of the prophecy that Israel would be restored in the promised land.

The Book of Mormon is scripture transported: brought across the Atlantic, naturalized, made agile, made American. Viewed as scripture it is "another testament of Jesus Christ", and rather lacks the bite of the King James Version, but viewed as fiction it is an early 19th-century novel. Written in the East, it survives in the West, a proto-Western. It has none of the props Charlie Russell or Zane Grey would have recognized, notably the horse. The costumes are different and the characters speak cribbed King James. But its action and its literary intentions are Westerly. In a decade when a writer like Poe was producing strenuous European fantasies, Joseph Smith chose to set his melodrama squarely in America, an act of literary courage, whatever its other merits. It is also, in keeping with the practical spirit of the New World, a simplification of history and religion, a simplification of the past in the service of the present, a mere fifteen books to master instead of sixty-six, an easier Bible. Simplified too, as in a Western, are the good and the bad (the bad are the ugly) and the working out of their fate. If one took the original Bible as an Ur-novel, then here is the condensed book with, as a bonus to subscribers, a Further Adventures bound in.

It was past 2.30. I was driving a stolen car. There'd be a barricade any moment now manned by the combined Montana and Utah State Police Forces. Also there would be the Royal Canadian Mounted Police, who'd been tracking me ever since 1981 when I skipped the country with an unpaid ticket for jay-walking. The motorcycle cop who slapped it on me would be waiting. Ten years would have made him an angry man.

There was no barricade. I slipped off the freeway into Salt Lake City, my week as a celebrity ended. I took Sora to a carwash and hosed him down till the caked yellow came off, and turned him in. The Californian boy who dropped me back downtown said it had been rough coming to Utah.

"Like, *culture* shock, man! What's India like?"

Unemployed Californians flocking to Utah were only following the example of the Utah state bird, the Californian gull. The story of the gull was this. When Brigham Young's settlers first arrived their crops were threatened by a plague of locusts. They prayed for deliverance, and the gulls turned up and ate the locusts. There's a statue to commemorate the event, and the gulls sit on that too.

On Main Street I stopped at a hot-dog stand. The woman who served me was a Lamanite, of my kind.

"Hold the onions," I said in Hindustani, to test her.

She held the onions and we began to talk. She was from Pakistan. She asked my name. Christian? I made an open gesture. Christian, she decided. In the subcontinent you had no choice: you were what you were born, if it killed you. A friend of hers came up, a girl from India. Both had relocated from California. Salt Lake City was safer and cheaper and cleaner. In San Francisco there was danger, there were blacks. I should settle here, both advised me. Neither had been married long. We stood and talked, a Muslim, a Hindu,

144

and a Christian from the subcontinent and I imagined I could feel the Nephites bristling. Still, a hot-dog stand was healthier than a Multicultural Social Center. In Canada minorities, coddled by the state, risked becoming feeble and picturesque.

The other American races suddenly surfaced in Salt Lake City. The janitor at the motel, a lanky old man in frayed white cotton flares, was the first black man I'd come across in a thousand miles. Montana had only cowboys and Indians. There were Hispanics here too. *Migrants*, the brain is programmed to respond until it remembers that Utah was theirs for four centuries until their forefathers' title deeds were annulled by the US government. Before them the land belonged to the Utes, from whom the state took its name.

Brigham Young's statue stands at the city crossroads from where all numbering starts. So completely does he dominate the city I began to see his name even where it didn't belong. Brighton Ski Resort the eye read as Brigham Ski Resort; Bingham Copper Mine, Brigham again. At Young's shoulder was his church, the Temple, forty years in the building. It occupied a whole city block, a campus of grey stone buildings with cement walks and turgid gardens. A single weed, one felt, would bring down the government, if not a thunderbolt. I sat in McDonald's opposite the south gate (the fajitas were still on special) and watched the people go in and out.

"You know, it seems like they're always doin' somethin' to that Temple," said a boy at the next table, lifting his hamburger to the steeple. The Temple was clad in scaffolding. Up on the steeple a golden angel lifted his trumpet to the sun.

The table was wiped down and occupied again.

"He's a cowboy?"

"He likes black tea."

"The thing about Becky is she's shameless."

The next day I returned to Temple Square. At the gate stood guides of all ages, ready to greet the visitor and lead him around the campus. The church fathers had chosen delightsome and efficient guides. Parties of visitors flowed from building to building down white paved walks, through arbours, past white statuary on flawless lawns. I moved about unmolested, wondering why I felt I'd been there before. And then I saw it: I'd strayed into a picture of Heaven from my childhood prayerbooks. The shrubs,

145

the clipped hedges, the lawns, the cool white statues of abstract virtues, all pointed back to an early idyll of piety rewarded. Even in childhood it was a chilling encounter. I slipped out for a fiery lunch of Szechuan chicken wings (still on special) and made for the Beehive.

Brigham Young's private residence was built in the 1850s, when he was president of the Church of Latter Day Saints. After Temple Square it was warm and welcoming, designed by a man accustomed to comfort and aware of the dignity of his position. Its honey-coloured timbers wore a worldly glow, but the governor was no sybarite: he ate two meals a day, worked hard, and prayed hard. He led the settlers into the valley, chose the site of the city, and on the very first day tilled the soil with his people and planted corn. When he came to build seven years later he remembered the Jaredites' bees and topped his roof with a beehive.

"Welcome to the Beehive!"

The guide, a radiant woman of thirty with pale honey-coloured hair, interrupted her talk to greet latecomers. She too was from one of my prayerbooks, the blonde girl in a circle of praying children:

> Red and yellow, black and white,
> All are perfect in His sight,
> Jesus loves the little children of the world.

The only blemish was a Band-Aid on her index finger, at the nail. Afterwards I asked her about the Mormons' ancient history in the Americas. I should read the *Book of Mormon*, she said, and produced a copy. I said I was trying to travel light.

"Let me make you a present," she said anyway. "I'll pay for this copy and you can have it."

I protested, but she had already signed the flyleaf, *Paula*. And if I had any more questions there was her telephone number. Her brother had been a missionary.

I stepped out into the evening and climbed up State Street to the capitol on the hill. It was not as pompous inside as the Montana capitol, Mormon thrift replacing boomtown flash. I'd been so Brigham Younged since I set foot in the city it came as a surprise to find the man accorded a mere niche in the central hall. The murals told pioneer stories: *Father Escalante*

Discovers Utah Lake, 1776; *Peace with the Indians, September 1852*; *Pony Express and Stage Coach*; another *Golden Spike Driven In*. A plaque above the constitution altar told of how the pioneers established the commonwealth, *framing its government according to the orderliness of their lives*.

The orderliness is evident as you look across the city. It was laid out in ten-acre squares with streets 132 feet wide so a wagon hitched to four oxen could turn around comfortably. In those days the territory of Utah was called Deseret, from Joseph Smith's revealed word for the honey bee. It was like Brigham Young to go for counsel not to the ant but to the bee, to sweeten the harsh desert life. It softened that orderliness and gave, I thought, an attractive touch of worldliness to the Mormon character. But it would have been short commons for the first year or two.

Every arrival in the New World had to improvise a menu. The Indians ate what they found on the beach or on the plain: grilled buffalo-hump ribs and soapberry sherbets were later refinements. A thousand years ago Leif Eriksson's men drank the dew on the grass of America and found it "the sweetest thing they had ever tasted". Further up the coast were "bigger salmon than they had ever seen". It was Trykir, the German in their midst, who found the vines by which Eriksson named the country Vinland. (He was so amazed he brayed German at his fellow sailors; then, calmed, he told them in plain Norse of the grapes.) They filled up a canoe with the fruit and towed it after them on their journey, getting their vitamin C a full seven centuries before Captain Cook dosed his crew with greens and lemons. The lemons were typical, tart reality after that misty feast of salmon, grapes, and honeydew. Today on Main Street the Pakistani woman sold hot dogs, but she would have brought her recipes with her on the PIA flight, adding her native cuisine to the wide American table traduced by fast-food chains.

I went down to dinner by way of Memory Grove, a chill canyon where a Grecian Chapel of Meditation stood locked in uneasy dialogue with an old armoured car. DON'T MESS WITH THE US! said Desert Storm graffiti. At the Royal Taj restaurant was Harry Saini, debonair part-owner and waiter. He kept an eye on the other tables while we chatted. He'd been to my hometown. In fact the chief shrine in Dehra Dun held the remains of a Sikh saint the Sainis especially revered. Saini was a popular host. His good looks and slight swagger turned heads. The earring in his right ear was not Indian, but he talked nostalgically of Home.

The simplest book of Indian cookery I know is by an American. I learnt to cook Indian food not in India but in America, and my guides were two: the recipes my mother sent me in every letter (letter recto, recipe verso) and Mary Atwood's *A Taste of India*. It was a book after Ben Franklin's own heart, if not his stomach: the ingredients listed without fuss in the order in which they went in, the method advancing with Euclidean clarity. And if the virtual QED lacked passion, that came with growing intimacy, as in an arranged marriage. (D.H. Lawrence, who berated Franklin for "using venery", would not have got far with another Indian recipe book, the *Kama Sutra*.) Americans began the use of simple measures rather than weights in recipes, putting an end to all those baffling gills and pints and quarter ounces so beloved of British cooks. Any man – Everyman – could understand half a cup or a teaspoon, and that was the spirit too of the old claim that American farmers were the only farmers in the world who could read Homer. Tocqueville found and read *Henry IV* in a log cabin on his travels, and although 150 years on the taste in log cabins runs to videos, the post-literate world has sprung from a democracy of knowledge.

Back at the motel I rang Paula's number. Her mother answered and there was a long silence. Paula came to the phone and almost at once got bogged down in doctrine. It was hard to explain on the phone, she said, but we could meet at Temple Square next morning.

In the middle of the night I woke to a strange high-pitched sound above my head: *tweak*, and then at 15-second intervals, *tweak*. I called the desk. Reach up and take the battery out of the smoke detector, the man said. I couldn't go back to sleep so I read the *Book of Mormon* and dropped off at dawn.

Paula was waiting at the information centre. Black sunglasses gave her a sophisticated look. She led me to a library where I picked two videos, *America Before Columbus* and *Christ in America*. We found a booth. She loaded the video – her nail was healed – and we watched in silence. The opening shots were Mayan and Aztec; temples and artefacts, straight archaeology. Then the camera began to dwell on certain symbols: were they crosses or weren't they? The video cut to epic paintings by Arnold Friberg, who did the sets for *The Ten Commandments*. Heroic scenes of battle and prophecy, luminous visitations, baptisms in Yellowstone National Park; the men handsome and preposterously well-built, the women looking like Paula. Friberg was the Charlie Russell of the proto-Western. We turned the lights back on and I asked my questions. I began to scribble as usual on the back of a map; it was a way of domesticating the foreign, and it cut down on weight. Paula would not hear of it. And over the next thousand miles the canary-yellow pages of her note pad kept cropping up as reminders of Salt Lake City.

"What was the original language of America?"

"We believe it was a kind of Egyptian. It was both spoken and written. It was engraved on plates of gold and brass and translated by Joseph Smith as the *Book of Mormon*."

"Which counts for more, the Bible or the *Book of Mormon*?"

"They go hand in hand." She produced her copy of each book. The *Book of Mormon* had been underlined in red throughout; the Bible had a more pristine look. She smiled at the disparity and said, "I *do* cross-reference." There were other books too, she said, such as *The Pearl of Great Price*, but the *Book of Mormon* had a special place. It came to earth in this way.

One evening in September 1823, an angel came down from heaven and told Joseph Smith, a farmer's son, of a hill in Ontario County, New York, where certain metal plates were deposited in a metal box. These plates, "the voice of a people speaking from the dust", Smith was empowered to translate. When he had finished the messenger "called for them" and Smith, having shown them to his family and friends (eleven of whom, including Smith's father, signed a testimony that they had "seen and hefted" the plates), delivered them up. His translation was published in 1830.

"We believe the Bible," Paula said, "to be the word of God as far as it is translated correctly. But the Bible has been handed down and changed along the way. Joseph Smith's translation was more direct."

American arrival stories intrigued me: they invariably became family sagas, but I hadn't expected the saga to enrol heaven. "We believe," Paula said, "in a Heavenly Mother as well as a Heavenly Father."

"Do you address any prayers to Her?"

"No. It's sufficient to address the Father, through our older brother Jesus Christ. In the spirit world you dwell in families. In the next life we will be with our families. We believe it was a celestial world once, but now it's a time of wickedness. We say it is the Saturday evening of Time."

It was noon, motel check-out time. Paula said her mother had packed a picnic. At the motel I put my bags in her car and we drove to a green hill. Over fruit juice she explained about Mormons and coffee. It sounded like a life of rules, Man made for the Sabbath. In the car she turned off the radio: no rock music on Sundays. We passed a garage sale: she loved garage sales, but you couldn't spend money on a Sunday. I saw Franklin cheer and Lawrence fidget in the back seat. But as she drove me around her city she could clown at the wheel. After dinner she shook my hand firmly.

I got out of the car feeling slightly drunk, on fruit juice and nine hours of Paula. Her marriage had come apart, she'd lost custody through a legal quibble, but beelike, she was rebuilding her life. The whole hive helped: university, job, family. A people who dwell in families in the next world – whose household gods have families – look after their own in this. It was the rules that mattered after all. As far as I could tell, the score was Franklin 1, Lawrence 0.

Bandaloops Café served stiff coffees. It was a good place to sober up and kill time till the train. The crowd were mostly young, in raffish black. Here the men wore the earrings and the women smoked cigars. Two men at different tables had been in jail; both had learnt chess while doing time. A card game was in progress.

"I keep getting aces, sorry!" gloated a zeppelin-shaped woman smoking a pipe. I began to feel at ease. One of the jailbirds checkmated a very tall cowboy. "History is written by the victors," said a baseball cap drinking a Diet Pepsi. He took on the jailbird next. The cowboy used the word *existential*.

At midnight I walked back to the station past melancholy brick terraces with faded names and functions. American railway stations were always at the dead end of town. A historical society had taken over the old Rio Grande station with its fine cravat of windows; the actual Amtrak station was a frumpish affair next door. The train was late. A bag lady, sleeping sitting up, shared the waiting hall with me. She slept fluffed up like a bird, with her nose tucked into the folds of her sweater. Her hands were clasped somewhere behind her and a single button, under strain, fastened the coat that contained her. Homeless, she inhabited her clothes. She smelt of Goodwill shops, a smell I recognized from forays I'd once made there myself. It haunted me for years after when I passed it in the street, a cheesy, grey-green, maudlin odour I came to think of as the smell of defeat, compounded of grudges and muddle and regret. But it was probably no more than sweat. It was the way most people smelt, most of the time, until the mass market deodorized them.

The hall began to fill up. "I remember when you could set your watch by the train, to the second," a man grumbled. Three young Japanese backpackers stole looks at the clock and then at each other. The bag lady got up and left in a huff at the mounting noise in her bedroom.

My ticket was to San Francisco, but half of me wanted to go the other way, to Denver. My original plan was to go down the centre of the continent, or just west of centre. But there was a visa to pick up, a bag to drop off. I lawyerized it to myself as time out, a West Coast loop; I'd pick up where I left off and continue on down the middle.

Unlike the bag lady I didn't sleep well sitting up. There was a soup kitchen and flophouse across the street from the station. She'd gone that way and I had half a mind to follow her example. I knew what to expect from nights long past: the sergeant major stomping down the men's dorm whacking the bedsteads, herding inmates into the showers before they got into the clean sheets; the racking coughs and troubled dreamers all night long; the breakfast of "live" food the Salvation Army truck had picked up on its rounds of restaurants; and then the glare of the street as you filed out into the day. It was like boarding-school all over again. Amtrak was better.

The train was two hours late. There were no blankets on board. I put my jacket on backwards and lay back. A full moon came over and eyed me coldly as the track curved around the calm salt lake.

12

West of West

Daylight brought Nevada and a powdery moondust that showed why Utah was only the second-driest state in the union. A mantle of sagebrush carried the flight as far as the mountains but then withered away as the black rock rose up like final desolation.

Presently feathery trees appeared, then cattle, and just as I began to see the Gangetic plain, Reno. Reno was the main stop, the first major town in 500 miles. The station was deserted. (Where were the tea vendors and cigarette boys and sweetmeat carts and short-order barbers and masseurs and pickpockets and beggars and pilgrims and vagrants and monkeys?) And then, just as we were pulling out I saw the elephants. A cow and her calf riding in a cage on the back of a truck. They were circus beasts, creatures of another era almost, like the train. The highway ran mockingly alongside the track. We were, after all, entering California, the state where an oil company and a tyre company conspired to run the railroad off its tracks and into history.

We were running three hours late. The conductor went by with a radio crackling in his back pocket. *We got two engines now . . . crackle, crackle . . . so we can do seventy-nine instead of seventy with one.* In the forest by our house elephants manage short bursts of high speed.

The track climbed steeply, tunnelled through sierra and pine, and overhung a cobalt lake. In the winter of 1952 the train got icebound at 5000 feet in the Yuba Gap and the passengers had to be rescued, the Amtrak host said, by "mountain men". He made them sound like another species, Bigfoot or Sasquatch or Canadiennes.

The mountains fell away, the coast appeared, and urban sprawl. JUNGLE FEVER *Coming Soon* said a movie billboard as the train threaded thickets of refinery pipes. Smog and evening fell together, blood-red where the sun slipped into the sea, deep purple the other way where a round moon wobbled up behind stacks of flimsy apartment houses. We plodded into Oakland, the circus come to town, and transferred to the San Francisco bus.

The YMCA café was closed. To get dinner I had to run a gauntlet of panhandlers. The night belonged to the workless, although in a sense they worked the night shift. They arrived punctually at dark, just as the day shift were leaving, and stood on an assembly line, their hands shaping the air.

Outside my burger bar I saw a long-haired white man struck down by a black man. He fell at a stop light in front of a row of cars and was hit again on the ground.

One block along I saw a squad car up on the sidewalk. A black cop had one of the white workless up against the wall; his deputy, a black woman, stood back looking uncomfortable. One-on-one was the rule since Rodney King. I'd been in town half an hour and already I was seeing things in black and white. A Martian reporting back would have said whites were an oppressed race in this country.

Next morning the workers were back, the street reclaimed. CONGRATULATIONS! NEW CITIZENS! *Register to Vote Republican* said a banner outside the Federal Building. I saw no takers at the booth and wondered why. The explanation was upstairs in the YMCA where English classes were held: the words were too big. A display board carried specimens of new Americans' writing:

I live in Hong Kong 35 years. Hong Kong's weather is not cold, not hot, have mountains and ocean, too much market, too much people, too much boat.

Yin WONG

My house 2 windows, 1 door, 2 bedrooms, 1 kitchen, 1 bathroom, 1 living room. My house is in Saigon. Color is green. There is a tree next to my house. 6 people live in my Vietnam house.

My Phuong LAM

Guatemala y San Francisco is much different.

CARLOS

The car from Continental Rent-a-Car (the old Continent; they were Slavs) was a rubber-band job that juddered all the way to Walnut Creek. Dinner tonight was going to be a cut above last night's chickenburger. I was going to meet a man I'd corresponded with for some years. He had a collection of Anglo-Indian literature I wanted to see. Like me, Bert Payne was an Anglo-Indian. Like me, he went to a boarding-school in north India. Unlike me, he was a millionaire.

His wife opened the door, a small woman of Czech ancestry. She'd been a nurse in Chicago when she and Bert met. Bert was on his way home, she said; his office was just up the road. I met the children. Bert walked in, a thickset, light-skinned, engaging man in accountant's glasses and an expensive suit. He showed me around the house and garden and said he'd booked me into the Doubletree Hotel – I swallowed hard – as his guest. He put up all his company guests there. I said I was quite happy sleeping on the sofa. "Suit yourself," he said, "but we have four kids and this is not a big house." It wasn't, but he had plans, behind the sofa. He reached down and came up with an architect's drawing, mounted, of his house-in-progress, one better suited to the family's needs and his own ideas. It was in a special neighbourhood, even more exclusive than Walnut Creek.

Bert and Rosemary started Starcare International in 1981. The company, which audits hospital accounts, brought together their separate backgrounds. There was no office up the road in those days. The computer was in the living-room and the typewriter sat on the dining-table. Rosemary did the secretarial work and managed their first child, Bert plugged away at the computer. When the second child came Rosemary gave notice. Now there was an office block, a whole team of employees, and a fourth child.

"I'll show you the office," Bert said, and we climbed into the BMW while Rosemary turned Indian cook. There was someone working late, Bert noted approvingly as we drove up. But the curtains should have been drawn. He would have to have a word with the secretary tomorrow. Bert's desk was big enough to land a helicopter on. We went from room to room switching lights on and off. It was not a hierarchy; every individual had his division and the divisions had been worked out by Bert. There were shelves

154

of binders, blue for one type of client, red for another, white for a third. Nothing was out of place, except those curtains.

It was now dark. The cockpit of the BMW had more lights and needles than a small town in the Deep North. Bert called his eldest daughter's room to check on a point of homework. Julie's voice filled the car as we swept into the Ygnacio Valley traffic flowing out of San Francisco. We did a tour of Walnut Creek. It was America as America was meant to be: shops, malls, restaurants, cars, trees; healthy, smiling people, girls walking dogs on lamplit streets.

"This is San Francisco," Bert said. "Where's the crime? Show me!"

I couldn't. He drove me past a car lot where every car was worth a quarter of a million dollars.

"Guy who owns that is a Sikh from Oakgrove." Oakgrove was Bert's school in India. "It's the biggest Ferrari dealership in the world."

We cruised home. "The company can handle itself now," Bert said. "I'm like the builder, I'm secure. There's no threat. No one can demand partnership, because they don't know enough. You know, they're either the plumber or the carpenter, so they can't go out and challenge me – they're the electrician. Today I'm the medical expert for the state of California. And I've found no one's indispensable. Somebody leaves who was very good, you think, 'That's too bad.' But you'll find someone better."

We passed the Doubletree Hotel. The Motel 6 next door looked sad at $35. "See what you've given up?" Bert chuckled.

That night I pored over his collection of Anglo-Indiana. He'd compiled a bibliography too. I slept not on the sofa but in Philip's room. Little Philip turned over once and mumbled something in his perfect sleep. He was dressed for school when I awoke. The sun topped green Mt Diabolo and flooded the living-room at 7.40. Rosemary was packing lunches, ice-water flasks.

"Julie, do you want a muffin for dessert?"

"Oh Mom! Today's Wednesday – today's *pizza*!"

"You don't need school lunch today. You've *got* lunch."

"Oh Mom!"

I drove the rubber band to Oakland. There were two shrines I wanted to see, one a fake temple and the other a half cabin.

The temple was the old Oakland Theatre, worked in brick, the Hindu details more or less right. A believer would have smiled at the thought of Hollywood movies shown under that tower: what are movies but a pious reminder of maya, illusion? The half cabin was Jack London's; the other half was in Dawson City.

London was born in Oakland into poverty and roamed the water-front as a boy before turning oyster pirate. Later he hauled in oyster pirates for the water police: he'd learnt their secrets. He drank with both sides and there were half a dozen saloons in Jack London Square that claimed to be his favourite. I steered clear of them – I could see each one with its resident ancient who remembered Jack well – and hunted for the cabin. I walked right by it once without knowing. The Jack London waterfront complex was immaculate. The shops and seafood restaurants sparkled like capped teeth and faced resolutely away from the embarrassing cousin with the decayed mouth. The cabin looked stranded and shame-faced; it knew where it would rather be. London himself, in bronze a toss away, put on a brave face. A passing derelict honked his nose in front of the bust, the kind of salute Jack would have appreciated. There was Californian grass growing on the cabin roof. It was hard to tell which timbers were genuine but a notice said the Yukon Historical Sites and Monuments Board had authenticated the cabin when it was located in 1968 at the north fork of Henderson Creek on Claim 151. Inside, in the gloom, were two pairs of snowshoes, a couple of old stools, an axe, a frying pan on a stove, and a blackened coffee pot on the table. Against the wall was a neatly sawn stack of firewood. On the floor in the dust were the pilgrims' coins.

The Mediterranean, Saki once said, produces more history than can be consumed locally. The United States consumes more history than can be produced locally. So it imports London Bridge and London's Cabin. London himself contributed to his historicizing; if a part of him approved of the nose-blowing derelict, another part approved of the bronze. A painstaking writer, a writer of long and punishing apprenticeship, he played down the wick and played up the waterfront – and the sea-dog, and the prospector. (So the cabin had it coming.) London belonged to and helped shape a durable tradition of American writerly macho, of would-be mayors and big-marlin men who just happened to write. He ran for mayor himself, but Oakland wasn't ready for him in 1901, or again in

1905. Now it was: it gave him a whole square and forgave him his socialism. That was part of his glamour.

From a window seat at the Oakland Grill I watched the city's fruit and vegetable supplies being moved. The wholesalers, open since dawn, were closing up shop. Felix Cohen, opposite, pulled down his shutters just as the Grill put theirs up to catch the sun. Two waiters approached my table, waved a set of dowelling wands and at the count of three the wall beside me disappeared and I found myself on the sidewalk, the innermost table become the outermost. The air, suddenly bucolic, carried green whiffs of celery and trodden coriander. Cartons of green peppers and corn, Spanish onions and aubergines climbed up trestle-work, teasing the traveller with visions of tranquil home kitchens. A blond giant moving bananas backed his fork-lift truck at high speed through an intersection. An old black man danced nimbly out of the way balancing a ten-pound watermelon. Lightning forked down on the city across the harbour and a thunderclap put all the pigeons in a panic. I ran for the car and drove back to San Francisco in the rain.

In the afternoon I bought a small tape-recorder at Macy's sale to replace the one that broke in Pocatello. Outside, a man followed me saying, "I'm haangry, I'm haangry," but he was lying. There were half a dozen places where you could get a free meal in town and he would know them better than most. In one doorway a derelict woman sat with her legs stretched out across the sidewalk eating stir-fried noodles out of a styrofoam box. Shoppers had to step over her, and she liked that. Two doorways down a boy was asleep on his side, Calcutta fashion, his feet drawn up so he fitted in crosswise. I ate in a Vietnamese greasy spoon on Leavenworth, a vast lake of beef noodle soup whose placid surface hid tripe and nameless strands of glutinous flesh that I left at the bottom.

Laughter, morning voices, drifted up seven floors through the mist. The workless were still down there, more foreshortened than most, clocking out. A few workers walked briskly to early jobs. In between, in fluorescent orange bib-waistcoats, moved the janitors, like a special race of worker ants belonging neither to the day nor to the night.

The Mexican consulate gave me sixty days. Expecting thirty, I was well pleased. On the way back to the Y a lady drew me into a Scientology centre. "Would you like to do a simple test?" she said.

I was given a pencil and asked to answer a series of multiple-choice questions. My answers were fed into a computer and the result was a graph that was interpreted for me as follows:

A   *You are an unstable character. Your decisions are unreliable.*

B   *You are extremely depressed. There is a problem going on in your life.*

C   *You are in a complete state of nervousness and highly irritable. Almost anything sends you into a state of distraction.*

D   *You are undependable as a person, and have very little self-confidence. Your judgement is poor.*

E   *You are doing a little more than you can handle, a sign of your instability.*

F   *You are incapable of handling people openly.*

G   *You are utterly irresponsible. You feel sorry for yourself and believe life has victimized you.*

H   *You are hypercritical, making you hard to be around. You pretend you are being frank but basically you are being mean.*

I   *You are quite heartless and unable to project yourself into another.*

J   *You are badly withdrawn, and either shy or dislike people or both. There is something about yourself you would like to hide.*

I was classed as an urgent case. Fortunately, Scientology could help. Level 1 was straightforward; by Level 2 I'd start to see positive results.

It took the thrill out of my Mexican visa, and that bothered me: what bothered me was that I was bothered. I felt mugged, scientifically; in fact I'd got off lightly. Supposing I'd grown up in a country where being liked was imperative, where there was a science of being liked, how would I be feeling? Here, in Ron Hubbard, was the other face of Dale Carnegie. And people, mostly the workless, already softened up by the San Francisco streets, were drifting into the Religious Technology Center all the time.

I lunched at the Y. "The whole course," a black woman at the next table said, nodding at my printout, "could set you back $100,000. At Level 30 you learn that Hubbard is God."

*

WORLD RELIEF, the door said, with a logo of four hands of different colours uniting to form a cross. I went in out of curiosity. The receptionist, Nguyen Ai, was not too busy to talk. Ai told me his nickname was Quan, or Soldier; Sailor would have been more accurate, or Boatperson. He was too young to have seen fighting in Vietnam, but he had made ten escape attempts by sea before he got away.

"How old were you the first time?" I asked him.

"Twelve years old, then fourteen, then fifteen . . . now I'm twenty-three." He was slight of build, with a low breathy voice and an earnest look. I could not imagine him shouting, even for help.

"What happened the first time?"

"The police came, but we threw away the compass. We had all the documents to prove we are legal. They could not find the compass so they had to let us go." He laughed. "And the next time the weather is very bad and we came back. We threw everything into the ocean. The police saw the empty boat and said, 'You are fishermen. Where are the fish?' We said, 'The weather is very bad so we threw everything away.' "

"Fishermen don't carry a compass?"

"They know. Fishermen don't have to go far from the coast. That's illegal on a small boat to carry a compass." He laughed again at the memory. He related it like an adventure, and when he was a boy it would have been. I asked him where they got the boat.

"My older brother who stays with me now, he has like an adopted father in Vietnam, and he's a very rich man. He wants to help young people leave because there is no future even if they study. He bought a boat for our family. It's about nine metres long and one and a half metres wide, a small boat."

On the night of 22 April 1986 Ai and three brothers put out to sea for the last time, making for Malaysia. Their motor broke down and they floated towards Thailand. The next day help appeared in the shape of a boat. The boatmen offered them rice but threw the brothers into the sea and took their motor.

"I don't know what country the pirates were, I'm not saying Thai. Next day another boat give us some food, but my oldest brother who went to get it, he drowned. Then after two days

159

another boat came and said, 'We will take you to Bangkok.' So we put our things in that boat and then they hit us and took our things. We floated for four days without food. We had some sugar, so we mix that in seawater to drink. We prayed and read the Bible.

"Then we saw land! Another boat came and we were scared, but they gave us rice and fish. Then the Thai police came and made us swim to an island. Next day a boat took us to another police station. From there they took us to the camp."

Ai and his brothers spent four years in the refugee camp. Now their father and sister were there, waiting on a green card. Their mother, old and unable to work, was in Saigon with her family. They sent her money every month. I asked Ai if he would go back to Vietnam, supposing the government changed.

"I became a Christian on the ocean," he said. "Now I would like to be a missionary. I work here two days a week and I go to college. I study English and Math and my major is Nursing. A missionary must have a skill. But I will go anywhere in the world. In Vietnam you have to have a licence to preach, you have to fill out a form. They ask for the religion. If you say *Christian* they kick you out. *Buddhist*, OK, no problem. But most Buddhists they don't know anything about Buddha."

"Is it hard living here?"

"At first . . . it was very hard for me. The first week, the first month . . . was very hard." He cast his mind back but would not elaborate.

"How long before your father gets here?"

He brightened up. "Three months maybe. And my sister!"

On the street I began to notice Vietnamese faces. It was tempting to stop them and see how their arrival stories measured up. Were they in their first unspeakable week, when the city was a fun-fair run amok?

I walked up O'Farrell. The painting in the gallery window was a kind of greedy fisheye lens that took in the whole West Coast urban jungle. It was zany in a Californian way, a Hollywood streetscape of fiendish complexity and startling innocence.

"He's Californian?" I asked the girl in the gallery, suppressing the *I suppose*.

"Fazzino is from New York," she said.

160

The Hollywood cut-and-paste job had Marilyn Monroe at its centre and a spaghetti junction of roads and cars and signs and sidewalks wriggling over every available inch. The pop-up sections were adult-complex and child-simple. Compared with other modern streetscapes, such as Lowry's bleak Lancashire towns, it radiated happiness and wonder. But part of its charm lay in its complexity, and that, in the real world, could just as easily confuse. As long as you made the connections in that opulent bizarrerie, as long as you cherished those icons – Marilyn Monroe, Mickey Mouse – they were benign. For those who couldn't connect, that world could rear up menacingly, as it did on Nguyen Ai.

Carole was from LA. She had worked in the art trade for five years. She'd studied art history but didn't finish university. "I got my knowledge on the shop floor," she said.

"Who's the best West Coast artist?" I asked her.

"I'm not even going to try to answer that. There's a lot of good work being done here."

"What's special about it? What makes it Western?"

"It's probably more open. You get a sense of space."

"Except there." I pointed at a teeming Fazzino.

"That one's New York!"

"Is he a good investment?"

She smiled. "I *try* not to think of art in terms of investment."

"You were toying with that calculator when I came in." As I said that the other girl in the gallery picked up the calculator.

"We don't give the stuff away."

"Has the recession made a difference to art prices? Have prices fallen?"

"They haven't fallen, they've levelled off. I would say, if you like the image, now is the time to buy. If you like the work you hold on to it and it'll weather the changes in the market." Her boss came in. "Now," Carole said, "what can we mail to India for you?"

"I'm trying to jettison goods, not take them on."

She caved in. In the world's most acquisitive society the Indian who strikes a renunciatory note gets instant and unlimited credit. A whole century of spiritual hucksters from the east has made no difference. Her boss went out.

"Is LA ahead in the trade?"

"They like to think they are. They have more galleries, they're a bigger city."

"Is there more money there?"

"There's money here too. Keith Heering around the corner is selling OK."

I'd noticed the exhibition.

"He died young," she said, "of AIDS, in New York last year. And they've been dancing on his grave ever since."

I strolled back to the Y down Leavenworth, downhill. The city stood up like a painting. Police and ambulance sirens made arabesques at its fringes like an illuminated border. The workless were back, prowling at corners or standing still; the well-off were hurrying home. It was evening in America.

Next morning I saw a familiar face in the paper. SEVENTH ANNUAL MAHATMA GANDHI FESTIVAL, *Sept 28 and 29, 10 a.m.–8 p.m. Featuring food booths, Indian fashion show, Live Music and Dances.* It was tempting. (It was my second encounter with the Mahatma: in Edmonton there was a bronze bust by the library, with a dent in the head.) But it meant waiting a whole day. I turned the page.

On the 2.30 bus to Salinas, YOUR OPERATOR, Sr E. Guttierrez, SAFE, RELIABLE, COURTEOUS, rapped idly with his ring finger on the gearshift. We were on a six-lane freeway, but the traffic out of the city was, as the *Examiner* editorial put it, "running, not flowing". Also running, for mayor, was a spread of candidates whose names were instructive: Agnos, Alioto, Hongisto, Hsieh, and Jordan. All had plans for the homeless, all had splendid homes. I went between the paper and the billboards. Serial killer and ex-US Marine Corps survivalist, Charles Ng, had been flown in from Canada under heavy guard. GREAT AMERICA! *Network with us!* Traffic arrows flew thick and fast. *Adopt-a-Highway!* AMAZINGLY LOW PRICE! Emergency Call Box. LOW LOW! *Don't!* Early that morning a man had leapt to his death from the Golden Gate bridge.

On such days Nguyen Ai (and perhaps Charles Ng) must wonder why he left Saigon.

My only American relative lived in Salinas, a cousin I'd last (and first) seen twenty years before. I'd just hitchhiked across America and it was my last ride. A soldier coming home on leave had his taxi stop for me and paid the driver to drop me off after he got out himself. It was the only time I ever hitchhiked by cab. The driver dropped me at my cousin's door, into a dinner party.

This time I checked into a hotel. In the morning Jenny and I sat over fat omelettes and ticked off cousins. Next we put headstones on uncles and aunts, and lastly we turned to Steinbeck's valley. Jenny teaches English, mostly to Hispanics. There was rising tension, she said, between newcomers and old residents. The population was now "fifty-five per cent minority". On every government form you were required to state whether you were Caucasian, Black, Hispanic, or Asian. Caucasian did not, any longer, include East Indians: they were Asians, though Asian generally meant Orientals of Mongolian stock. In effect, Asian Indians were an invisible quantity, sometimes lumped with Chicanos (whom they once married, when their own women were scarce because Californian law forbade them a white wife). I'd once heard a Spanish American describe them as White Indians to distinguish them from Red Indians. Generally they were "achievers", or by American standards "overachievers", a kind of nuisance category, hominids with round eyes, dark skins, and high grades. Locally, Jenny said, the Patels were known as people of substance, and Sabu the Jungle Boy had a restaurant in Monterey. As for the Hispanics, their politicians cynically manipulated them with talk of the old New Spain. The other, the original, Indians didn't even figure. And latterly there'd come into the valley a people called the Hmongs, aborigines from the border of Cambodia and Laos, boat people who now made a living from market gardens and undersold the established farmers at roadside stalls. The Stone Age had moved next door to Silicon Valley.

There was a train to LA at 11. One track was better than six lanes, I reasoned. We drove to the station. The train was Amtrak late: it would now come in at three. We drove to Monterey through sea mist and scrub oaks and dunes clad in iceplant. ARTICHOKE CAPITAL OF THE WORLD, said an arch we passed under. In those fields Cesar Chavez rid the West of the short-handle hoe. I took the bus back to Salinas. The train limped in at 3.30.

"When I think of Salinas I think of lettuce."

Alison got on at Salinas, but it was only a train station –

and a lettuce bed – to her. Her mother lived in Carmel and her clothes spelt money. She drove a red Nissan turbo, she said, and collected speeding tickets. Her black T-shirt said CORVETTE in mobile gold sequins. But there were complications: she was a vegetarian, she rescued cats off the freeway – dogs too. She didn't take her sunglasses off until dinner. Dinner – courtesy Amtrak, for the delay – was Salisbury steak or nothing.

"But she's vegetarian!"

"I'll just have some broccoli."

"No, ma'am. We'll see what we can do." And he came back with vegetarian lasagna.

Since her husband died Alison had lived with her cats. All three were strays, one had an eye missing. Piece by piece the red turbo, the speeding tickets floated away. I was surprised at how easily the Californian dream came apart. Underneath was an introvert who had once read Spanish literature. Mexican mangoes she simply adored, but was allergic to: her face swole up once. Papayas too, she loved – and the Mexican gardenia!

"We have a gardenia bush at the gate in Dehra Dun," I said.

"You must send me some."

But then there was a lull, and the lull lengthened into silence. At Santa Barbara the train stopped. The conductor hurried down the aisle. A voice on the intercom asked for any available crew to go to his assistance. Presently he rushed back going the other way. "We had to put him off the train," he called to us as if we'd had our eye on the culprit all along. "Too much to drink," his assistant glossed. The train moved on without the drunk. Just short of Glendale we stopped again. Six squad cars raced up to the train and parked at crazy angles, lights flashing. An ambulance arrived, its siren dying. For twenty minutes the streets on either side pulsed red light. The conductor came through again. "Molestation," he said, hammily, *and* the victim had had a fit. "Epilepsy," said the assistant, and dashed offstage. The cop too was buoyant; American men preferred wheeled toys, and the more wheels in one place the better.

Alison got off at Glendale. "You'll enjoy Guadalajara," she said in Spanish and went home to her cats.

The Share-tel hostel on Venice Beach stored luggage. It was the only place in LA where I could leave the gear bag for a month, free. In the morning I walked along the beachfront. With me was an army of strollers who in their other lives drove red turbos and collected speeding tickets. Today, a Sunday, they'd climbed down, stepped out, were trying on their legs. That narrow strip of concrete was the only part of California where walking was respectable. Even there, feet grew wheels. A Rastafarian on rollerblades glided by with a giant white turban and an amplified guitar. That was his life. In a little eddy off the promenade, watched by the curious, there danced the rollerskaters with headphones, each dancer moving to a private music, black men and white women, the sexual currency of the West.

The dancers intrigued me, more than the psychics and palmists and holistic healers with their glass prisms and mystic horns. Whenever I went by, coming or going from the Share-tel, I looked out for a black woman or a white man. And then I saw one: a white man. But he was middle-aged, with thinning white hair and gym muscles running to flab. He wore white body hair and red silk shorts with a Walkman clipped to the waistband. He was handsome and moved easily among the younger dancers. They were too young to guess his age, but he was a figure of fun with the watchers – uneasy fun, because he was one of them, the unsexed: white but not a woman; a man, but not black. In Salt Lake City at that moment, Temple Square was filling up with worshippers in Sunday suits, but this too, under the palms on Venice Beach, was a kind of worship. I saw the man preparing himself all week for this ritual: he lived for it, and judging by his ecstasy, he lived by it too.

In the earliest maps California appears as an island, and something of that insularity remains. More than any other state it is seen as a distinct entity, its wealth quoted as a GNP among nations, its signifying appetite so great that all the American myths – including that of the West – have to come here to be reinvented. So heavily does the scent of careless power hang in the air, so lightly do the natives wear their assurance, that the foreigner becomes perversely foreign. I found myself becoming woefully ignorant, wilfully unAmerican. I began to play a game all colonials play in the metropolis; Carthaginians would have done the same in Imperial Rome. Usually I played it with children: "Mutant Ninja *What*?"

165

or "Bart *Who*?" In Los Angeles I could use it on adults with the same effect – "Dances With *What*?" "Kevin *Who*?" – and treasure the looks I got.

The India shelves in bookshops had only mysticism (so it worked both ways). I asked for *Mother India*. At one time I'd seen copies of Katherine Mayo's 1920s bestseller in every secondhand bookstore in America. Mayo was the Kitty Kelly (Kitty *Who*?) of her day, a journalist who visited India in a spirit of enquiry and raked a rich vein of muck for the moral delectation of the West. Poverty, ignorance, filth, famine, wretched hospitals, child-marriage, suttee: they were shamefully and irrefutably there, in the country and in the book, but only the book profited by them. It went through dozens of printings. The many rejoinders included *An Englishman Defends Mother India*, but Gandhi's stood out: here is a book no foreigner should have written and no Indian should fail to read.

Footsore, the only walker in Santa Monica, I stumbled into a café where everyone was drinking watermelon juice. The patrician-looking Armenians at the next table gave me an interested look; Calcutta's dwindling community had lost another family. School-girls in white – fashion, not uniform – sat singly at the other tables over schoolbooks. Gothic black was washed up in LA, and I'd never seen homework brought to town before.

Back at the beach I went looking for a lifesaver. It seemed the quintessential Californian job, sitting up there in those frag-ile Martello towers and gazing professionally out to sea. But the tower I picked was closed, and so was the next. I was destined not to exorcise my horror of beach culture. But the sea, to some-one growing up a thousand miles from it, was always something theoretical, requiring proof. I scooped up a little of the Pacific. On the rocks was a strand of Venus's necklace that I carried away. Then, recalling that seaweed rots, I dropped it and checked out of the Share-tel.

On the Downtown bus I was suddenly in another city, minority Los Angeles – only, as in Salinas, LA's minorities were the majority. Nothing dates an LA novel like *The Big Sleep* more than the charac-ters' names: Sternwood, Wilde, Geiger, Regan, Brody, Mars, Ohls, and Marlowe, all northern European. Raymond Chandler would not recognize his city today. Anglos, once the overwhelming majority (90% up to the War), are down to a third of the population, with

166

Hispanics heading for half and Blacks and Asians dividing up the rest. The most common name among young Los Angelenos is Jose. For the country as a whole, Hispanic Americans will displace Blacks as the largest minority by the turn of the century. Their eateries and alteration tailors and pentecostal chapels lined Venice Boulevard. At every stop more Hispanics got on; the bus was America. The streets darkened steadily as the bus approached the centre, walls and faces contributing to the twilight at high noon. I had to remind myself that large chunks of a smarter downtown LA were owned by another invisible Asiatic group, the Japanese.

The last stop was the train station. I bought a ticket on the Southwest Chief and checked my bag in. I had eight hours to kill. My name was Philip Marlowe. I recrossed the grand marble hall where the floor took more wax than a dago's moustache, and stepped out onto Alameda. I wasn't looking for trouble, but I bet a dollar on a Canadian dime the dame would find me. Right in front of the train station is old LA with its Spanish-style buildings. The mick church is straight ahead beyond the treed square. On the right of the square facing the pavilion is the Metho church with some fancy stone scrollwork and a yellow Arab dome. There was a crowd of spics milling about the church, but when I came up I saw they were milling about the building next door. That was the Institute of Mexican Culture. They were waiting for the President of the United States of Mexico.

California was important to President Salinas. After the US, Mexico's second biggest trading partner was the nation of California; there were besides ties of history and steady migration. Salinas was important to the US too: the success of the Free Trade Association depended largely on his staunch advocacy. How they treated him now, and Mexico after the world's largest trading block was formed, would be of interest to the rest of Latin America. South American leaders would be watching, because a unified North America, from the Yukon to the Yucatan, was presumably the first step towards a larger zone stretching from Bering Strait to Cape Horn. So Mexico was a test case. The peso might be a lousy bet – lousier than a Canadian dime – but the stakes got higher.

Not everyone was happy to see Salinas. In San Francisco there'd been Mexican human rights activists and American dolphin advocates protesting against Mexico's record. Outside the

Institute of Mexican Culture the crowd was in two camps with a squad of black-uniformed Los Angeles Police Department officers in between. The pro-Salinas group was nearer the church, dressed up and waving flags. A space the size of a tennis court was cordoned off in front of the institute with yellow LAPD tape and the cops stood in a line inside it with their hands clasped in front of them facing the crowd. I worked my way to the front till I was up against the tape halfway between the two groups. Also inside the clearing was a line of charros, Mexican gentleman cowboys in their braided dude outfits and sombreros. And along a red carpet stood two lines of Chicana schoolgirls in duenna dresses with flowers in their hair.

Salinas was late. The Mexican director of the institute and his very blonde wife fussed with ribbons; behind them two charros stood at attention holding the two national flags. The press corps huddled under a flame tree. On my right the anti group began to chant slogans; the pros returned *Viva Mexico*s and waved the paper flags a government man was handing out. The chanting grew impassioned, punctuated by savage bursts, while the pros kept up a sort of bland tintinnabulation. On the street the anti side was growing. A family turned up with a Salinas effigy and a length of rope. There were placards calling for human rights and for an end to political assassinations and torture. WELCOME SALINAS! VIVA MEXICO! said a long banner on the other side. The opposition unrolled one that said, SALINAS USURPER! and *Repudiate the Fraudulent Election!* The loyal charros looked like they wanted to spit. Some of them leaned up against the black-and-white LAPD squad cars (called *black-and-normals* ever since the police chief said famously that blacks didn't bleed like normal people) and chatted to the cops.

I'd been noticing the names on the officers' badges – Ludwig, Waldron, Reed, Ishida – but couldn't make out the one glittering right in front of me on a fair-haired, delicately put-together man with large pink hands. I thought of him as Heinz, and admired his composure. He stood with his hands clasped in front of him, one foot slightly forward, unlike Andrews next down the line, who had his feet apart like a boxer, balanced and ready. Heinz had a small neat moustache on a small neat head that he held at a slight tilt as if considering the crowd and withholding judgement. His eyes, like those of every other cop there except Andrews, were hidden by sunglasses, but it was the nose and the mouth and – especially – the moustache that seemed, mouse-like, to do the seeing.

A Mexican journalist in an expensive suit flashed his press card and tried to get beyond the yellow tape. Heinz gently ushered him back. A drunk ducked under the tape and did two press-ups for the crowd. The crowd cheered. Heinz let him finish and shooed him back. Down the line from me was a woman in a pink polka-dot dress. With her round face and short permed hair she looked the model housewife. In a lull in the chanting she made a trumpet of her placard and screamed in Spanish, *"Cancers of the Fatherland!"* The crowd roared approval. She went on screaming till her voice cracked: *"Murderers of the Nation! Bandits of our Patrimony!"* Young Andrews, standing two feet away, stared at her with frank distaste and then looked the other way at the flag-waving brigade, whose enthusiasm was at least comprehensible. Heinz turned his moustache on her and sussed her out. His face registered no emotion. As he turned I saw his badge. Fair-haired Heinz was Gonzalez!

At 3.15 there was a sense of urgency. The plainclothes men with walkie-talkies began to walk and talk faster. Everybody was looking a different way. A helicopter landed somewhere nearby and several cop cars appeared from nowhere and blocked off the street. A long black car rolled up and no one got out of it. The girls in costume fiddled with their flowers; the red carpet glowed on their sweating faces. A woman in a long black gown with a white sash tiptoed up with a bouquet. "Fuck you, Wilson!" someone from the gay party shouted. There were many irons in this fire.

At 3.25 the director and his blonde wife reappeared. The government man handed out more flags. Andrews faced the crowd and pulled on, with great deliberation, a pair of black kid-leather gloves. Beyond the polka-dot lady was a grandmother who carried a sign that said: SALINAS! US COPS ARE MURDERING MEXICANS AND CHICANOS.

At 3.35 more cops in black lined up and faced the crowd. The welcome party faced the other way, their backs to us. Another black limousine rolled up and Salinas got out. A small, bald man, looking older than his forty-three years.

The crowd erupted with jeers and screams and cheers and vivas. Salinas was hustled into the institute. While he was in there the chanting continued; the pros revived their fatuous trilling like cicadas. The Salinas effigy dangled from a tree. Salinas emerged ten minutes later and the crowd erupted again. He ducked and smiled like a boy caught in mischief, then waved and was tucked back into the car. The car glided away down the drive and it was all over.

The cops took down their yellow tape — would it be used again? — waited till the crowd thinned out, then went home. I went to look at the institute but they were closing too.

In the square where Los Angeles started I sat and cooled my heels and imagined Heinz–Gonzalez cooling his. For two hours we'd stood facing one another. His moustache would have picked up a pretty clear picture of me too. I watched the family that hanged Salinas carrying him home in two pieces. Had they lost a son in Mexico? They looked as deflated as the dummy. The air in the plaza had that stunned, emptied quality that follows an explosion. A few young men lounged on the benches around the pavilion; in a few hours they might be dangerous, but for now it was still light. A white woman with long matted hair conducted an invisible orchestra. The bells of the Catholic church began to toll, candid Spanish bells rocking out in the open.

The Church of Perpetual Adoration was built by Franciscans to serve the town of Los Angeles that had sprung up in the 1780s by the village of Yang Na. Today it stood marooned in the city's traffic, cloistered against the present, secluded but never tranquil. Mass was in progress when I stepped in and took a seat beside a matron whose fierce prayers competed with the priest's. The mass was in Spanish and I strained to hear the priest over the torrent of sighs and whispers beside me. A drunk shouted "*Amen!*" A young woman agitated the water in the font with such force I could hear the ripples at the back of the church over the matron's earnest soughing. Hispanics brought their energy to prayer; Anglos went jogging down Venice Beach.

In the flagstoned cloister were jardinières of hibiscus and bougainvillaea and black wrought-iron benches with a crest in the middle that showed a conquistador with a church and a cross on a hill. The motto was SOBRE TODO LA FE. A door at the end of the verandah said: *Artículos Religiosos*, relics for sale; in the yard was an empty hot-dog stand with limp bunting. In the City of the Angels the church medieval was biding its time. A cool breeze stirred, a helicopter went over, a pious policeman crossed himself at the gate.

I strolled along Main Street past the court house and City Hall, gigantic stone-faced structures that fitted in the eye only when you crossed the street. In Little Tokyo I came on a Japanese curry house where the shrimp curry came with Japanese pickles: deep red radishes, angelica-green cucumbers, and tiny white onions. There was a little glass of what I took to be complimentary sake. I was about to drink a toast to Master Basho when the waitress told me it was syrup for the cold coffee.

Night had fallen. The streets were empty at 8.15. A Hispanic boy stepped out of the shadows and asked for money. He looked lost and frightened and grateful for a dollar. The plaza in front of the Institute of Mexican Culture was dark and deserted. It seemed impossibly quiet, that scene of so much fury. A few sodium street lamps made pools of mournful amber light. It was a curious light that bled objects of their colour. The sub-orange bird-of-paradise lilies looked unnaturally stiff in their beds. I sniffed a khaki rose. A lone man sat sideways on a bench and arranged a newspaper over his legs. He was in bed too.

I crossed Alameda to the railway station, got my bag, and boarded the night train to Arizona. Philip Marlowe was fast asleep.

13

Indian Red

On the Southwest Chief was a woman reading Umberto Eco's *Travels in Hyperreality*, and chuckling. The paperback showed where American intellectuals had been shopping for more than a decade: on the Continent. A whole generation of Anglo-Americans had abandond their empirical virtue and — like the painters and musicians and writers of an earlier generation — gone on a trans-Atlantic spree, a kind of whoring after foreign gods, the wages of which was the French distemper. Now it was Italy's turn; anywhere but home. Signor Eco plays kittenishly with the fluff of American reality. His wit sweeps you along like sparkling table talk, a delightful Higher Chat that will, after the fourth bottle, pass for philosophy. I borrowed the book briefly, and unearthed a notion of my own, Higher Cow.

The average visitor to India is going to remember cows. Whatever else he may see — slums, degradation, the famous Colour — his lasting impression is of cows in the street. As a visitor usually from the advanced industrial world, the world of the automobile, he registers not so much a simple bucolic fact (cow) as a disjunction of two orders: cows (pastoral) *among* cars (industrial). He photographs it and goes on his way. Now there is another sort of visitor. He has read R.K. Narayan and Nirad Chaudhuri and V.S. Naipaul, Romila Thapar's *History of India* (Volume I), perhaps Stella Kramrisch on the Hindu temple. He has probably read other travellers too. He has in short read more on his subject than the average Indian. But he gets simple things wrong, he misses things that are staring him in the face, he sees things that are not there. He is seeing Higher Cow. And until he marries an Indian woman and lives with her in an Indian city or town or (less likely) village, he is destined to go on seeing Higher Cow. It was so with me in America. Twenty years ago, I'd had my chance. I'd come close to settling, and I'd let it slip. Now I was condemned to wander, along with every informed visitor, in the realms of Higher Cow, noticing an elevated order of things (or ordinary things in an elevated way) but getting simple things wrong, reading over, reading into, unable simply to read.

Hire Cow glances across the aisle of the Amtrak Southwest Chief. A woman has taken the window seat. She has her foot in bandages and has laid her walking-stick across the seat beside her. "I want special treatment," she warns the conductor, who laughs, black to white. (Black American men have the same feudal hold on Amtrak that Goan stewards have on P&O liners.) The conductor posts a GBA destination slip on the rack above her head. Enter a cowboy wearing two hats. The woman lifts first an eyelid and only then her stick. The cowboy nods mournful acknowledgment and stows his case overhead. He takes off his outer hat and lays it solemnly on the case, a wreath on a tomb.

A man from Kansas comes through the train spreading the good word: the lounge is open. "Then let's go drink," says the woman Susie, and the cowboy and Hire Cow follow. In the lounge car is a hippy from Denver reading Peter Matthiessen's *Crazy Horse*.

"But he's not your kind of Indian," he warns.

Susie prefers Linda Goodman's *Star Signs*. "I'm Sagittarius," she says. The cowboy is Gemini. "Too bad you guys are getting off at Flagstaff," Susie says, "or tomorrow night we could really party. Both my husbands were Taurus. You know, the people in my second husband's town were ignorant and inbred and hated strangers. They had bad teeth. My husband was smart and looked after his teeth. But it was a raw town. Once in a bar I saw a cockroach as big as a mouse."

"I'd hate to see their mice," Hire Cow says, and the cowboy cheers up for the first time.

Hire Cow borrows *Crazy Horse*. The Denver man would still like to clarify a point. "These Indians are *not* your kind of Indian."

Hire Cow returns to his seat. Susie's blue denim bag has a white cross and a stylized dove on it, with BETHEL on top and

WHERE CHRIST IS PRIORITY underneath. Wrong again: he thought he'd read her through. He dozes. When he wakes he finds Susie asleep with her head on the cowboy's chest, her leg drawn up across his knee. A socked foot peeps intimately from under their shared wrap. Her hand clasps his, a band of gold on the ring finger. In the soft focus of sleep it's a touching tableau: Domestic Bliss, or Tenderness. But overhead their star signs are crossed:

65 WINDOW GBA 1.   66 AISLE FLG 1.

The Southwest Chief was cold inside and out. The desert stars hung low and frosty, and a small brass half moon rode high up near Orion's belt like a buckle. The double glazing reflected a second, fainter moon, and at certain angles the ghost of a third. I was back where I left off in the middle of the continent, the coast a dream.

At Flagstaff I waited in the steely morning light to see if the cowboy would stay on the train. Would love conquer distance? But no: there he was on the platform in his two hats. He had small furtive eyes that looked sideways at me when he thought I wasn't looking. I looked back, but they slid away. We were strangers again.

I took a bus to the Grand Canyon. "Look out for the pinyon jay," said the gangly boy beside me. He told me there were two kinds of tassel-eared squirrels at the canyon: one kept to the north rim and one to the south. It was eighteen miles across, he warned; it took five hours to get to the bottom and ten hours to get back out and I'd need so many gallons of water per day because the evaporation rate was such and such.

The visitor to the Grand Canyon comes burdened with so many figures and expectations that the reality is bound to let him down, to look more like an inverted jelly-mould than the vision that stretched before Don Lopez de Cardenas, its first documentarist, in 1540. In the great hollow are other jelly-moulds, the right way up, and as the sun dries up the pools of shadow, the watcher's spirit sinks. It takes a whole day of wandering along the rim among the sun-struck chipmunks for patience to be rewarded. As the sun dips, the shadows return. They are the colour of the pinyon jay's wings, violet, but without the iridescence. The weathered rock takes on a pomegranate tint and starts to glow. The effect grows as shadow replaces light, until night fills the canyon like a lake.

The next day in Flagstaff I watched a man make stone. He was up a ladder restoring a red frieze of acanthus leaves that was badly weathered. His job was to make it new.

"You see that pillar behind you," he said. "All that's got to be done. We make a mould of the original where it's preserved like over there. We make a cast and we duplicate it."

"What is that stuff?"

"It's Portland. It's a kind of accelerated acrylic." He nodded at his wife. "We got our hands full with these three pillars." Talking, he changed hands on his jelly-mould and the acrylic bruised a little. It was my fault. His wife looked displeased but he shrugged it off.

The tortillas at Kathy's Place were so fine and soft and the bowl of chilli so enormous it seemed churlish to use my discount voucher. When the bowl was empty, a kind of lesser canyon, I wrote my Grand Canyon postcards. One was to our jobbing gardener in Dehra Dun. It was in Hindi, but he would still have to have it read. He would not have heard of the Grand Canyon. As I posted it I saw it looked like a picture of a hole in the ground and I imagined him puzzling over it. He spent his life digging holes in the ground.

The hardest part of the job, the stonemaker said, was matching the colours. You had to take a good look at the original stone and guess what your wet acrylic would look like when it dried. The colour he was after was a dull red, a colour very like the unused one in my childhood paintboxes: Indian Red. I always wondered about that *Indian*. (It was the same with Indian ink and Indian corn.) Our Indian or theirs? The ink, I decided, was ours. The corn was problematic – we grew maize in our back yard – but I let it go. Indian Red was the sticking point. As a colour it was drab; it lacked the frank appeal of the other reds, the scarlets, the crimsons; it lacked the rich lustre of even its brown neighbour, Burnt Sienna. It remained a flat cake of dull red earth long after the others were eroded away into fascinating canyons. In the end I gave it away. India was ochre, not red. The way Russia was black, as molasses and rye and orthodoxy; or the way Spain was a harsh high orange, and China a willow-pattern blue. The way, on this journey, Canada persisted as Canola yellow, in spite of the Yukon. Mexico was still open, but now that my time in the United States was almost over, I formally ceded to the union Indian Red.

Bill Earlycorn was no help. At the Flagstaff youth hostel (NO VICIOUS DINOSAURS ALLOWED) I asked the girl at the desk for a room without too many sharers.

"I'll put you with one of the residents," she said, sounding doubtful. "He's an Indian guy." She had no trouble with the two kinds of Indian.

It was a two-berth room, with bunks, but then not so long ago travellers in these parts slept three to a bed. Earlycorn had the lower bunk. He had laid out his things with a painful neatness, demarcating his territory in a room he was obliged from time to time to share with strangers. The closet held a hard-shell suitcase and a tidy row of shoes and shirts. On the suitcase was a bible. I was writing at the desk when I heard the key turn in the door.

Earlycorn was not pleased. He was a stocky man, a little shorter than my middling height, with a wide face that looked like trouble smoothed over. He nodded at me and said, "Bill." But because it was a small room we began to talk. He worked in town in a government office. On weekends he went home to the reservation. His was a large family, and they prayed together. I asked him about traditional Indian faiths. Were there people on the reservation who practised the old teachings?

"There are some," he said. "They say the earth is sacred, the sun, moon, animals, sea, mountain, river, stars. They call coyote God, the bear their uncle, the horny toad their grandpa. But the earth is not God. The Bible says there are only two powers, the Devil and God. I don't think the old way's gonna work. You can't ride horses, hunt buffalo today. They go to school — that's not keeping your belief. The best way is to get on with the modern way. Christianity is the world religion, for all walks of life, all races."

"The Muslims believe *theirs* is the one true faith, and the Jews . . ."

"I base my belief on what God says in His word." He reached into the closet and brought out two bibles. The English was more thumbed than Paula's *Book of Mormon*. But there was also the Navajo Bible, *Dyin God Bizaad*, Holy God's Word. " 'The people who have walked in darkness have seen a great light,' " he read.

176

"They follow the old ways because they have not been born again. But when you are born again" (he spoke very softly and earnestly) "the Holy Spirit fills you with *such* grace, it's truly the peace that passeth understanding."

I told him of my evening with Gary Oker, the Beaver Indian from Dawson Creek. "Do you think his Great Spirit could be the same as your Holy Spirit?"

He shook his head. "There is only one Holy Spirit. I know there are Indians who want to go back to the old ways. Mostly they're troublemakers, s-sinners. They s-*sin*." He gave the word a terrible susurrus. "I pray to God every night to touch their hearts."

He preached hard and long; then we turned in. He had to be up early to go to work, he said, turning off the light. In the dark he said he'd been a soldier in Vietnam.

"When were you there?"

"1966 to 1968. That's where God came into my life."

I thought it explained the mask, that glassed-off look that spoke of sights beyond belief. He would have been young then.

In the morning he switched on the overhead light and dressed for work. Then he switched it off and opened the door.

"Don't use my name in your book," he said and went out without saying goodbye. I was sorry about the name. It was much more vivid than "Earlycorn".

The bus depot was just around the corner, they said. At the corner was a Middle-Eastern restaurant. I dropped my bags and cooled my hands on a glass of guava juice. The Anglo woman who ran the place sold Asian foods too, to Saudis and Pakistanis and Indians on the nearby campus. One wall was lined with shelves of couscous, coconut, canned dumplings, chickpeas, tahini, tall jars of Poonjiaji pickles I hadn't seen for a while, the more familiar squat Patak's pickle jars, brown gunny sacks of Basmati rice, Persian Cold Wax Hair-Remover, Al Wazir's olive oil, Olga's Imported Greek Peppers.

"It's a dollar seven with ice," she said half-heartedly when I poured the drink into a glass. It was 99¢ straight from the bottle. "But you don't have to . . ." We pushed my dime back and forth on the counter. I could see she would never get rich.

It was a long hot haul to the Greyhound station. Some motel Patels pointed the way and I only just caught the bus. On it was Eddy, star receiver of the Arizona State University football team. He was the first American football player I'd ever talked to; in fact he did the talking. (Later, in following the Super Bowl, I learnt this was a trait in star receivers, tall, loquacious, mercurial men. But before Eddy I wouldn't have known a star receiver from a dish antenna.) My first thought was that he was too weedy to play football, nothing like the behemoths you saw on TV. It hadn't occurred to me to distinguish between runners and blockers, but the moment he made it, the distinction seemed fundamental, even primordial. All men, all microbes, were either runners or blockers. Eddy was a runner.

But he was resting up. Two months before, he said, as the bus ground slowly up a steep hill in first gear, he'd jumped to collect a high pass and two defence helmets had met at speed — with his knee in between. The *pain*, oh man, the pain! He'd have to have surgery, and enforced rest. He was ready to play now, but the coach wouldn't let him because the doctor wouldn't sign his release. So he'd gone to Florida to visit his mother and get the insurance papers: he was on her policy. It had been a long journey and his knee was acting up. He stroked it from time to time.

"The day I graduated from high school they were knocking at my door," he said. "My father handled all that. He's in California. I got offers from Notre Dame, and Michigan offered a two-year scholarship. But ASU made the best offer. I got their top scholarship — four years and a new Nissan."

He sketched a gridiron and showed me a series of complicated moves. The page looked like an old-fashioned battle plan. Later he noticed me looking at the organ pipe cactus that had begun to replace prickly pear in the desert.

"At Christmas time in Arizona," he said, "people put strings of lights on their cactus in the front yard and it looks cool." The way he clipped his *cool*, I saw goose-bumps come up on a cheerleader's knees. I took out my journal.

"I keep a diary too," he said. "I never miss a day."

He got off at a suburban stop. Across the aisle from me was a sombre, handsome woman wearing sensible black felt shoes embroidered with roses. I'd had the choice of those two seat companions when I got on the bus. I tried to catch the title of the woman's book. She didn't shut it till we got to Phoenix. It was called *The Quiet Answer*.

*

Phoenix had a shell-shocked look, as if an anti-personnel bomb had fallen downtown leaving the buildings untouched. The glass and steel glittered in the afternoon sun, perfect shapes without apparent function, like those elegant structures on science-fiction paperbacks. I walked the streets under a harsh sun, expecting multiple moons to loom from behind the next tower. The water in the drinking fountains ran hot, the potted trees looked Venusian. When I asked a man where the public library was he pointed to an empty lot and said, "It sits over there on Mondays," as one speaking of a flying saucer.

The youth hostel was overrun by aliens, mostly English, talking like Mr Spock. After dinner there was Higher Chat. Les was the only American in the room. He was a man of my own age with a slight stoop. He leaned against the wall the whole time like a stage extra with an empty coffee mug and listened without joining in. Next morning I saw a leaflet on food stamps beside his breakfast plate. He was studying it with the same baffled intentness he'd turned on the company the night before. I asked him where he was from.

"Chicago," he said, "inner city," and then, "not *inner* inner." He'd come to Arizona looking for work and found it at the air force base near Nogales. After three years the cutbacks started and he was laid off. He'd earned good money, he said, over $7 an hour. Now he worked at the hostel in exchange for accommodation.

"I've been to Mexico," he said. "Usually I go to Mazatlan. When I was in Nogales I met a Mexican girl who worked in an office. She took me home to meet her family. I've stayed with them several times, whenever I go down there, but it's been over a year now. We used to write, but her letters took so long to get here."

I saw a patient Mexicana, a disappointed family.

"Sometimes the Mexican authorities will bother you," he warned, "especially if you're travelling alone. But once I was harassed by US Customs coming back in. I didn't have a birth certificate so they kept me waiting a long time. They made me recite the national anthem in front of the whole queue. I got really mad and took out my Legion card. Then they let me in."

*

179

I caught the Tucson bus. At Casa Grande a green-uniformed border patrol officer came on board and took away a smuggler. The Mexican had two colourful bags and a big portable stereo. He climbed into the waiting van as if it were his limousine and they drove off into the desert. We were in a giant furnace. In the pay restroom the only faucet was marked, surreally, HOT. A mistake, I thought, and let it run a while. The water, cool at first, turned hot.

The Tucson Congress Hotel set certain rooms aside as a youth hostel. Sharing my room was Peter, a young German scientist attending a conference. "In Tucson," he said (he said *Tew-sn*) "you must see the desert museum." I made a note of it; he was a plant scientist. In the evening I felt queasy but made a feeble foray downtown. The heat from the buildings hogged the sidewalks; you looked up hopefully every time the slightest breeze rattled the palm fronds. At the Bookery Café I sat beside the Health & Diet shelves and knew I was ill. I took a single bite out of my sandwich and put it down. Its profile resembled the route of my journey: a diagonal from top left to bottom right with a bite taken out of the middle where I made the West Coast loop. In Shandean terms the way from the Yukon to the Yucatan would be:

I had taken up the straight line at the south rim of the Grand Canyon at the very longitude of Salt Lake City, so in a way the canyon was the bite.

The next day I made a phone call on a sore throat. It was to a man whose name I'd known for twenty years but whom I'd only lately read, N. Scott Momaday. I called him from the library, where I'd marshalled all his books, and we arranged to meet. I spent the rest of the day in the library, trickling out for meals when my mother's voice repeated: *Feed a cold, Starve a fever*. A Hare Krishnavite caught me at a hot-dog stand and offered to sell me a vegetarian cookbook. Swami Gobinda, alias Dennis, was also a photographer and his talk was a mixture of film speeds and salvation; he'd done a photo tour of India where the two lines appeared to converge. Gobinda was born in California to Baptists and almost became a Baptist minister, but couldn't control his sexual appetite. "How can you sleep with me and profess to be religious?" a girlfriend asked him, and got him thinking.

"Say a prayer for me, pal!" said a big Anglo, patting him on the back. He looked like a blocker. His friends sniggered. Gobinda bowed his pink shaven head and drew his lips into a tight line.

"Educated sudras!" he said to me. Sudras are the lowest of the four Hindu castes.

A girl came out of the library. "I've been reading your pamphlet," she said, "and it says here 'the infant is born with nine holes and a penis.' I don't have a penis, and I have *ten* holes."

"Talking like a golf course," Gobinda said when she'd gone. "Did she learn anything else from it? When people get blasphemous – usually Christians – I just turn away. I've learnt how to spot a Christian and I say" (looking at his watch) "'Is *that* the time!'"

After the library closed I was sitting at the bus stop when I noticed the lid was off the observatory across the street. In a starlit cabin was Jeff.

"Have a look at this," he said with his eye to the lens.

It was Saturn, glowing like no heavenly body I'd ever seen. It was the size and colour of a pearl, and about it spun, in sharply defined bands, the famous rings. A medieval astronomer would have given his fortune for such a glimpse; he would have travelled the whole distance I'd covered for this alone. Jeff poured out the facts. Saturn was a million miles away. It was not solid, it was gas, but really dense at the core. It might even be nearer liquid there. The rings were made of ice particles, mostly water ice . . . I let my tape recorder listen and gazed. Then we looked at other stars, but nothing matched Saturn. It fitted the stereotype, the familiar cartoon planet spinning over a bump on the head, and still it mocked the traveller's capacity to digest wonders.

I breakfasted with Peter the botanist. The night before we'd woken

181

intermittently to a savage bass guitar in the dance hall below. The beat shook the floorboards and bedsteads with tribal violence and died in the bedsprings under the pillow. Friday night was music night at the Congress Hotel and the cheaper rooms were above the noise. Breakfast among the ferns downstairs, on the Saturday morning sidewalk, was tranquillity itself. Peter was interested in plant behaviour, in the way plants accommodate themselves – their selves, their very shape – to their environment. Humans, he said, changed the environment because their own shape was determined in the womb. They might respond to external stimuli with small changes, like tanning, but their form was fixed from the start.

"With plants it's different." He ran a finger down the fluted vase between us. "The way their roots go depends on the obstructions they encounter; their flowering is in response to the length of the day. There's no controlling intelligence as in the case of the animal brain: the whole plant *is* the brain. All its cells do the 'reasoning'. What I study are the ways the cells change and the 'reasons' for those changes. It's one of the last unresolved problems in biology. We know about the nature of human cells, we've cracked the codes. But we don't know how, or why, plants respond the way they do. We tend to change the world; plants change themselves.

"Morphogenesis – the establishment of form – is an old problem but there's been really very little progress in our understanding compared with other fields. You see, shape is independent of substance. There are constants in a plant's development, but there are also random, unexplained responses. For example a flower might appear at the bottom of a stalk for no apparent reason. You take the morning glory. Normally it flowers in winter, so if you artificially shorten its 'day' it will respond by flowering. But if you deprive it of daylight it will continue to grow without flowering. It becomes 'immortal'. Once it flowers it enters mortality. At what stage does it 'choose' to die?"

He went to his conference. I took a bus to the end of the city grid. Where the straight roads gave way to curved ones (where the money began) I took a taxi to Momaday's house on Roller Coaster Avenue.

"My hacienda," he said with an apologetic laugh as I surveyed his demesne. It was a gullied stretch of yellow earth towards the mountains, saved from utter desert by scrubby palo verde trees and thorny cactus.

Natchie Scott Momaday was a big man with pale metis features and a dark woodwind voice. He was Kiowa Indian on his father's side and Anglo-French on his mother's. His father, Al Momaday, was an artist; his work hung beside his son's in the living-room where we sat on chairs upholstered in plum-covered leather. Momaday won the Pulitzer prize in 1968 for his novel *House Made of Dawn*, which draws on his earlier book, *The Way to Rainy Mountain*. *Rainy Mountain* retraces in distilled prose the Kiowa migration from Montana to Oklahoma. The effect is one of chastened pastoral, gravely beautiful, somewhere between eclogue and elegy.

"I grew up in this part of the world," Momaday said. "I was born in Oklahoma, but my parents moved when I was very small and I spent my growing-up years in New Mexico and Arizona. When I wrote *The Way to Rainy Mountain* I was living in Santa Barbara, about 1965–66. I just got in my car and drove up to Yellowstone and retraced the Kiowa migration route through several states where I knew they'd been."

The Kiowa are a small tribe. One story explains why. To enter the world they had to pass through a hollow log. One by one they wriggled through, but then a pregnant woman got stuck and no one else could follow.

"What's left of the Kiowa now?" I asked Momaday. "Where are they?"

"They are in Oklahoma. That is the centre of their culture now and has been since about 1750, when they ended their migration. There are about seven thousand."

"Seven thousand is not very many. Is the population increasing?"

"It's increasing. I don't know what it was at the turn of the century. I would say about two thousand."

"Is that increase true of the American Indian population generally?"

"Yes, I would say so."

"You've been quoted as saying you couldn't make sense of the term 'The American Indian'."

"Oh, it's true that there are so many different communities and they are so diversified you have to talk about individual tribes or locations. 'The American Indian' in quotes doesn't exist. Most tribes suffered a great diminution in their numbers in the latter

183

part of the nineteenth century: diseases, wars. You know, at the turn of the century 'The Vanishing Indian' was truly vanishing, but from about say 1910 on it changed."

I said, "In Great Falls I saw a painting by C.M. Russell which shows an Indian elder sitting by the roadside with his pipe before him on the ground and in the distance the locomotive is approaching and the city and industrial blight, and in the middle ground there's a white girl on a bicycle – a modern miss in bloomers and pumps – looking back at the old man. How would you paint the Indian today? Is that your work there?"

"That's my father's. The figure facing you is mine. I think the alternative to Russell would be to paint a blue-collar worker or a professional man or a student who is indistinguishable from others except for his features, the colour of his skin, and maybe he wears an Indian ring or a bracelet. The pow-wow figure is interesting and retains all the colour of the past, but that image of the Indian is not really useful. Of course the film industry reinforced that misconception."

"And also, Vine Deloria says, the anthropologists."

"Well, Vine, who is of course a friend of mine, is a little more volatile than I am. But I do enjoy his jibes at the anthropologists [*laughs*]. It's very funny . . . kind of a sport!"

"Sort of potshots at the Union Pacific?"

"Right, right! Have you met him, by the way?"

"No, I was hoping to . . ."

"He's gone back to Colorado."

Deloria has written caustically of the anthropologists' Indian. "Indian people begin to feel," he wrote in *Custer Died for Your Sins*, "they are merely shadows of a mythical super-Indian." By parroting the anthropologists' ideas young Indians have avoided facing "the need for adjustment to the modern world". Deloria argued for "modern tribalism" rather than the anthropologists' folk people.

I asked Momaday if there was such a thing as an Indian aesthetic.

"I think there is," he said. "You can see how it has evolved. The Kiowa are known as painters. They started with pictographic representations on skin, tipis, and saddles and shields. And then – I don't know if you're familiar with the Fort Marion experience?"

"No, I'm not."

184

"Well, there was an army man whose name was Richard Pratt and he had this great interest in Native Americans in the 1870s. He decided that the best way to treat the Indian would be to take him, put him in a uniform, cut his hair, teach him English, and give him a trade. One of his great slogans was *Kill the Indian and save the man.* He gathered up some plains Indians, Kiowas, Apaches, and Cheyennes, something like seventy-five of them, and took them to Florida and there in an old Spanish fort called Fort Marion he made a kind of school. The Indians there – it's a very poignant story – were physically dislocated, they were prisoners, they'd been taken in shackles, and he did indeed put them in uniform. And this is where Kiowa painting began. Those Indians got hold of ledger books – in fact Pratt gave them books and paper and pencils, coloured pencils.

"And so they began drawing, and they made ledger-book drawings that are really quite expressive and touching and they're now very rare and they're collector's items – but they're fine art. And from that early expression evolved the whole tradition of Kiowa painting, and that grew and grew and grew, and my father was right in that line of evolution. And it's still there. I think I'm in that line too. I've looked closely at early Kiowa paintings.

"You know there was a group of painters called the Kiowa Five in the 1920s. They were students at the University of Oklahoma. They did really fine two-dimensional things, things that would be related to pictographs, rock paintings, work with a wonderful vitality."

"But that," I pointed at a painting of his, a figure in yellow and brown, "would be a cross between a Western modernist impulse and a pictograph. What are the Kiowa elements there?"

"That's also, as I see it, two-dimensional. It's very simple, it's a line drawing in effect, and it has the lines of a pictograph more than other paintings you see around. But you're right, that's a departure from Indian art as well."

"Can there be a blend, a cross?"

"Certainly."

"What is the essence of that cross?"

"One of my own favourite artists is Emil Nolde. I hope I've incorporated something of his vision into my work. Fritz Scholder, who is one of the pre-eminent Native American artists, admires Francis Bacon. So it's a reaching towards the universal."

"What would be the elements of an Indian aesthetic?"

"I think first of all a view of nature. The Indian sees very deeply into the physical world, and so he has a special regard for animals, birds, features in the landscape, so those things are delineated with a kind of devotion in the work that sets him apart, that sets the work apart. Also there's always been a very great sense of proportion and design and symmetry in such things as Navajo weaving and this comes out of a native awareness."

"You notice that proportion in Kwakiutl art as well."

"Exactly. I think that's very highly developed on the coast."

"Do you see an evolution, an increasing sophistication as the Indians moved southwards, peopling the Americas?"

"I don't see that. It would be hard for me to imagine anything more sophisticated than the prehistoric paintings."

"I was thinking of the surface evidence. For instance Eskimo art has a kind of simplicity to it. It's not as crowded with detail — a reflection of the landscape perhaps."

"Ya, well, if you take an Eskimo soapstone carving or a sealskin kayak, those are very pure and very simple, and then you follow the line down you do find things that are more complicated."

"I often think of that difference when I compare a Japanese painting with an Indian painting — my kind of Indian. There's a lot more happening on the page in the Indian one and a greater simplicity in the Chinese or Japanese. They're less fussed."

"I suppose there is a greater intricacy of design as you come down through time from the kayak to the northern plains quill work or bead work."

"Do you find a similar development in the literature?"

"In the oral tradition historically, the songs and prayers of the native Americans were very simple. Sometimes profound — very often profound — yet at the same time very concise and simple. And you look at Native American poetry now, and it's more complex and there are many — often technological — images."

"I was looking through the university telescope at Saturn last night. It was so beautiful, and yet it could also be seen as just an angle of light. There's a magical way of looking at things, and then there's just a plain planet. Do you think something is lost in the transition?"

186

"Absolutely, yes. I believe the efficacy of language has been lost. We do not in our times, in literate times, have the same belief in the power of language. We put something in the computer and it's there when we get back. But the storyteller in the nineteenth century knew that if he didn't get it in his head and speak it on his tongue it was lost. So story, prayer, any kind of verbal construct was more precious."

I asked Momaday about his most recent novel. It had, he said, a strong sense of place, the place where he grew up. "New Mexico and Oklahoma, because that's really where I set down roots in my most impressionable years. I think that's all you really have to write out of."

"Are you a regionalist?"

"Well, you know, Wallace Stegner is a great spokesman for this part of the world, and there's Thomas McGuane . . . so many others."

"Do you see yourself as part of that tradition?"

"I don't like geographical labels for writing. But I think the Western experience, this lived experience, is an important literary subject. People who live in the West are concerned to reflect this landscape. And it's not really new to American literature, but till recently the West was seen as something very exotic."

"Well, here's one outsider who never thought that way! I always felt that because the East set itself up as a mirror of Europe, a New England, what was valuable in American literature – what was American in it – would be found further out, out West."

"Oh absolutely, that's just right. A couple of years ago I wrote a chapter for the *Columbia History of the United States*, the initial chapter, called 'The Native Voice', and I made that very point, that we have been taught – *I* was – that American literature was a derivative of English literature. When you looked for the origins of American literature you thought automatically of the Puritans and New England and so on. And I made the point that American literature really begins with some illiterate anonymous paleo-Indian who takes a daub and puts a mark on the rock. Barrier Canyon, Utah, I think I used as an example, as one of the rock paintings of anthropomorphic forms in procession, two thousand years old, and I argued that if you really want to specify an origin of American literature – why not that?"

14

Ethical Cowboys

Sunday I swapped Momaday's tawny Mercedes for a small white rental Geo and headed for Tombstone. Before Momaday went I got a photo of him on Oracle Avenue where he dropped me. I still had a cold and Alan, a Canadian at the Congress Hotel, had the remedy.

"Ten drops of this stuff in a glass of water and you can gargle the phlegm away. Chemists usually sell you hydrogen peroxide at 3% strength so I had to send away for the real thing. This is 30%."

I was ready to clutch at straws.

"I do things differently from normal people," he said while I gargled. "I picked up a firewood truck for three hundred dollars and drove down from BC to meet a man who makes adobe huts. He uses the rammed-earth technique. Feel better?"

"Much." His faith was so patent it seemed cruelty to disappoint him.

"I had four sessions with a doctor in Idaho who administers it intravenously. It's in the blood for twenty seconds and it does its cleaning real quick and leaves by the lungs. See, I had a colon problem that a medium told me about. She went into a trance and told me – in a man's voice, eh – that my colon was fucked and needed cleaning out. So I had two enemas with hydrogen peroxide and all the crud came away along with a white mucus and I had a clean colon."

"Wonderful!"

"My girlfriend has an allergy to apples so I took her down to my doctor too. If my mother ever got cancer I'd take her away from the chemotherapist and clean her out with hydrogen peroxide."

I rented the Geo next morning. The downtown rentals were closed so I had to go out to the airport. At the Laos Transit Center I appeared to have strayed into Mexico. A chicana icecream girl trundled a cart that said *Moreliana Paletas* and nothing at all in English; her little bell tinkled in Spanish. All along the road to the airport were signs in Spanish proclaiming lawyers' oficinas and cantinas serving fine Mexican food. The squat brick houses huddled together in the heat, their top-heavy verandahs the only cool-seeming space about them. On one verandah two old black men sat on tilted chairs and stared into the afternoon.

The Eggs in Hell at breakfast hadn't scoured my throat either. I stopped at a superpharmacy and bought some potent capsules in red-and-yellow motley. Next door I got a gallon of water and a yard of fiery sausage, desert food, and got on the freeway. The freeway signs said Benson for miles. Tombstone is out on a limb on Highway 80, past Apache Peak. Beyond Cochise, the one-time Butterfield stage route crossed Apache Pass into New Mexico, through mining towns with vaunting names like Lordsburg and Shakespeare.

Tombstone, another mining town, owed its origin to silver but its reputation to its cemetery and to a few square yards of yellow earth fenced off as the OK Corral. Here in 1881 Wyatt, Virgil, and Morgan Earp, and their friend Doc Holliday, shot dead Billy Clanton and Tom and Frank McLaury in the most famous gunfight of the Wild West.

"Murder" was how the Boothill Cemetery pamphlet – no revisionist tract – describes the killing, and the word takes some of the shine off the Earp halo. The Clantons and McLaurys were cowboys in the literal sense of the word, cattlemen, and therefore almost by definition occasional rustlers as well. In the Huston movie *Gunfight at the OK Corral*, with Burt Lancaster as Wyatt Earp and Kirk Douglas as Holliday, the good guys are the other sort of cowboy, professional men in cowboy clothes: the lawman with a star pinned on and the urbane doctor, sharp shooter, but also sharp dresser. As I remember it, the lawman's hand is forced, his kid brother killed by the Clantons, while the doctor's faithless mistress is the cause of his delinquency, if not his whisky cough. A complex social stand-off becomes a morality play: the Clantons get what's coming to them and the good cowboys win.

The Argentinian Borges, heir to another sort of cowboy tradition, once distinguished between his own country's celebration of the lawless gaucho and the North American elevation of the virtuous cowboy. The Good Cowboy he attributes to the "ethical" penchant of the Puritan; the Hispanic motives he leaves sadly unexamined, merely stating that good and evil were secondary qualities in Argentinian Westerns. His obsessive Anglophilia apart, it's hard to imagine why Borges, so sure out East, should lose his grip in the West.

A simpler reason suggests itself. The gory reality behind the United States' primary myth, the settling of a continent, had constant need of moral justification, especially after the fact. After all, a sizeable Indian remnant persisted – chiefly in the West – an undigested lump in the body politic. In Argentina, where the settlers made shorter work of the aborigines, there was no noticeable remnant to stir the mythmakers to righteous indignation – or to vindication. For American writers the division between good and evil (the conquerors and the conquered) was out in the open. (Romanticists of the Noble Savage simply reversed those moral poles.) And just as the Good Indian could become an honorary white – *Kill the Indian and save the man* – the Bad Cowboy was a lapsed white. Bandits, cattle thieves, horse thieves, were simply displaying classic Indian behaviour, and deserved the same rough justice. In Indian stories Coyote was sometimes wrong; in cowboy lore the hero had to be right. The new Americans had to make the good guy win, if only by making the winner the good guy.

In the Huston film Earp is a curiously colourless figure, rather like an American president, who need not be distinguished but must be blameless, judged by what he is not, rather than what he is. It's Holliday who catches the eye and the imagination, even with that unconvincing cough. His genre accomplishments apart, he is a more complex figure than Earp: a professional who scants his profession (this doctor kills, goes for the wrong bottle), a responsible man gone off the rails. He got the clothes right but he's in danger of backsliding (he falls more than once), of becoming a Bad Cowboy. The film must rescue him: hence the mistress, the cough. It's a pity. He comes to the brink of complexity and backs off. He must, because the ethical cowboy is a simple soul. He gets

190

his virtue not by thinking but with his mother's milk. Complexity is as bad as cattle-rustling. The whole point about ethics is that it comes instinctively, naturally. Some have it, some don't.

After my journey I went back to a childhood book, *The Wild West*, for the facts of the famous gunfight. Three abreast, the book said, the Earp brothers started down Fourth Street towards the OK Corral. Doc Holliday, carrying a shotgun, ran after them and insisted on going along. Here there was an illustration: *They made a grim but splendid sight*. The picture, in black and white, showed four men with square jaws and long coats in perfect step, a phalanx of avenging angels bearing down on the wicked. (Huston's camera angles did much the same ten years on.) "Without breaking step the four swept around the corner." Moments later, at the Corral, "Wyatt had his Buntline Special spurting flame. A slug from his revolver ploughed into Frank McLowery's stomach, pitching him forward." And so to Boothill.

KILL SADDAM INSANE, said the graffiti, but the Earps of the day botched the job. They did so partly because policing the world had become an embarrassment; when you are self-conscious you don't shoot straight. True, with modern gunfights there are more people watching at the window, but the fact is ever since independence the United States' dealings with outsiders (with Canada for example) have been a matter of amnesia or caprice: brusque truculence punctuating bouts of self-absorption – anything but diplomacy. About foreign policy the common feeling was: the less of it the better. The consequence was a Tom Sawyerish view of the world, a stolen circus-tent glimpse of "A-rabs and elephants". The conflict between peeping and withdrawal produces a combustible anxiety. From this charged closet spring military adventures better suited to Frank Powderhorn's *Book for Boys* than to the late 20th-century organum.

The verbal correlative of the ethical cowboy is a literature that oscillates between boyish wonder and a few gruff words, between Salinger and Hemingway, with one extreme sometimes infecting the other. At bottom is the man of action's impatience with words, an impatience that voluble Jewish writers have hilariously parodied but never shaken. The impatience appears in another classic Western, John Ford's *Fort Apache*, where the gallant but pig-headed colonel (Henry Fonda) leads his men to certain death against Chief Cochise's force. ("I can't see him any more," says his wife on the battlements, "I can only see the flag.") Afterwards it is the disciplined John Wayne, who warned him, who must deal with the journalists. The wordlings sit around in the former colonel's office (Wayne prefers to stand) heaping praise on the misguided hero, already enshrined on the wall in a painting, telling tales of his prowess, puffing, inventing copy. Wayne listens tight-lipped, and then says – deafeningly – nothing.

Nothing! It is what everyone in the audience would like to say. It is what American writers long to say, hence the tradition of writers-by-accident, hunter-writers, boxer-writers, killer-writers. *American Psycho* is that muscle gone to flab. It's a necessary progression, since the original, American Macho, is now so easily imitated that women from the land of Gandhi acquire it at Creative Writing Programs.

I lingered on Fourth Street without the expected sense of *déjà vu*. In a ghost town it might have been easier to let the imagination roam. In modern Tombstone there were billboards proclaiming the OK Corral that would have sent Doc Holliday scurrying for cover. In the county museum, once the court house and jail, there was a collection of barbed wire (patented seven years before the gunfight) strung out and labelled like barbaric jewellery. Joseph Glidden's product quickly replaced all those thorn bushes and cactus hedgerows and sealed off an epoch as decisively as the British closure of the commons. Almost by the way it helped deter old-time rustling more effectively than Earp's Buntline Special. (It also meant that once and for all beeves or "white-faced cattle" had replaced the Indians' buffalo across the entire West. By the end of that century all the buffalo of the Great Plains would have fitted into a couple of OK Corrals.) In other glass cases were the weapons of the West – but also Chinese porcelain, perhaps the property of Mrs Ah Lum, who was born in China and buried at Boothill in 1906. In the walled yard below was a gallows that could accommodate two men at once.

I took a last walk down Main Street past men in dude boots and ten-gallon hats that would have gladdened the heart of John Stetson (who died the same year as Mrs Ah Lum). You had to pay to get into the famous corral, where they staged the gunfight at intervals, but a historical society sign said the real corral was over a bit, so I took a photo of thin air and drove to Boothill. There, on a stony hillside that must have taken some digging, were the graves, wound about with (the pamphlet said) "the true crucifixion thorn". Billy Clanton and Frank and Tom McLaury lay there, and Old Man Clanton, killed on a cattle drive by Mexicans. There also lay the less notorious dead: Mrs Campbell, restaurateur's wife, who died of suspicious stomach cramps; Delia Williams, coloured innkeeper, who took arsenic; Quong Kee, popular proprietor of the Can-Can restaurant. And Wells Fargo agent Lester Moore:

> *Here lies Lester Moore*
> *Four slugs from a .44*
> *No Les, no more.*

Suicide, jealousy, revenge, smallpox, wagers, even leprosy, carried them off. But no memorial so poignant as:

> *George Johnson*
> *Hanged by Mistake*

On the way back I turned left off 80 and drove west along a lonely road. Highway 82 skimmed across barren uplands creased with dusty mesquite valleys and knobbled with red rock. I ate my sausage by a creek among startling yellow and blue avens that might have distracted an unwary mammoth from the early humans creeping up on the steep bank. Back on the road the beggars' banquet resumed: a bare table of caked yellow earth spread with silvery sagecloth and lit with stark candles of yucca that dripped clusters of white flowers just out of reach. I stepped warily in the brush: all I remembered of my first Western, *Cowboy*, was a fatal rattler incident and a rocky grave and the wagons moving on against the horizon. It's easy to forget that the desert bristles with far more deadly strikers. Ever since Montana, in fact, I'd been travelling over missiles of increasing obsolescence but sufficient venom to make Boothill look like a lively corner of the globe. As a boy I kept clippings of Atlas and Minuteman missile stories that lovingly documented trajectory and payload; it was the next step up from six-guns.

But the strangest part of going back to *The Wild West* as an adult was the realization that I had never read the book before. So the story of the gunfight, of all those gunfights, had been etched on the memory by that grand template American Comic Book that reached halfway around the world. Adults could succumb too. Once in a remote corner of our poorest state I came upon an Anglo-Indian manufacturer of soft drinks whose everyday hat was not the British solar topi or pith helmet, but a stetson as wide as Texas. When he died, and was buried in the small Christian cemetery, I knew there was one corner of an Indian field that was forever America.

Driving west on 82 I was hoping for a vast ketchupy sunset complete with saguaro cactus and table mountains. The sky offered marmalade instead, with the fruit sunk to the bottom in shreds of golden cloud. The barbed wire, with me all the way, now fenced in large ranches. Early ranchers in these parts would connect their telephones to Joseph Glidden's patent wire and talk to neighbours.

The cactus was at the Desert Museum, next morning: saguaro, the sequoia of the cactus family, organpipe, hedgehog, Stetsonis, with thorns as big as darning needles, beavertail, fish-hook, pincushion, prickly pear, like our cobra-hood, its smooth green flesh inlaid with rubies. Indoors was a room that jumped and skipped like a silent movie, the hummingbird cage.

Old Tucson was right next door. It adjoins the Saguaro National Monument and can't get enough of the cactus. It was built as a set for the movie *Arizona* in 1939 and was one of Hollywood's earliest "locations", a notable stage in the history of illusion. Scores of Westerns have been shot here since, including *Gunfight at the OK Corral*. From here, cowboy pictures went international: spaghetti Westerns, curry Westerns, noodle Westerns.

Built as a replica of the Tucson of the 1860s, Old Tucson encourages a double suspension of disbelief. "I thought it was the real Old Tucson," writes one conniving visitor, as if the original signs would have read OLD TUCSON GENERAL STORE and OLD TUCSON STAGE LINES. It's this happy double-think that gives the place its charm and popularity. I was eating a coyote dog when a roadrunner broke cover and ran across the dusty street. I photographed it at once. I wasn't sure it was a roadrunner, but it looked about right and I was happy to make up the difference. Some of the painted signs made life even simpler. PHOTO HERE, they said, and people obliged. When nothing is real (even the red chillies hung out to dry in the Mexican plaza were cunning plastic) photography is freed from vicariousness and becomes a sort of creation. Creation by rule, to order, along preordained vistas: Front Street, Kansas Street, The Reno Track, The Old Mexican Chapel, classical models all. No graffiti at Old Tucson

– not even in the toilets – but every handmade adobe brick cried out BIG JOHN WAS HERE and EASTWOOD FOR MAYOR. The old trumpet-led film scores poured from concealed mono speakers in a torrent of crackles, as if the Origin were not an orchestra but an honest-to-goodness scratched soundtrack. I taped a minute of it out of an old orange crate by the Sheriff's Office, music now at three removes, and left wishing I could stay for sunset. They would tint the sky if they had to, but they would get it right. The coyote dog had even left a spot of ketchup on my shirt.

I was late returning the car. The steak fingers at the bus station weren't up to much, but we headed south for Nogales with a dozen live lobsters on board.

15

So Far From God

The road to Mexico runs south through industrial parks and ranch-land, past orchards with fruit stands and mobile homes stranded on parcels of desert land. The border ahead is quite unlike the one I crossed a month ago. It is not a crossing into more of the same. It is not notional. Nowhere else is the contrast between two sides of a frontier more marked: the richest nation on earth faces a poor nation, and now the two are thinking the unthinkable: a kind of merger. Not a merger of peoples, though that will come, but of markets; goods, not individuals, will cross this border freely. The crux of the problem is how to encourage the one without the other. So far the approach has been to widen the gates while raising the fence.

An association of North American neighbours has always been a prospect, if only because of geography, but lately it is history – and not always local history – that has provided the motive force. Developments in Europe and East Asia have had as much to do with the fate of this border as developments on either side of the present line of demarcation. A united Europe, a Japan-led Pacific: these are the spectres haunting North America and driving latinos and gringos into one camp.

In the row in front of me, across the aisle from one another, sit two heavily made-up girls, one a latina who has painted her nails black, the other a ginger-haired Anglo whose arms and waist show smoky white through a blouse of black silk and gauze. The two heads, and the space between, are what the border is about. It's a racial divide as well as a cultural one (unlike say at the border between Hong Kong and mainland China), although there is dark hair north of the border and fair hair – rarer and more startling – south. The Mexican presence to the north is of longer standing (it *was* Mexico once) but browns are nevertheless a minority. In New Mexico, for example, statehood was withheld from the former captured territory until it was "settled", that is, until Anglo majority was achieved.

The sunscreens are down on the right side of the bus. Outside are rocky ridges clad in mesquite, the pink rock showing through green gauze like flesh. A blue Chevy stands abandoned on the road shoulder, its trunk lid up. Dirt roads sun on the hillsides: red snakes. The air drips in dazzling ropes from the sun like eggwhite.

At Nogales, USA, the bus disgorges lobsters, luggage, passengers. I take refuge in the small depot. My visa is in order but I feel like a fugitive. It's a little like my arrival in Inuvik, in arctic Canada, those initial moments when one stands looking out through the protective glass and wonders: What now?

I take up my bags – suddenly leaden – and walk.

ENTERING MEXICO/ENTRADA A MEXICO. I don't need the 14-foot clearance. I could keep straight on – most pedestrians make the crossing twice a day – but I must seek out immigration. A Mexican officer points the way, as to a good boy. I feel I am doing something wholly unnecessary.

"Entering Mexico?"

"Yes."

The official nods adult approval. I have done *well* to come to him. I present my passport.

"India!"

"Yes!"

"On holiday or on business?"

"A little of both."

He stamps the curious passport. "To Mexico City?"

"Eventually."

He loses interest and wanders off. He would go straight to Mexico City. My dismissal, or abandonment, conjures up officialdom in India.

Immediately I feel the need of pesos. I haven't yet grasped that in Nogales – in Mexico – the US dollar is common tender. I stand on the sidewalk among the expectant idlers who gather at the edge of forbidden places. Taxi drivers, touts, offer their services; I check

197

my makeshift security vest. Down an alley I find a cambio. Ten years ago I got 30 pesos to the dollar; today I get 3000; next year they will drop all three zeros. I still have no hotel. Where are the hotels? Again the stranger's panic. Then, over my shoulder, music from a radio: familiar Mexico surging back.

The radio was in a jugueria, a fruit juice fountain, one of a row of three furnished in pink and white and blue laminates, with the familiar tropical fruit painted as in a child's picture book on the price board: banana (shake), mango (shake), papaya (shake), watermelon (juice), and so on. The jugueria was classic Mexico. I could recall no other nation so devoted to the cult of liquid fruit, with shrines at every corner. I slipped into a booth opposite the counter, a kind of public confessional. The girl brought nachos and melted cheese and a papaya licuado. She sang along with the music:

Dance, dance!
Let me be your fancy man.

I stayed longer than I needed, then stepped out, remade. The sun had gone down. I trudged up an endless street in the papaya-coloured afterlight. The hotels, it turned out, were one street over, all along. I took a room for more than I paid anywhere in the United States. By 9 p.m. only one cantina was open. Behind the once-blue mesh doors were once-yellow walls and a picture of the Sacred Heart, once-red. A 40-watt bulb cast its wan light on the oilcloths of four tables. I asked for dinner. The woman who lived there stood undecided, then nodded and set a place: plate, knife and fork, earthen bowl of guacamole, tortilla basket.

"Refresco?"

"Si."

She returned with a cola. Then she was gone a while, scraping and clattering. I got the feeling I was to share her dinner. She brought three flour tortillas and a dish of beans. I made short work of them. More scraping and clattering. She brought a plate of meat scraps in gravy. I had hoped for more tortillas but none appeared. The meal cost more than my chicken in mango sauce at the Congress Hotel.

Next morning I looked in at the Barberia Mochis. Francisco Medina was sitting in his barber's chair reading the *Voice of the*

North, a local daily. He was a stocky man with hair like steel shavings. His wife snipped those. He took out a pink polyester cloth so brief it was more bib than barbersheet. But the fabric and the close fit — and the hot pink — made a warm day stifling. I was a prisoner.

"Quite short," I said in a show of authority.

Medina took no notice. He drew a tissue from a box and tucked it lengthwise around my neck as if he had all day. He would teach me to interrupt the *Voice of the North*. He took a crank and lowered the chair a fraction.

"You can't afford to lose too much on top."

"No."

"I'll cut it short."

"How long have you been cutting hair?"

"Twenty-three years in this city. Before that I was in Cananera."

"Do you get many foreigners up here?"

"No, mostly locals." Barberia Mochis was on a side street, a short way up a hill.

"Has Nogales changed much?"

"For sure. It's more expensive. Much more. I've watched the price of things double and double again in the last ten years — the last *five* years. The paper says they're going to rebuild the Gateway of Mexico. They expect traffic to double once they sign the Free Trade treaty. They're saying the Treaty will create more jobs, increase our Buying Power." He put big capitals on the last two words. A long-staple brush I never saw but felt gently flicked at clippings that got under the tissue.

"No, ours is a small family. We have three daughters but they're all married and settled in other parts. Now my wife and I live alone. They're good girls. They come and visit us." He wet the tips of his fingers and marked out a line above the ear with gentle prods. Next he applied dabs of hot foam. I didn't feel the razor at all. "You must be from far away," he said.

"Yes, from India."

"Far away!" he repeated in a melancholy refrain. I might have said Outer Mongolia and he would have sighed "Far away!" Trussed up in his chair, my eyes shut, I felt the enormity of distance weigh on me like the globe. The latitude was the same for Mexico and

India – I had left behind that sea of vacant blue eyes – but I was on the far side of the earth.

I bought a copy of the *Voice* to read about the Treaty. Tratado Libre Comercio is how the Free Trade Agreement is rendered in Spanish; its acronym, with sweet irony, is TLC. On the tender loving care the verdict must wait, but in the Notimex report from Los Angeles a vice-president of the Bank of America was saying American companies would go where wages were lowest, with or without the TLC. And he praised the maquiladores, that string of factories set up in a corridor along the US border.

The maquiladores have been a source of contention ever since they started. Working conditions there are the main irritant for Mexican tourists; the very notion of unionism is thought to be endangered by their presence. There is also, for traditionalists, something of the stigma of mere assemblage about the maquilador: the word carries connotations of making up, rather than making, as if the real factories were elsewhere. For countries like Mexico and India, once ideologically committed to a model of self-reliance symbolized by heavy industry, the expansion of the maquilador sector represents a paradigm shift. As processors the maquiladores work with materials temporarily imported and then returned to the country of origin. The proof that they are not assembly lines is less in their products than in their unfortunate by-product: pollution all along the border. Only thirty out of a thousand border companies took their wastes back to the United States in 1991. The rest of the poison stayed.

Parasites, not pollutants, were my own worry. Even Mexican travellers, I noticed, took along bottled water. (In Nogales one in three citizens did not have running water at all.) And so I bought and carried the standard 3-litre flagon of purified water, a precaution surely comic in a citizen of India. But I lunched at Gloria's taqueria, a hole in the wall run by a beauty. She shaved meat off a gyro, a little boy served, and his tiny sister, asleep on her feet, stood by the cash register polishing it in her dreams. Her futile pawing was more troubling than real work from a child.

The city bus was packed; at the railway station I popped out like a cork. The station was deserted in a way no Indian station ever was, but it wore a familiar air. It was the way something new, a fancy concrete-origami structure, had been allowed to run down.

A makeshift board blocked off the ticket hole at the counter; the grim food stall, also abandoned, carried a sign that might have been translated from Hindi: MONEY IS NOT LIFE, BUT NO DINNER WITHOUT IT. Four dusty boys sprawled on the platform, leaning up against a door fastened with a twist of wire: urchins, not street kids. An old crone came by. With her mutton-chop sleeves, she appeared to have stepped out of an old engraving.

Mexican poverty, unlike American poverty, has an archaic quality to it. The American poor wear clothes from a decade ago; they look like, and often are, relics of another generation. The Mexican poor, even when they wear contemporary designs mass-produced in maquiladores, seem to belong to the last century. It's not simply a matter of race. Asiatic poverty, more acute and endemic, has a radically different garb; it can plead cultural distinctiveness. For Mexicans, ever since sandals gave way to shoes and peon pantaloons to trousers, the shelter of cultural otherness has vanished. There is only the difference of shabbiness. It means that their norteamericano cousins see them through a time filter, as they see hillbillies, and respond with Goodwill parcels, once-used tea-bags, and old roller-skates, with pity and contempt.

It's the denatured form of an attitude older than the border. When California was Spanish, visiting Yanquis like Richard Dana saw the inhabitants as a shiftless remnant, undeserving of the land they failed to exploit. Ten years on Parkman found more Mexicans lolling in the shade and in the way. Not for long. When he got back home the Mexican War was underway, and by the time *The Oregon Trail* appeared the border had been redrawn. "One of the most unjust wars ever waged by a stronger against a weaker nation," wrote an interested observer, but not everyone agreed. "Let our arms now be carried with a spirit that shall teach the world that while we are not forward for a quarrel, America knows how to crush as well as how to expand." The first voice is that of a soldier, Ulysses S. Grant, who would find his just war in time. The second is that of a poet: Walt Whitman.

Later Americans were either jocular ("Do not confuse Mexican cakes with pieces of iron ore") or rhapsodic ("I can feel the superiority of their contentment"), while occasionally reverting to the common denominator ("dust and Mexicans and a heathen chatter"), Stephen Crane all three. By the early 20th century all

Latin America had become a painted cloth against which quite ordinary adventurers like Richard Halliburton might perform feats and pranks. A wealthy young man, Halliburton climbed Popocatapetl in winter, twice dived into the Well of Death at Chichén Itzá, swam the length of the Panama Canal, stormed Lima, and went on to write *New Worlds for Adventure*. (He was later lost at sea.) Mexico remains a gringo proving-ground even in so shrewd a modern Western as Cormac McCarthy's *All the Pretty Horses*. And in a recent Hollywood film, *The Border*, the plot merely serves the American border guard (Jack Nicholson) who helps a Mexicana cross over because he would like some day to remember an unselfish act. With mass tourism the circle closes, as Mexico becomes for its rich neighbours a place of ruins and scenery and obtuse waiters.

After an hour the station began to fill up. Four traders appeared, small businessmen from the cut of their suits, with forty pieces of luggage between them: cases, boxes, trunks, bags, parcels. Queues began to form at blind ticket windows. An engine driver crossed the track, leapt onto the platform, and shook off his heavy work gloves like a boxer. (The day before, Raul Perez of Mexico had become the world bantamweight champion, the latest in a long line of Mexican battlers.) People peered up the track towards the locomotive yard. When an engine did come through there was no train attached. The queue grew restless. I got hungry. Across the way a man was selling pineapple-filled cakes from the back of his pickup truck. I bought two and went scouting for water.

The bus depot was right there, and the contrast with the train station was telling. Four gleaming kiosks did a brisk trade, and there were bright souvenir shops, bookstalls, newsstands. Mexicans travelled by bus if they could help it.

I returned to the dismal railway station. The train was late. I sat and ate bus depot sandwiches, drank bus depot water. Then I ate highway pineapple cakes. They were mild to blandness – to boredom, almost – like Chinese cakes, but finally the penny dropped. I left the queue, slung my bags about me and crossed the highway.

At the bus depot I stood below a timetable and looked for Hermosillo. There were half a dozen bus companies, each with its timetable painted in the company colours. It was competition as Adam Smith would have wished (and as it did not appear to exist at American bus stations, where Marx's theory of monopoly applied) but only the mildest rivalry existed between the windows. At the gold window, under a gold board, stood the cowboy.

"Adónde?"

He spoke with the natural arrogance of the tall and the handsome. He and the ticket clerk behind the grill had been studying me while I studied their board.

"Hermosillo," I said.

"Vamos."

"When does the bus leave?"

"It's leaving now."

"Right now?"

"This moment."

But he was in no hurry. He leaned against the counter smoking a cigarillo. His whole manner suggested a man with time on his hands. I felt I was being toyed with. I would buy a ticket and find myself on a ramshackle bus. Or on an empty bus — leaving this moment. A moment was a long time where I came from.

"Aire acondicionado?" I was playing for time.

"No, es segunda clase." He stated it matter-of-factly, waiting for the stranger to blink. This was how it ended in a Tombstone saloon; it was how the territorial apes sparred, and probably turtle doves. I slowed down, asked more questions. He answered coolly; dynamite would not budge him.

"Bueno," I said with a show of speed. The clerk scribbled out a ticket. The cowboy unbent a fraction. Still leaning, he added a seat number and pointed the way. He and the clerk shared a few amused words as I went through the door.

A brand-new bus stood there. The passengers were all boarded and waiting; I took the only remaining seat. The cowboy appeared, not hurrying. He was, I realized, the driver. His co-driver made way and then stood in the stepwell making jokes, much the sidekick. The cowboy took the driver's seat and looked down the bus.

"The dark one, did he get on?"

I caught his eye and lifted a finger. He nodded, and we rolled out of Nogales, past the static railway station and onto the highway. I felt ridiculously happy: it was like starting out from Inuvik again. It was the first bus since Inuvik that had windows you could open. For half an hour I hung out of mine, sucking in the smells of the Mexican campo and marvelling at the prodigal drifts of orange calendula.

Then the sun grew hot. This was the sun I had longed for in Canada. It came around and shone in my window with special malice. The girl beside me got off at Imuris with her Nogales shopping. I took her seat, warm in a different way, and papered the window with the *Arizona Wild Cat*. The paper worked loose. I held it up against the sun, then began unconsciously to flap it and realized I was performing the tropical act of fanning oneself. The heat was official.

WAVE DWELLER, said a surfing T-shirt, cryptically on a second-class Mexican bus, the foreignness more important than the message. In Nogales I'd seen I'M THE BOSS on a woman, which was refreshing but hard to credit; still harder was OHIO LESBIANS CLUB on a man. Across the aisle a brown skinhead wore a black T-shirt that said PURE FUCKIN ROCK. The shaven head had a filter-tip cigarette tucked behind its ear, where Indian clerks tuck a pencil.

But it was the cowboy my eyes kept returning to. He sat in his saddle and spun the steering wheel like a lariat. He had a red bandanna draped over the seatback, and above the windscreen, where American Greyhound drivers had their SAFE, COURTEOUS, DEPENDABLE sign, he had a sticker that said: I ♡ DRIVERS. His lizard-beige uniform was carefully pressed; a personal touch was the chestnut brown silk waistcoat. He had grey in his sideburns but a good head of hair that he built up high in front and plastered down at the back in long strands that curled at the tips. He used an ivory cigarillo-holder and talked through the side of his mouth, through smoke. The mouth stayed slightly open and the eyes slightly closed, but at Santa Ana, a dusty depot township where a road splits off to Mexicali, that half-grin dried up. He sat in the cantina with his legs straight out and gloomed at nothing.

I'd seen his original in a dozen movies set in the very desert we were traversing. He was the sharper who never lost a game unless he meant to; the wry lines were his; he mounted up without bending a knee. He would have made a good Doc Holliday. But why would he swap his bus for an MGM job lot? He had his Virgin of Guadalupe up above the dashboard, where Hindu drivers have Kali, and he ranged over the desert, his own man. The bus left when he was ready for it, when he had finished his cigarillo, the passengers penned up like patient cattle. He loved drivers. He loved his cattle too. No, he would not go to Hollywood. He had a lawless streak. He was a vaquero, not an ethical cowboy.

After Santa Ana, the halfway stop, the co-driver drove. The vaquero, who for the last twenty minutes of his spell had been talking over his shoulder to a young woman travelling alone, now took the seat beside her. I watched his head listening, nodding, advising, cajoling, leaning intimately. Gradually he sank down in the seat – the girl did too – his boots climbing higher and higher on the rail. As it grew dark all I could see was his profile, and sometimes hers, in the gap between the seats.

We barrelled through stunned townlets. Magdalena was a dream from my childhood: twilit games in the hot dust of a railway town that was the whole world; children shrieking like birds in the dusk by a gleaming track that flew to the horizon. San Lorenzo, Santa Ana, Benjamín Hill: the towns slipped by, named for saints and generals, the saints remembered, the generals forgotten. With Santa Ana you couldn't be sure. Was it kind St Ann, or the general who lost a leg defending Mexico and gave it a burial with full military honours? The sun went down, the air cooled off, the bus emptied with every stop, and in the end we were skimming through the dark with half our human ballast gone.

All along the highway tin crosses mark the site of road accidents. Grieving relatives remember *Estebano Principal, aged 17*, or *Cecilia Mendoza de los Angeles, aged 36*, with a wreath of plastic flowers. At sharp bends, especially in the mountains, the white crosses sprout in clusters, like lilies. Drivers are inured to them, greater fatalists, apparently, than Hindus. The crosses are at least a local reminder; in India even such frail tokens are lacking. The bus goes over the bank with sixty pilgrims. They vanish, cleansed.

The crosses actually start north of the border, a southern import. Culture has always ignored the border, and in recent years, despite the T-shirts and baseball caps and American TV, the flow has gone predominantly northwards – an astonishing achievement. In an increasingly Americanized world, Mexico must be the only country with which the United States has a net cultural deficit. Mexican food and drink, latino music, and the Spanish language have changed American habits to a degree that Canadian nationalists must envy. For that matter the Mexican vaquero (from vaca, cow) and his trappings moulded that all-American hero, the cowboy. The reverse conquest is something Mexicans are aware of, and it's a mark of their security that they are quite as avid consumers of American food and drink, music, movies, and the American language. They have not absorbed, or even noticed, the norteamericano stereotypes of the Mexican, and rarely go out of their way (as colonials will) to disprove them.

"Chickens," or illegal migrants, are a notorious Mexican export, but the country is also a destination. The day I arrived in Nogales President Salinas welcomed fifty-one new Mexicans: eight Cubans, seven Spaniards, five Argentinians, four Nicaraguans, three Frenchmen, three Lebanese, and five stateless persons among them. The other nationalities included Peruvians, Yugoslavians, Chileans, Moroccans, Guatemalans, Koreans, Iranians, and "hindúes" – Indians.

Culturally Mexico should be a secure member of the new trade bloc. Its fears, as always in Latin America, are economic. When the United States first invaded Panama, in 1903, the Nicaraguan poet Ruben Darío's response was a heated poem that represented the US president, Roosevelt, as a Great White Hunter. Dario pictured men with "Saxon eyes . . . possessed of everything, lacking only one: God!" He posed an inherent conflict between the United States and "naive America". It's a just polarity, but the poem is spoilt by a bravado that makes it unconvincing. Worse, Darío the diplomat was prevailed upon to recant. He apologized, in verse.

The bravado typifies Latin American foreign policy in the face of a vastly superior antagonist invariably disguised as a friend. Free Trade presents other ways of getting even, but it's still a gamble for Mexico. The country could become a dumping ground for US industrial wastes. It could become a "trampoline state" for goods coming from elsewhere. It could be forced into "rational" measures that hurt the poorest Mexicans. If the TLC does Mexico more harm than good, the shade of dictator Porfirio Díaz will spend another aeon in purgatory, sighing as it goes: "Poor Mexico! So far from God, so close to the United States."

16

The Black Ruby

The four o'clock bus from Nogales arrives in the Sonoran capital
after dark, and Hermosillo, picked out in white and yellow lights
that spiral at the centre up an improbable hill, might just be the
Little Beauty its name promises. The hill, a lava cone rising out
of the plain, is the Cerro de la Campaña, once sacred to the local
Indians. But daylight finds the hill crowned with radio towers
and ringed about with barbed wire, perhaps the Seri Indians'
true crucifixion thorn. In India one does not photograph sensitive
installations – even bridges are forbidden – so I turned my camera
on the cathedral.

Church and state face one another across the city square,
or zócalo, a park whose shade trees have grown tall enough to
obscure the one or the other, depending on where you stand. I
stood nearer the seat of power, the Palacio de Gobierno whose
labyrinthine innards I had traversed the night before, and took
a picture of the cathedral. Two fretted icing towers appear in the
photograph, and little else.

The sun was already hot so I turned my back on the lava hill.
In a square lined with park benches men sat in silence. Shoeshine
stands with vivid awnings enfolded customers involved in morning
papers. I circled the square looking for a seat in the shade. In the
farthest corners of their empire the Spanish took pains over public
seats. Even a modern concrete bench was a deep, dignified recess.
It might be topped with simple scrollwork or ornamented with a
glazed-tile street scene from Europe. Here was a culture of noonday
rest and contemplation whose peculiarities busy men from temperate latitudes never stopped to fathom. Their snoozing Mexican,

half sombrero, half poncho, took in the cactus but left out the sun around which the working day revolved. (The temperate park bench is an afterthought, a prim skeletal perch designed for men embarrassed by ease.) In Mexico I was never tired of the public squares. The very word was tinged from my childhood with romance: there were no squares in our north Indian towns, simply crooked streets and crippled parks remorselessly punished, like freaks.

Julio's was the only available seat. I climbed up onto it and he rolled up my cuffs. My boots had their first wash in 6000 kilometres, a proper shampoo with a pink liquid soap and water. Julio towelled them dry, then piped a line of gel along the rim of the sole and worked up a rich foam. He might have been brushing his teeth. He would not talk. Silence rang in the square like a gong.

In the Loncheria Fredy I found more tongueless company: Fredy himself, a pinup girl, twelve disciples at the Last Supper and an empty mirror festooned with rigid ivy. Outside I sought out the shade, but walking towards me were three men in fur-lined jackets and snowmobile gloves: workers in an icecream factory. They rippled silently, like a mirage.

At the Calinda Hotel two girls drew me a map to show me where I could get a map. But fate had other plans. At the other end of the counter a swarthy man was leaning over a page making rapid calculations.

"Just give me a minute," he said in English, "and I'll show you the way."

The girls exchanged looks.

"I know this city well," he went on, "though I come from Tecoripa. My family are well known here. We have businesses in the city – hotels, restaurants, fast foods." He went back to his chart, a cost estimate, I felt, for a hamburguesa franchise.

"I'm doing a star chart for her." He smiled at the girl who had drawn me a map.

I had a closer look at his page. It was covered in arrows and loops and hearts and stars. The writing was a thing of flourishes, with serifs like fishhooks and circles for dots.

"I've studied law," he said bashfully.

Ah! I thought: the lawyer in love.

"But I work for the government, as an advisor. Come on, I'll show you my office. It's here in the Palacio de Gobierno. I help them out, but I have many interests. My name is Enrique. Allan? Pleased to meet you."

We shook hands.

"I have many plans," he said, "but one master plan. I'm an ambitious man. I like power. I respect people with power. I know my capacities and I know that within twenty years – fifteen years – I can be president of this country. Not *can* be. Will be. In fifteen years I will be president of Mexico."

We had not been together ten minutes. At the door of the Calinda he hesitated.

"Would you like a drink? Be my guest."

We took a corner table in the restaurant.

"You see, I have a dream – no, not a dream, a *goal*. I'm not like Martin Luther King, I have goals, not dreams. You have to have concrete objectives. But also you have to have a strategy. You can't do it all at once, you go by stages. Stage one, stage two, stage three. Stage one you enter politics. You have to have a degree. Most politicians have the licenciatura, what you call the bachelor's. I have that. Let me give you my address."

He wrote out his name, with the prefix *Lic* which Mexicans commonly use, the way Indians at one time wrote BA (Pass) after their names, and sometimes BA (Fail) to show they had tried. Underneath he wrote his address and followed *Hermosillo, Sonora* with MEXICO in capitals, the *I* dotted all the same – with a circle. Then he wrote his nickname, Riqui. The *i*'s were dotted with hearts.

"My mother says. 'Of all my sons, Riqui, you are my cross. We send you to the United States, you get an education, a green card, and you waste it.' But I have a plan. She doesn't understand that. It can't happen overnight. First, enter politics, then – stage two – Governor of Sonora, *then* President. I'm the right age. I could be the next president but one. Salinas has been to Harvard, but has he been to the University of Southern California? That's where most Mexicans are. He hasn't been to the school of hard knocks. I've been a grape-picker, an orange-picker, a shoeshine boy. When I was a kid we were poor."

"When were you in the United States?" I didn't doubt he was there; he spoke fluent Californian.

He produced an identity card with his photo from the 1970s. It showed an innocent with curly black hair getting on for long.

"*Enrique Velasco Ramirez*." The words had not lost their music, whatever the years might have done to the face. He gazed at the photo as at a former lover. "My biggest mistake was coming back," he said. "I can't tell you how they got me here. They locked me up, my family. They kept me by force. They said I'd become a hippy, that I was *nogood*," (the two words had fused in his mind), "that they'd straighten me out. They shaved off my beard, cut my hair. I was all drugged out. I tell you I almost died. My friend who's a doctor saved my life. He said to them 'Can't you see, he's dying?' And then they saw. It was that close. I can't tell you what it was like."

He was sweating. I said he'd done well to survive.

"I have a temper, but I know how to control it. I know karate. I walk around, looking, learning. I know life on both sides of the border, I've seen it all. That's why I think – I know – I could be president. Salinas hasn't lived there. I know where they're coming from. This Tratado Libre Comercio," (he waved at the cover of a magazine, *Nexos*) "they want cheap labour, that's all. They want a parque industrial in every city. We've got Ford right here in Hermosillo. You want that magazine? You keep it. No, no, it's yours. I know their politicians. I've worked for the governor of California, Edmond Brown Jr. You know him? The boyfriend of Linda Ronstadt. I love politicians, politics. Come on, I'll show you my office."

He paid with a credit card.

"Right now I'm staying in the hotel – till my money runs out." The Calinda was one of the top hotels in town. It cost four or five times what I was paying at the Amigo. He turned to me. "Where are you staying?"

I told him. He hadn't heard of it. The Amigo was a hollow Moorish recollection with fountains down the middle and tiles of Ottoman ultramarine up the sides. Potted palms poked through the white railings on the balconies. In the toilet the shower recalled Indian plumbing, the materials blameless, the joining at fault, as if a modern idea had not been grasped completely.

"It's close to the bus station," I apologized. "It's very convenient."

"That's right, that's why you chose it. If it's convenient you stay there. But if you like you can be my guest here. They know me. I have a room on the tenth floor. I go home to collect my mail. Do you want to see my home?" He hesitated as soon as the words were out. "My mother might be there. We'll go to my office. I'll show you the Palacio de Gobierno."

We set out. Half a block down was another hotel.

"We'll just look in here. There's a beautiful girl at the desk. I think I'm going to marry her."

The girl he wanted was on the telephone. Riqui introduced me to the other girl at the desk, then waited. His girl smiled at us but stayed on the phone.

"We'll see her again," he said, and we stepped back out into the street. We crossed to the zócalo and came to a verandah by the Palacio. Groups of men stood there in the evening light chatting. We stopped at the first group. Riqui introduced me, an author, his friend. The men bowed as they were named. We walked on as far as the next group. I was introduced, the author; the men were named. At the Palacio door were more men. Riqui knew them all. More bowing, hands shaken, polite words. We went up the steps and turned a corner. There was an official he would like me to meet. The official met, we crossed an inner court with trees and statues and came to a grand stair. Murals in the style of the Mexican 1920s covered the corridor walls and the stairwell.

"You see that fist? That for me is power. That's politics."

I asked how old the murals were.

"These were done when my uncle was governor."

Immediately the deference in the men we'd met became comprehensible, even when they suppressed a smile. Kinship was a wild card in Indian politics too.

As we climbed the stair I looked for the inevitable eagle with the serpent in its beak, Mexico's symbol since Aztec times. The Aztecs travelled to the site of their imperium by much the same route as the one I was following, a rough northerly tribe on the make for generations. Somewhere in the present vale of Mexico they saw an eagle swoop down on a snake and carry it off to a cactus bush where it sat and feasted. They took it as a sign and built their capital there, at Tenochtitlan. It's a moment celebrated in countless murals throughout the land, a moment not

211

of deliverance – as with the seagulls that saved the Mormon harvest from locusts – but of conquest. The American eagle of course has better credentials, but its gender is in doubt. "It's a hen eagle," Lawrence scoffed, taking the long view. The Mexican eagle is not a hen. Its wings are clipped, but if it could grow testicles it would.

"You've got to have balls," Riqui said. "You've got to have guts, ambition, will."

At the top of the stair we turned right and travelled along a corridor that overlooked the patio. By the outer pillars stood jardinières whose increasing grandness suggested the approach of high office. I prepared myself to meet the current governor, but we got no further than his antechamber. The young man on duty there stood up more out of deference than a show of authority. His was not the chief desk in the room; he appeared in fact to be minding someone else's desk. I recognized his class from Indian officialdom, and his quandary: we might be men of power. He smiled uncomfortably and said the governor was not in. Chance intervened for him too. Riqui, who had been outlining Mexican history as we travelled along the murals, got entangled. He turned to the young man for help.

"The Revolution was in 1910, but what happened in 1810?"

It should have been a moment of triumph for the peon class, but the man spoke with caution, merely reminding his betters.

"1810 was the Shout for Independence from Spain," he said. "1910 was the Revolution of the People."

"That's it!" Riqui jabbed the air.

We continued around the corridor.

"I'll just grab my case," Riqui said as we came at last to his office. It was in fact yet another antechamber, with two desks on either side of a significant-looking door. At one desk was a smartly dressed middle-aged woman, at the other a bulky police officer of some seniority. Riqui introduced me, the author of many books, his friend from the old days at the University of Southern California. The officer inclined his head. The woman gave a steely smile. Riqui went to a table and picked up his attaché case. He opened it, not on the table but in the air, crooking a knee for support. It was not enough support. The case was full of audio-cassettes. One or two fell out. The officer followed my gaze and looked away. The woman looked at all three of us from a great distance.

"It's all Mexican music," Riqui explained. "I've been away so long, I have to catch up. You get out of touch."

I bowed to the officials as we left. The officer dipped his head without looking up. The woman was in a state of deep meditation. The honour of Mexico had been compromised.

"Just a minute." Riqui ducked into still another waiting-room. There were a dozen people in there, petitioners seated in armchairs along the wall. Riqui knew one or two, but introduced me in a general way: author of books, his friend.

I said, "Riqui," and stepped back over the threshold, but a woman sitting by the door leaned forward, interested.

"India! What sort of books?"

We talked over someone's head, then she got up and joined us. She was a pale, elegant woman, small-boned and delicately fleshed, a royal water-bird at ancient Luxor. Mariana was the editor of a humanitarian periodical, *Mexico Moderno*.

We came to the Department of Social Communication. The offices there were glassed off but there was a passage that had been turned into a waiting space with a couple of soft blue sofas. Mariana began to explain her mission. I asked for note paper and Riqui snapped open his case and produced index cards. "You can rest on this," he said, and laid the case on my knees. He disappeared behind the glass and returned with coffee. Mariana refused hers; she drank only water.

Mariana was a follower of Maestro Thakar Singh. She believed that one lived in order to experience the divine, and in order to do that it was necessary to have a guru. With his help the spirit – which otherwise rushed pell-mell into the world through the external faculties – was concentrated in its proper seat, behind the eyebrows, and only then did it illuminate the true self. When the spirit penetrated the upper reaches it entered a zone fraught with peril. Those who ventured there alone were beset and deceived and led astray. Hence the need for a master. In Yoga Surat Shabda it was impossible to overstate the importance of the Master.

Mariana lived in Hermosillo but had a foot in Mexico City, from where her periodical was published. I wondered if she missed metropolitan life. She said she was now committed to the Northwest because she saw the country undergoing a grand transformation. The three northwestern states – Chihuahua, mineral-rich and the largest state in the union; Sonora, Mexico's granary and ranchland; Sinaloa, the country's kitchen garden – formed a mystic triangle, a kind of pyramid at the nucleus of a New Jerusalem she saw rising in Mexico. *Sonora*, she reminded me, meant musical.

She reached into her bag for the latest edition of *Mexico Moderno*. Across the top of the tabloid she wrote down two titles I should consult: *The Thunder that Will Destroy the World*, and *The Architecture of the Universe*.

"What about Baja California?" I asked her. Baja is the most northwesterly of the Mexican states. It had always struck me as an anomaly, that withered tail pinned on the rump of the richest state on earth.

"Baja," she said, "has no place in the trinity. It will sink without a trace into the sea."

We agreed to meet for breakfast at the Calinda the next morning. As she left Mariana dipped into her bag again and came up with a gift. It lay on the palm of her small white hand. It was a black ruby. Black rubies are fragments of volcanic rock. This one had a shiny igneous look and was from a certain mystic lode in Chihuahua.

I put the stone away. An old peon took our coffee mugs. Riqui disappeared behind a glass screen; there was a secretary there he wanted to talk to. I leafed through *Mexico Moderno*. I could hear his voice over the partition and see moving shadows through the frosted glass. I grew restless. The peon went to the door and coughed. "The señor is waiting," he said. "Coming!" Riqui called, but didn't come. I went to get him, was introduced: author, old friend. The girl, who'd overheard the whole waiting-room discussion, seemed anxious to correct certain impressions I may have gathered of Mexico. Hers was, after all, the Department of Social Communication. She gave me the latest issue of the government magazine with the air of a physician dispensing bitter medicine. But the magazine was called, for all that, *Sonora Magica*.

Downstairs it was dark. I sketched the elegant patio with its trees and statues. The statues were of two 19th-century generals, illustrious Sonorans. Riqui copied down the inscriptions for me on index cards, murmuring "*served with distinction . . . great patriot . . .*" We looked in at one more office. A blonde secretary was just

214

locking up. She smiled a tired smile, pleaded haste, asked us not to take offence. Riqui let her go.

"You hungry?" he said to me.

I was. We returned to the San Alberto Hotel. His girl was on the phone again. A meeting was about to start in the convention hall. We looked in there. It was the Amway Marketing Corporation, now in Mexico. An exquisitely groomed man came up. Riqui knew him too. Miguel Angel y Lourdes Molina turned to me and spoke earnestly of Amway's unique network marketing method. No, not a second job, he corrected me: a second income. There were two basic principles, he said. He counted them off on manicured fingers, but although he went over them twice I forgot them immediately.

Riqui had been talked to for four hours in his hotel room by an Amway man. "My neck was sore," he said, "but he convinced me I was going to become a millionaire. 'With your brain,' he said, 'you could be a millionaire by May!' "

Miguel had glided away. He had a speech to make. Coiffured women were selling tickets at a table. Through a door I could see young people immaculately turned out, standing in twos and threes brimming a fearsome will. Their poise was a palpable thing.

Riqui was back at the desk chatting up another girl. Dinner looked a long way off. I said I'd see him at breakfast. He found me a taxi and bargained a higher price than I would have got on my own. At the Amigo a group of young men, the hotel staff, were sitting on the steps. They were dressed plainly and wholly free of that crippling, and enabling, poise.

I woke at cock-crow, before my wake-up call. The cock crew again right outside my window as I sat up in bed. In the heart of a capital city that call was like judgment. Early for breakfast, I strolled through the zócalo. "All the monuments in Mexico," Graham Greene complained, "are to violent deaths." But on the way back to the Calinda I chanced on, in the cool of the morning, a tiny square with the statue of a pharmacist.

Riqui was waiting, Mariana was late. She arrived full of apologies and ordered orange juice. Riqui had been in the Palacio, where someone had upset him.

215

"Such ignoramuses," he said in Spanish, "so inept, such conformists! You and I who don't conform, who spend our time searching, we're crazy!"

"The crazies are the ones who change the world," Mariana said soothingly. Riqui began to translate automatically. "But they're helpless because this is the age of . . . of what – ?"

"*Kali Yug*," Mariana repeated.

"The Black Age," I translated for him from Hindu cosmology.

Riqui resumed: "She says actually the Black Age is finished. The Golden Age has begun."

"When did it begin?" I asked.

"January 1976," Mariana said.

"And when will it be completed?"

"When we have a mind to come together as one we can start to live in peace."

"With God the Father, the Virgin Mary, and the Holy Spirit," Riqui added off his own bat. Mariana let it by.

"And Jesus Christ," Riqui put in, encouraged.

"*Not* Jesus Christ!"

"OK, God the Father?"

"We have to prove God, scientifically. Human beings have a little tape recorder here." She tapped her chest. "In there these eyes, these ears are no good. You close them," (she closed her eyes and placed her fingertips on her ears) "and He comes in and the tape starts rolling. And you ask yourself: 'Who am I? Where do I go after I die?' Come back again to earth? Forget it – there's too many crazies!"

Mariana's laugh was a wide-open mouth that showed all her even teeth. She leaned forward and tilted her head back. Riqui's was a flatter laugh, a sharp staccato fire delivered with a straight back.

"We have to pay for our time on earth. We're here in this restaurant, Calinda – Kali India! – and we eat and drink. We can't go out without paying."

"Cash or credit card," Riqui said.

"If we want to leave the earth and we owe, who picks up the tab?"

"God the Father?" Riqui asked.

"Look," Mariana said, "the Higher Consciousness is our Father."

"And that's why I say – excuse me," Riqui broke in. "I tell you

216

– allow me – I've walked the streets of Hermosillo at night, one, two, three, five o'clock in the morning, alone. I've met all sorts, cocaine addicts, marijuana smokers, drug dealers. I say to them: 'Que tal?' 'Oh, Hi! Good day!' They're my friends. My mother says, 'My boy, don't go wandering.' I say to her, 'Mother, let me be.' 'But I'm your mother!' 'Mother, forgive me. You are my mother, that's all. But I have a father and a mother and a brother in God the Father and the Virgin Mary and Jesus Christ.' "

"Sonoran mothers!" Mariana said, speaking as a metropolitan. "I was born in a small town of only a thousand people. They used to call me crazy too."

"My mother says, 'Riqui, why are you the only son that I have that doesn't concentrate on what he's doing? You get money, you give it away. The seven cars you had you gave them away.' I say to her, 'Mother, because the Bible that you taught us says *If you want eternal life give away all your belongings and follow me.*' "

Mariana turned to me. "Let me give you an address." She wrote on one of Riqui's index cards. "This man will give you five words."

"Five words?"

"Yes. They are a passport, a visa you will need to travel through the five celestial planes."

"What are they?"

She laughed gently and continued writing. "This person in Culiacán will tell you. With those five words no one can touch you."

The strain of rapid translation was beginning to tell on Riqui. Mariana spoke in great sweeps, never losing her thread or her grip on him. He kept his eyes fixed on her and delivered the English instantly. The sweat stood on his forehead; she remained cool.

"What's the significance of the Cerro de la Campaña?" I asked her directly.

She smiled. "It's a long story. Have you read the Book of Enoch?"

"No."

"It says there that the Aztecs who went to Mexico City were from here, from Sonora. Their Tenochtitlan is from T-*enoch*!"

"They're guachos down in Mexico City," Riqui interrupted. "They're like this." He snapped his fingers rapidly. "They don't like it when you call them that. They get mad! You must use that word in your book, *guacho*!" He sprayed us with machine-gun fire.

"Is that the opposite of a gaucho?"

He turned to Mariana. "What does it mean?"

"I don't know, a guacho is a soldier."

"She's got beautiful eyes," Riqui said. "You should see her daughters." He tapped the glass of grapefruit juice I'd squeezed with the greatest difficulty out of the waiter. "Is that stuff good for you?"

"It cuts the grease."

"I weighed two hundred forty pounds," he said. "I was big, huge, like an elephant. But I lost it walking."

Mariana used a Spanish expression.

"She says I get my strength from the cat in my stomach. She says Jesus Christ did all his curing by the Dead Sea. Salt water cures, she says. Three days on just *water*? Jesus Christ! The worms came *out*? He cured hundreds, but then he got pissed off and he said, 'I'm gettin out of here, man, I'm starvin!' "

Mariana caught the improvisation and rolled her eyes up to heaven. He asked her, "You're Catholic, no?"

"No," she said at once. Then she shrugged. "By birth, of course . . ."

"She says she doesn't have no religion, like you. She says the generation of 1962 are going to build the new world with their knowledge."

"What is this knowledge?"

"Spiritual knowledge from the masters of India. Her master has seven schools. Faros? Lighthouses. Seven schools of light where they teach practical knowledge. From three years old the little ones are taught music. Everything in the world has its vibration. Everything is alive, rocks, plants, everything. So they're taught to play classical music. Sitar, flute, bongos, wow! And they learn gardening – you know, watermelons, radishes – and respect for nature."

"Where do you go from here?" Mariana asked me.

"Ciudad Obregón," I said. The second city of Sonora is three hours south of Hermosillo.

"There are many Indians there," she said, "at the agricultural institute. This year the state prize for agriculture went to an Indian,

Ramachandran." I said a Mexican hybrid wheat variety had made India's Green Revolution possible.

"She says God moves in weird ways. We think we act but everything is done through us. Like I met you and through me she met you. She says she was expecting you. When you finish your journey, after Yucatan, she'll take you to Chihuahua. You have that rock? That's where a divine thunderbolt struck. There's a man there who has a galactic museum. She can't go right away, she has a family. You should see her daughters. You know, if you're interested we could sit down together, you and I. You have the words. I'll give you my thirty-five years —"

"Look!" Mariana cut in, "you *have* the power."

"That's true. She says I can tell my own story. I met a guy last night who said to me: 'You're smart, but the thing that's wrong with you is you're too noble.' Let me tell you the word: 'You're too *stupid*. You want to help everybody, you don't help yourself.' My parents, my family don't believe in me. They think I'm fuckin' mad, that I'm a worthless person."

"You should concentrate on one thing, something that interests you."

"Law."

"Whatever."

"OK, that's good advice — even though I'm versatile?"

I returned from the restroom to find him writing on index cards. Mariana was telling him about the Hindu trinity of Brahma, Vishnu, and Shiva.

"The Creator, the Sustainer, and the Destroyer," she dictated. "Nature is an illusion, Maya. Maya is Maria, the Virgin Mother Nature. We call someone *indio* and he gets mad. But indio means *en Dios*, in God. India is the oldest country in the world. All knowledge . . ."

"All knowledge," Riqui wrote, repeating the words, "is . . . concentrated . . . in . . . India."

"When the culture of ancient Mexico unites with the culture of New Spain the new humanity will be born, the new race, the new Indians, Amerindia, Amer-India."

I asked Mariana how long she'd been in Hermosillo.

"One year," she said. "I had to come. I lived twenty years in

Mexico City. I don't know when I'll go to the other side. When I finish my work, I suppose."

I asked her what I should see in Hermosillo.

"The Cerro," she said.

"It's full of gold," Riqui added.

The gold of the New World was only part of its lure. The quest for El Dorado led more than one voyager to a sticky end, but the stronger magnet, the mother lode, was the newness itself. Every man who ever dreamed of starting afresh, of cancelling the old life and re-inventing himself, would have been stirred to the depths by the rumours from across the sea. But once transported, once there, he felt keenly the loss – and the lure – of the old. He needed at least, if not to go back, then to legitimize the new by invoking the old. Hence the naming, or the renaming of the new land: New Spain, New England, New York, names that look backwards as well as forwards, embodying the painful division. Hence Joseph Smith, discovering in New York state old plates – plates of gold – which hallow the new. Hence every orphan who ever invented a lineage. And not until the new outdoes the old is the pain in the name soothed; compare even today the bold sound *New York* with the melancholy cadence of *New England*. Only when the very echo of the old has died down is the usurper at peace.

Mexico is no longer New Spain, but it still has a frontier, the North, where things may be made new. Up in its Deep North, in Sonora, the deposits of civilization are thin on the ground. Hermosillo was not founded until 1742. The colonizing of the northwest was an 18th-century achievement. Its exploration was an earlier adventure, but even that came a whole century after the Vale of Mexico and the East (Mariana's "other side") were pacified. The job was just too hard, the returns too poor. It was not just the distance from Mexico City, it was the bleakness of the land. Not since the Dempster Highway in the far north of the Yukon had I passed through a harsher landscape. The Sonoran desert had been tamed in patches, but there were still tracts that resembled the face of the moon. If ever a land wanted re-inventing, this was it. The very Yaquis who lived there for thousands of years needed the solace of peyote and chiliastic myths. And Baja California was still crueller. No wonder Mariana saw it disappearing into the sea.

I never got to the Cerro de la Campaña. Mariana went off saying she would be at the Restaurant Jung around lunchtime but we never met again. The banks were closed. Riqui led me back to the Palacio insisting he knew someone who would cash a cheque. It was a farcical replay of the night before. This time the people were not so patient. One man, a high official, cut him dead. It was the only display of ill grace I saw in Mexico. Riqui pressed on undaunted. In the end I broke away and found a cambio.

In the evening I strolled in the belly of a great white whale. The supermercado Blanco woke memories of a ritual from my first year in the New World: simply wandering awestruck among inert products beautifully packaged and stacked in multiples that stretched to infinity, a promise of plenty impossible for a visitor from a poor country to discredit. The Blanco was not quite up to the American mark. There were gaps, some bare shelves, too much of one line, too little of another. There were whole bins of avocados, some very indifferent potatoes. The apples, from the US, were not of the best – a sad contrast with the Mexican mangoes you found in the United States and Canada. (In India too we exported our best and got back their second-best.) Almost all the employees were children of junior- to high-school age; in Ciudad Obregon they would be even younger. The whole store looked overstretched, in seven-league boots. But the children were self-possessed. The boy pushing a dust-mop in diminishing rectangles had a spring in his step. The girl at the dairy counter showed not a trace of the servility of her counterparts in India. When I asked to try the Chihuahua cheese, she first nicked a piece off an old wedge, then of her own accord unwrapped a huge roundel and stuck the point of her knife into its heart to winkle out a moist bit.

The next morning I wrote a letter to Riqui. The girl at the Calinda desk promised to deliver it personally. On the way back I passed the Restaurant Jung and went in. It was decorated with Hindu oleographs from the lurid press of Sharma Pictures, Bombay: Shiva seated on his tigerskin; the boy Krishna stealing butter; others. The menu was vegetarian; a poster asked you not to smoke. In the open-plan kitchen stood four middle-class women working peacefully. One of them made and served my mango shake without a word. On my table was a photocopied article on the miracle of royal jelly. It had a photo of the Future Queen in Pupal State.

17

The Day

of the Race

Highway 15 drops like a plumbline down the 111th meridian as far as Guaymas on the Gulf of California, then swings in to continue its long trek along Mexico's west coast. In southern Sonora the land is not so forbidding as up north, and towards Guaymas the approach of the mountains and the sea on either side lifts the spirits of the desert traveller. The sagebrush and whiskery turpentine bush yield to knotty mesquites whose green pods make succulent fodder for the cattle droves. After Guaymas creeks give way to rivers and irrigated valleys. The highway speeds past the newest crop of iron crosses, impromptu truck-stops, and thatch ramadas where people bundle out for shrimp and cockles and Coca-cola.

Ciudad Obregón swelters very nearly at sea-level but is a good way from the sea on the silt fan of the Yaqui River. The Yaqui, having risen in the Sierra Madre not far from Tombstone, Arizona and travelled for much of its long southerly course among mountains, flops onto the coastal plain, and ends in fenland. The marsh has been drained by a network of canals and the land is now worked by small agriculturalists, many of them Yaquis who, until the Spaniards arrived, preferred hunting the whitetail deer to growing corn.

The Yaquis had warning. Their elders tell of a speaking tree that long ago foretold the arrival of a dragon from the north. The dragon appeared and pillaged at will until the villagers enlisted the wizard Chapulin. Chapulin bathed in green tea, put on razor-sharp spurs and struck off the dragon's head. But the beast's head had a dying prophecy to make: Chapulin will not always be with you. In the latter days there will come pale men bearing weapons that spit fire. Take care.

You get what you pay for, and my room at the Colonial Hotel cost half of what I paid at the Amigo. The toilet flushed from a bucket and there was no shower head, just a pipe that spouted warm water. The walls were painted a milky green and a bare electric bulb hung from the ceiling on a fly-blown cord. But what set the room apart from an Asiatic flea-pit was the air-conditioner: it was aged and feeble and throaty, but it worked. I demanded fresh sheets from the laundry and drew comfort from contemplating Master Basho's lodgings at Iizuka: "a filthy place with rough straw mats spread out on an earth floor . . . not even a lamp in the whole house . . . the noise of thunder and leaking rain . . . the raids of mosquitoes and fleas . . . and a horse urinating all the time close to my pillow."

I made a dinner of the Chihuahua cheese and avocadoes and went down to the corner pharmacy. The pharmacist, a blanca or fair woman of sixty, was sitting with her assistant, a moreno or dark man of thirty who was laughing professionally at her jokes. In Mexico you are either dark or fair. Fair is better. As I leaned on a glass cabinet, waiting, the woman froze and pointed at me. Her assistant jumped up, ran at me, and brushed an earwig off my shoulder.

The Colonial Hotel was across from the bus station, the reason I took a room there, the reason it was built there. Across the road the other way from the station was a row of cheap taquerias, taco joints where the clientele sat on wooden benches at laminate-top tables and ate chopped meat rolled up in flat cakes. Served in batches of four, the tacos bore no resemblance to the American taco, but might have passed for the kebab rolls you can buy anywhere from Cairo to Calcutta. I smelt the tropics and perked up. In a gym up the road a temperate import was not doing so well: jazzercise. The instructor rapped out the steps on his mike, the music belted out a rhythm, but the dancers, in fluorescent leotards, were a sorry lot. You saw similar groups in Bombay, prancing listlessly. It was simply too hot for violent exercise; merely to walk was to raise a sweat in Ciudad Obregón.

I sat in the San Juan taqueria, my stomach cured by, and sick of, supermarket food. On the TV was baseball.

"*Twenty-two!*" the cook echoed as a score was called. He came

223

over and stared long and incredulously at the box, then returned to his griddle a broken man.

Four bus operators, one of them blond and boyish, were flirting with the waitresses. A fair waitress was summoned to the ship men's table – she came obediently – and the three older men pointed her at the blond boy. The boy grinned, the waitress turned away with a laugh. After dinner the men boarded the bus they'd parked, like a car, in front of the taqueria and began to back out into the traffic. It was a tight spot, requiring much back-and-forth manoeuvring. Meanwhile the crew crowded the windows, looking out like sailors at portholes. The waitresses lined up to watch the ship go out. There was now a barrier, glass and steel, between them. The men began to say the things they couldn't say face to face. The remarks became catcalls; the bus filled with cries and whistles; the driver took longer than he needed. The girls giggled at the antics, at the things said, at the things they would like to say back, and perhaps do. Then the bus pulled out and it was quiet again. The baseball match went on, there were tables to clear.

The next day was 12 October, Mexico's Day of the Race. It is Columbus Day in the Americas (and Master Basho's death anniversary in Japan) but in Mexico the pageants commemorate the arrival of Cortes and his conquistadores. Blond villains cross wooden swords with dark-skinned heroes, but what is being ritually remembered is not so much that distant clash of arms as the union of two races to produce a third. An abstract festival north of the border has fleshly connotations here. Here every individual is a living reminder of the historic encounter, a crossing of breeds more than of swords.

On a city bus I saw ranged along the same bench the whole Mexican spectrum, from "pure" Indian to "pure" European. In between, a girl with fair hair and dark eyes seated beside a sister with identical features but dark hair and light eyes. At the centre of the spectrum colour and features show signs of settling down ("homozygosity" is the ugly word) to a uniform type, the "pure" mestizo. In northern India the strain has settled down, but it has taken 3000 years. Successive invasions from the Aryan heartland and Tartary, overlaid on the original "Indians", have produced the

224

race of today, but one still comes across green-eyed throw-backs to Alexander and lesser conquistadores. Mexico has had only half a millennium to digest the invader, and it shows. Until the process is complete (on that Final Day of the Race) the spectrum will remain, and include, beyond the two extremes, still another variant: the white Indian and the red European, with features entirely "pure" but their colours switched.

Leaning on the common balcony outside our rooms was a salesman who travelled regularly to the United States. He'd just gone thirty-six hours without sleep.

"I never thought I'd live to see a traveller from India!" he said, pumping my hand slowly. "Why, you're from the other side of the world!"

Armando's company made many things, including clothing. He was in charge of women's panties. The panties were made in Mexico but sold only in the United States. They went from Nogales, Sonora to Texas, to North Carolina, and then to the department stores, including stores in Nogales, Arizona.

"Duty!" he explained wearily.

It did seem absurd. I remembered the border guards at Nogales, USA looking askance at suitcases coming north: they might be full of women's panties.

"Yucatan!" Armando said. "It's beautiful. Our company is relocating there from Nogales."

But before he could tell me why, Nesto the night clerk arrived to let him into his room. He shook my hand, asleep already. Downstairs I chatted with Nesto, who was getting ready to go home. He was a student of accountancy at a college outside town. He broke off and ran to the door to call out to a passing friend.

"He's also at my college," Nesto said. "He speaks perfect English."

Orlando, from Belize, stood there smiling. He was a short, pale-skinned man in his mid-twenties, with sleepy eyes and an alert, hawkish nose. He was on his way to teach English to a group of lecturers from his college.

"Why don't you come along?" he asked.

The streets were holiday bare and we walked many suburban blocks in the sun. Then, by a small iron gate, we entered the house of Teofanes. It was a bachelor's house, stocked with a fridgeful of beer, the science-fiction of H.P. Lovecraft, and a rocker in front of the TV. In a tiny back yard Teofanes grew pineapples, grapes, and a single citrus tree with grafts for oranges, lemons, and grapefruit. He was a brooder, a tough, balding man of fifty-two or fifty-three who lived alone and taught accountancy. He wore jeans and a white linen short-sleeve shirt with a pen in the pocket. With him was Victor, a dark-skinned agronomist they called Indio. He was more demonstrative, with a softer, more yielding face, a custard-yellow T-shirt and a baseball cap he kept on. There were two teachers missing, so the English lesson came to nothing. We sat at a table on the back porch and ate pine nuts and drank chilled Pacifico beer. Teofanes told of a visit to Álamos, the picturesque capital of the old Northwest.

"This happened when I was a young man. A friend invited me to go there in his car. The place was full of Americans. One of them came up to us to ask directions. 'Senorrr, don-de pu-edo irrr . . .' " Teofanes rolled his "r"s farcically and hunched his back a little. "My friend said, 'You see that road? You just take that and keep going north as far as you can.' "

It was the bitter humour of vanquished peoples. Indians would have told similar jokes about the British when Britain was a power. I produced my map of Mexico and spread it on the table. The map included American states just north of the border. Teofanes bent over it.

"Mexico," he said. His finger rested on California. "Mexico," he repeated, pointing at Arizona. "Mexico, Mexico, Mexico." He took swipes at Texas and New Mexico and beyond, towards Utah. "All Mexico."

Mexicans have not forgotten. If American filibusters had had their way in 1857 there would be a fifty-first state: Sonora, Mexico's granary. Even so, in a last-minute bite they got Tucson. Now the border was breaking down in a wholly unexpected way.

Teofanes thought free trade would make local industrialists pull up their socks. Before, they took government subsidies and invested them for quick returns, never in new plant. One brewer in Ciudad Obregón simply dismantled an old brewery in Canada and shipped it home.

"Here in Mexico," Teofanes said, "the minimum wage is thirteen thousand pesos a day. It's not in fact enough to live on." (13,000 pesos was just over $4. My hotel room cost 40,000 pesos.

226

A kilogram of flour cost 3,000 pesos.) "So in the United States today *American* workers are agitating for an increase in the Mexican minimum wage – so their companies don't relocate to Mexico."

It was not just industrial flight, Victor put in. The US government was pressuring Mexico to reduce its bank rates to prevent money draining south. At the same time Mexico was changing its laws to encourage Mexicans to invest in Mexico. At the moment the richest Mexicans sent their money abroad.

Another lecturer came in, Agustin, a mechanical engineer. He was younger than the other two and had a long, well-fleshed face that wore a droll, slightly bored look.

"You know," Victor continued, "American corn is dearer, so people immediately think it's better and buy that, if they can afford it."

"As long as the product has an English name, a marca gringa."

"It's the same in India."

"One of the points that Mexico is raising in the trade talks is labels. We want at least the words *Date of Expiry* to be in Spanish."

"Or we could all expire!"

"Now American farmers can simply rent land here and send the product back, so they have a sure market. But the danger is they'll simply exploit the land. They use high-tech equipment, and it's private enterprise so the technology is not transferred to Mexico. The package is sealed."

Agustin joined in. "You know, the gap between the rich and poor was always there, but it actually was closing. If they tamper with social programmes it'll start growing again. In the early days politicians used religion to sway the people. Then they used money. Now it's trade talks. But people aren't fools, they judge you by your actions. What did the rich do when the peso was devalued? They put their money in the stable dollar. If some of that money comes back, well, the talks have worked."

He went and switched on the TV and sat down in Teofanes' rocker. "Here is a symbol of free trade," he said, pointing at the screen. "We're free to become slaves!"

"There will always be ruler and ruled," Orlando said, quoting the norteamericano Emerson. "You can keep eliminating people, but even if two remain, one will dominate the other."

Agustin ran through the channels to show me Mexican TV.

Several had American programmes. The narrator on a nature show was saying that the lion ate first, then the cubs, then the lioness.

"Same with Mexicans," Agustin said.

"And Indians."

We left the table and sat around the TV. The Atlanta Braves were playing somebody else. Braves supporters were waving red plastic tomahawks. The camera closed in on Jane Fonda.

"Mexicans invented the Human Wave," Orlando said, and was amazed when I didn't know what it was.

It was time to go. We stood at Teofanes' door saying our goodbyes. Victor gave me his note pad as a souvenir. "He's more Indio than I am!" he said to his colleagues.

"Watch your step!" they called. "There's a hurricane loose on the coast."

Returning, we passed a statue of a one-armed man. "Who is that?" Orlando asked a boy scout. He enjoyed accosting strangers.

"It's General Obregón," the scout answered, adjusting his woggle. "He lost an arm in battle against Zapata."

We went into the municipal buildings past an armed guard. There were more improving murals and a stained-glass window above the chief stair. At the centre of the window was the torso of a Yaqui medicine man wearing a scarlet amice crowned with the head of a stag, a figurehead that is the state symbol. (The scarlet in the original would have come from the Yaqui's famous cochineal, got from the female of a desert beetle, but many Indian weavers preferred to unravel trade baize for their colours.) The antlered medicine man is a happier symbol than the eagle; one variant shows the medicine man blindfold with the stag doing his seeing for him.

On the wall were some lines from Norman Borlaug, whose research into high-yielding varieties of wheat won him the Nobel Peace prize:

> *If you want peace*
> *Cultivate justice,*
> *But at the same time*
> *Cultivate the fields*
> *To grow more food.*
> *By no other means*
> *Can you have peace.*

228

"I'll show you my college," Orlando said. "Or better still, I'll show you Pueblo Yaqui. We'll pass my college on the way."

Orlando's college was an agropecuario institute, that is, it took in animal husbandry as well as agriculture. Orlando himself had travelled from Belize on a scholarship to learn the newest techniques. He was one of the bright young men of his small country (a knuckle on the thumb of the Yucatan peninsula) and had already studied in Costa Rica. Already he saw himself as leading others, as no longer young. A foreign student, he had nevertheless stirred up the local student council.

We took a city bus out to Pueblo Yaqui. The road left the city behind and lit out across the flat green campo. I felt keenly the exhilaration of a detour for its own sake. The land was densely cropped and the roads across it followed the grid of the canals. At crossings – there might be a small brick house with four fruit trees, two cows and a dog – the bus would let people out. At one time the land belonged to absentee landlords; in 1977 under popular pressure it was parcelled out to small farmers, but not before seven people were killed.

"Every year," Orlando said, "on the 18th of October the people of San Ignacio and Pueblo Yaqui honour the martyrs of '77. I'll show you the memorial when we get there." He spoke of the land with a sense of attachment, as someone who belonged. In fact, he said he felt he'd become one with the local people. He spoke their Sonoran dialect and was in love with a local woman. I felt a bond with him that took me back twenty years.

Across the aisle from us sat a startling beauty in a tatty yellow dress. I called her Susana for the Black-eyed Susan and told Orlando about the flower I'd followed south all along the Rockies. He looked hard at me and said, "Black-eyed Susan, eh?"

We got off the bus at a crossroads in what looked like a village. On one side of the road was San Ignacio, on the other side Pueblo Yaqui. The Yaqui side was said to be rougher but you could take your pick. We sat on San Ignacio benches and drank refrescos. It was evening and the young men and women of San Ignacio were coming out to promenade. A teenager sat on a motorcycle and revved it for his friends. Two men lolloped by on horseback, big groomed horses – one white, one skewbald – not the ponies I'd seen so far. Groups of girls went by, five and six abreast, looking sideways at the boys. The boy on the motorcycle went rigid and sounded his horn. Across the way was a liquor shop with a naked light bulb already on and several dusty old men dancing around it like moths: liquor had carried them well past women, but they could still heckle. The girls wheeled about somewhere and came back; knots of boys barred their way and made them go around. There was high tension in the air, made up of dust and sweat and approaching darkness. I felt the menace like something coiled and waiting. An evening in small-town India was altogether different, slack to limpness; besides it was usually a family affair, people strolling, the day's tensions spent. In San Ignacio it was strolling with intent. The air crackled, and the players were young. Older men might bawl from the sidelines, but theirs was a toothless challenge. The girls had a way of blotting them right out.

We crossed the road to Pueblo Yaqui. There the air was softer, less charged. It was more village than town. The occasional pickup truck went by, raising a flat white cloud of dust, low cumulus, that settled on the roadside bushes like talcum. Dark groves of trees overshadowed the adobe huts. Shaggy palms stood silhouetted against a yellow sky. Under one, a Yaqui woman had lit several small fires that she was tending in a cloud of blue smoke. Her young son stood in the middle of the road and watched: that was excitement.

At the edge of the village, where the cornfields began, we came to a small, flat-roofed concrete house. It had a little garden with a scarlet flame tree. A group of men was sitting under the leaf-fans, barely visible in the dying light. Orlando said he knew them but wasn't sure we should look in. We had gone past the house when he turned back.

"Come on," he said. A small man, he worked by daring.

The men greeted him warmly. I was introduced in the dark. La *India*! The name Gandhi sounded. Someone went for more chairs, another bottle of beer was opened. The men were science teachers at the local high school, gathered at their favourite watering hole, the principal Andres' house. Andres held court, a quiet man of fifty; the garden was his domain. His wife, a stormy philosopher (Orlando said), was down with high blood pressure, indoors. In the circle of chairs I made out Manuel, heavy, Fidel-bearded, and bespectacled; David, young, fair-skinned, and clean-shaven; and

Rudolfo, a smouldering figure beside me, with the edgy bearing of a boxer.

They dredged up what they knew of India, dwelling on its riches, not its poverty. Then they put their questions. Orlando settled back into his role as interpreter, but selectively, as he saw my Spanish return. The beer loosened my tongue, I ventured discourse. Manuel leaned forward earnestly. Had I and my fellow students at university belonged to the right or to the left? (His beard told his own story.) What did I think of recent events in the Soviet Union? In Eastern Europe? What of Cuba? The United States? I imagined earlier discussions under that flame tree, with Andres' wife holding sway. I said we had belonged to the left and had since watched the world unravel our ideas. He nodded ruefully. But Cuba, Cuba could still be a lesson to us? Surely the danger was now an orthodoxy of the right?

"And what do you think of Mexico?"

It was everyone's question wherever I went. I said it was a country I could live in. It *was* India in many ways: the people, the heat, the houses, the food, the dust, the disorder, this tree. Then I asked a question.

"Don't you celebrate the Day of the Race? I expected to see some festivities."

Manuel answered. "Alán, the reason we don't celebrate El Dia de la Raza is that we don't know whether to laugh," (he counted on his fingers) "or to cry, or to remain silent."

It sounded like Octavio Paz. I asked what they thought of their Nobel Laureate.

"Paz es loco," Rudolfo said. He stated it flatly, like a law of chemistry.

Paz mad! I asked why he thought so, but he glowered and shucked off the question.

"What do you want to see of Mexico?" Manuel asked.

"Just what I'm seeing now."

"Alán wants to see the mystical Yaquis of Carlos Castaneda!" Rudolfo said with his taut smile. "Peyote, no?"

"Not so!" I said and held up my empty glass. David refilled it, beaming. He said very little but from time to time called "Alán!" from where he sat and held up a bottle. Presently he and Rudolfo went off in Rudolfo's van to get more beer.

When they got back we were already crying out:

"Viva Mexico!"

"Viva la India!"

"Viva Belize!"

Manuel went off casually to piss in the cornfield. When he came back he sat and fondled his glass and said, "Alán. Is it true that the women of India are the most beautiful in the world?"

"Of course!"

They laughed uproariously, and glasses were raised to Indian beauty. I saw my mistake. After a suitable pause I said in an all-things-considered voice, "The most beautiful women in the world are Mexican women."

I stated it as a natural law. I believed it. There were howls of assent. Even Andres raised his glass.

"To Mexican women!"

"The women of India!"

"The women of Belize!"

We got noisier before the beer ran out again. By then it was late. We stood up. I thanked them for a raucous evening. Raucous? they said. No, no. This evening they'd been especially quiet because Andres' wife was ill.

Orlando decided he wanted to spend the night in San Ignacio with his girlfriend. Rudi would drop me back to Ciudad Obregón.

"Don't worry," he said. "They're my friends."

I wasn't worried. I'd known them a long time. We got into Rudi's van. He would drop off Orlando and David in San Ignacio, then Manuel at his village, and then we'd drive back to town.

In San Ignacio Saturday night had got jumpier still. Riding its dirt roads – I had the front seat – we explored the ruts I'd missed on foot. Villages in India had such roads, but no cars. (In Mexico one in ten drove; in India not one in a thousand.) The van plunged and reared. Our beam fenced with the lights of approaching cars. Nobody gave way – the earth did. Then the other car shaved a horseman's flank and we skinned the shanks of a motor-cyclist and his girl. The girl's red hair streamed behind her and caught the lights of the refresco stall where we'd sat. A taqueria had sprung up next to the liquor shop. Smoke from its grill seeped through the thatch and filled the street with the reek of charred fat. It got in the eyes of the drunks struggling to prop up a crucial verandah pole.

Rudi slowed the van to a crawl.

"Alán. The girls of Mexico . . ."

"ARE THE MOST BEAUTIFUL IN THE WORLD!" was the chorus.

The girls were walking ten abreast now, with linked arms so the traffic had to go around them. No one minded. Prowling boys and wizened men, too young and too old, ogled and smirked and hooted, but they were nothing. The young men who mattered stood about or sauntered past going the other way. There was no San Ignacio and Pueblo Yaqui now: the border had been breached. Mestizo and Yaqui — Yaqui girls in pink Mickey-Mouse T-shirts — walked arm-in-arm. Horsemen galloped past raising dust, horns sounded, men whooped, dogs howled at the moon.

David got out.

"Alán! My house is your house."

We said goodbye. Then Orlando got out. He would see me at the hotel in the morning. I noticed there were no seats at the back of the van. Manuel sat on the floor with his son, a boy of nine or ten who leaned on the seatback and made shy conversation. We picked up speed in spite of the ruts. A black dog ran under the wheels. Rudolfo slammed on his brakes. I jerked forward. Manuel flew forward and struck the seatback, grabbing his son, who was flying towards the windscreen.

"Did you see the dog?"

"I saw it."

There was no serious damage. The dog got away. A Coke bottle that had been rolling about was smashed. We got out and Rudi picked up the pieces. There was a roadside cross on a mound by a canal. I asked if it was a real grave. No, they said, the real grave was elsewhere.

Manuel lived some miles from the main road in another settlement. "A polvoron," he joked. A polvoron is a cookie but also a dustbowl.

I said I grew up in a dustbowl, but I saw what he meant when we left the main road. The dirt road ran along a canal bank. The embankment had been gouged and fissured by rainwater that ran off one way into the nightblack fields and the other into the canal.

"Bad water," Rudolfo said as we pitched perilously on its bank.

233

It smelt bad. It was impossible to tell in the darkness at what depth the canal lay. There was a factory upstream, Manuel explained. There were no lights other than our own and we appeared to be heading into outer darkness.

At the next junction a truck loomed up, parked half on the road, its lights off. When we came up to it we saw it was two trucks parked nose to nose. The drivers and passengers were drinking. Rudolfo stuck out his head and cursed them for taking up the road. We would have to inch past. The men looked at us without moving. One of them spat out a few words and Rudolfo snarled back. We began to edge forward. The men sneered as we drew level. Rudolfo stopped and returned a sneer. I saw no way out. I had not been in a fight before and wondered how it would end if they had knives. The men growled among themselves. I counted five heads. They would have seen four up front with possibly more in the back of the van. Little by little we got past, words flying between us now. Then we broke away with parting shouts on both sides.

The dust was of a quality entirely familiar. It lay white and inches deep on the road, it coated the broad leaves of a roadside milkweed, it rode in a column behind us. A pair of headlights behind us – truck lights? – were orange in the pall. We plunged into black pits, skidded a bit at the bottom, and sprang out at an oblique angle. Once, on our way down, our headlights fell on the surface of the canal and it glittered evilly, like pitch. At points the road simply veered out into the fields around a ravine. Finally it left the canal and skipped across cropland. Dimly, beyond a copse, a short row of streetlights appeared. The lights were out at Manuel's house. I imagined sleeping bodies inside. Manuel's son looked sleepy. Manuel apologized for not inviting us in. It was an awkward moment: we both had more to say that would be left unsaid. Rudi swung the van around and we waved goodbye.

We now had to backtrack along the canal road. Once when the engine failed Rudi switched off the lights to start up again. We looked to be in deep space.

"Alán," Rudolfo said, in the only English he used that evening, "don't be afray-id."

It had not occurred to me to be. I told him so.

He said, returning to Spanish, "I have two tapes here that

234

I listen to a lot. One is Mexican, one is Vivaldi. Which would you like to hear?"

I said, "I hear Mexican music all the time. Put on Vivaldi."

He was delighted, as if I had passed a test. "Now you are Mexican," he said, and put on the Vivaldi.

We bounded along the canal. A truck covered us in dust, but the ostinato cut through it and the cellos poured out into the silent fields. As a boy I'd travelled such roads on remote inspection tours with my father. Then, I wanted every jolt to be more jarring than the last.

The main road returned, and then the lights of Ciudad Obregón. We sat in the San Juan taqueria. Rudolfo ordered wheat flour tacos for me and maize ones for himself.

I asked him again why he said Octavio Paz was mad.

He said, "Because I cannot understand a word of what he writes. Others I can understand a little. Him, not at all. A poet should communicate." He laughed ironically. "Paz is mad – because I cannot understand him."

He asked me what I had studied at university.

I said, "Mostly literature," and added ritually, as one does in the presence of scientists, "nothing useful."

He would have none of it. "Literature is crucial," he said, and was going to mount a defence of it when he checked himself and smiled haughtily: "But you know that."

He held himself very still when he spoke. When he wasn't speaking he was even more still. He ate neatly, almost invisibly.

"Now you try maize tacos," he said, and ordered a batch for me. He watched me eat them like a poisoner.

They were stronger, earthier. I delivered my verdict.

He nodded. "Those are tacos."

I had read somewhere that the distinction between maize and wheat was once a class division in Mexico, like brown rice and polished rice in Asia.

"I would like to go to India," Rudolfo said, his eyes lighting up. "The land of Gandhi. Of Buddha." He formed and sounded the syllable "OM" with the same distant smile. I sensed a turbulent spirit. He had read *Siddharta*, Hesse's greatest book, he said. He could name the boatman, the prostitute, Siddharta's boyhood friend.

"Govínda," he intoned, "Kamála, Vasudéva."

I asked him about himself. He said he lived alone. He had twice been married; his child lived with the mother. He lived out of his van, had no real home.

It was closing time. I paid before he could and he was upset.

"The guest is sacred," he said, but I felt the muscles in his hand tense as he tried to take the change and pass me his note. I wouldn't have liked to fight him.

"You've just driven me forty kilometres," I protested.

He yielded with an effort, but said, "That's not the way, Alán, not the way."

He walked me back to the hotel because he said dangerous types hung around the bus station at night.

There was a girl at the desk hardly into her teens. Young Marta showed me to a new room because I'd asked for a change. When the light didn't go on she fetched the bulb from the old room and clambered up onto the bedside chest-of-drawers with it. She had skinny brown legs and ginger hair.

18

Amo Vaqueros

Ciudad Obregón is Sonora's second city. If Hermosillo is the frontier's Athens, Obregón is its Sparta, a tougher, rougher, newer – and slightly jealous – encampment which refuses to ponce but is not above preening. There are more hats and boots here than all the North might need, but no more than it wants. It was here that I heard Mexico's king of country music, Ramón Ayala. Strictly, Ayala is King of the *North*, but then norteño and country are synonymous. Norteño is a style as much as a direction, and even those who don't wear hats wear it in their hearts.

Orlando was late and full of his woman. We went looking for a particular boteria, or boothouse; they were sure, Orlando said, to have tickets for the Ayala concert. They did. The owners had their hats on indoors.

The boots stood in ranks on shelves that went from floor to ceiling. They were protected from the Sonoran dust by glass, like specimens in a museum, except the glass gave them an unfocused look that their sameness multiplied: two became four became four hundred. In a shoe shop the eye might wander and rest; in a boteria it ricocheted off cabinet after cabinet. Every boot was identically shaped: the variation was in the stitching. The standard pattern gave them a winged aspect at the top of the shank that, along with the lifted heel and pointed toe, suggested a creature poised for flight but frozen behind glass. It was the colours that quickened them: rich tans, dove greys, oxblood, butterscotch, even a spumy aquamarine. Also, for the brave, white, and for the dateless, black. They were not cheap. The cheapest cost five times as much as the tickets – and *they* were not cheap. Two tickets cost a week's wage.

237

If you were taking a girl and buying a pair of boots for the dance, it might be your outing for the year. So unless you were rich you would pass up the crocodile and snakeskin boots, which cost twice as much again, and merely linger over the still dearer tortoiseskin ones. Most expensive of all were the ostrichskin boots, horripilated where the feathers had been plucked out.

The hats, at sombrerias, were a simpler affair, and more emblematic. Their lines were cleaner, less precious, and carried a greater charge. A hat was not a statement, it was an icon: it stood for itself. Hats met a real need, unless you wore them indoors, and they were usually unpretentious. They were stacked on the very sidewalk, humdrum as egg cartons. There were fancy ones further in, behind glass, but most lived out in the open, leaning in their hundreds in anonymous white towers. There was a democracy in hats that boots could not, or would not, match. Only hatlessness was a greater leveller.

Orlando roomed in Rio Muerto with a family. We got on the Dead River bus and raced past fields green with maize and livid with sugarcane. I stood at the back door of the bus and inhaled the campo like a decongestant. Little hamlets stood on canal banks, clusters of tin-roofed shacks with washing hanging out and roosters scratching in the dust. A circle of empty chairs made a mushroom ring around a mango tree. Children tormented scruffy dogs and stole fruit; one leaned over a sinister pond to pick a purple water hyacinth.

Orlando's family's house was at the end of an unpaved street, a concrete cube with white verandah chairs and little back yard with fruit trees and the dungy smell of livestock. The family weren't home and Orlando was reluctant to take me in. He was going to dub a tape of Belizian music for me, but now said I could have the original. We walked back up the dusty street.

Just short of the local school, behind a fringe of trees, was a lime-washed shrine to the Virgin of Guadalupe, Mexico's Holy Mother in Indian guise. A few devotees, old and poor, sat on rough benches facing an open-air stage whose winged proscenium arched into a bell tower. Above the bell were a wrought-iron cross and a loudspeaker; below were orange and yellow pennants, paper flowers, and a string of naked light-bulbs. A set of barred doors

238

stood open: beyond was the altar with its relics. Blue and white floral chintz made up the altarcloth, and there was a vase of red and white plastic flowers in the centre. Propped up like missals were two large holy pictures framed in aluminium. They looked like push-out windows hinged at the top – and they were. The windows were the relics, and they were not pictures but photographs. They were recent photographs of the Virgin of Guadalupe.

One evening, quite late, a pair of schoolgirls was going home from the local school, just beyond the trees over there, when they saw a shining light. It didn't look like a streetlight, and all the classroom lights had been turned off so they went to see what it might be. It was the Virgin of Guadalupe. She remained with them for some time, they could not say how long, and then she went away. Naturally, when they told people what they had seen, no one believed them, until someone noticed that the windows near the place where she appeared had taken a picture – two pictures – of her. There, imprinted on the glass for all to see, was the outline of the Queen of Heaven.

"Go up and look by all means," the old folk under the canopy said, and we did.

There was plainly a rainbow swirl in the glass that ran from the bottom of the pane to the top and then swooped back down again: a peak between two troughs. Glass is like that. What was significant was that the wave was not upright but gently leaning. It was this tilt that matched the tilt of the Guadalupana as she is represented through the length and breadth of Mexico. There was a reproduction of the classic painting placed helpfully there to guide the viewer's eye. That was all.

As we were leaving a girl came up on stage and genuflected before the windows. Someone said she was one of the schoolgirls who had had the vision. I saw a lifetime of devotions ahead of her, perhaps a nunnery, and wanted to hear her story. But she stood unmoving before the altar. Orlando was for pressing on; he wanted me to meet another woman.

We rejoined the main road at the edge of town and walked along it into the setting sun. There were fallow fields on either side and a smell of burning stubble. A kilometre out of town we turned up a long dirt drive that led to a white farmhouse. A grassy mound ran along the track, stuck with utility poles and clumps of Blackeyed

Susans. The horizon was perfectly flat in every direction. The only trees were those that darkly framed the farmhouse.

Cathy had once been Orlando's girlfriend. Now they were each seeing someone else, but she remained a good friend. Her parents looked after the farm for a rich Obregón landlord.

"She's a good example of a village girl who's come up through education," he said.

But the meeting was doomed. When we got to the farmhouse there was a long car parked outside.

"That means her fiancé is here," Orlando said, a bit put out.

Cathy and her young sister greeted us. Their mother brought water, a smiling woman in an apron. They were always happy to see Orlando, I could tell. The fiancé was a sober accountant with a long face and sceptical eyes. It would be a very different match. Orlando excused our intrusion by saying I wished to interview Mexicans. I protested, but they were on their guard at once. We talked formally, pedantically, of American foreign policy, Mexico, Iraq. I said I had no more questions. The tension lifted like a veil. Cathy's sister, who'd been sagging, perked up. The fiancé told me he'd read Elena Poniatowska's novel, *De la noche vienes*. Cathy began to chatter with Orlando as if it were old times. The fiancé grew gloomy again and went and sat on the hood of his long car. When we got up to go it was dark, the night sky country-clear. I looked for the Big Dipper.

"The big dipper?" Orlando said.

"Or the Great Bear. It lines up with the pole star."

"The pole star? Let's go see."

The farmhouse and its grove of towering trees stood in the way. We could see clear to the west where the sky was still faintly yellow, but for the north we had to walk a short way into the fields. Cathy and Orlando walked together, I went on ahead. Orlando called back to the fiancé, "Allan's showing us the pole star. Do you want to see it?"

"No."

I pointed out the dipper, its bowl, the pointers, the North Star.

"You know me, Orlando," Cathy said. "Whatever happens, I'll always be your friend."

The two pointers, I'd read, were travelling in opposite directions at a million miles an hour.

I felt an invisible hand reach down and brush my face. I'd walked into a cobweb. We said our goodnights at the head of the drive. The fiancé didn't come out. We walked back into town in the dark. Orlando left me at the bus stop and went to dress for the dance. He'd meet me at the hotel.

"You'll see," he said, "the girls will look a man up and down before they agree to a dance. If he has a gold chain, a good hat and boots, Levi 501s, a good shirt, they'll go with him."

The bus started from there so I got a seat. I sat by an open window and felt the black night rushing in, the heat gone at last. The driver turned off the inside lights and we hurtled along the dark country road, stopping at blind corners to pick up passengers. At one stop two bleach blondes got on wearing skimpy dresses. They looked absurd on a bus, the dresses simply black silk négligées, but it was Sunday night. They were small-town girls travelling by bus to a bigger town for a dance. The man in front of me nudged his girl. They looked wordlessly at the blondes, then the girl laid her head on his shoulder and he slipped his arm around her. For forty minutes we sat in silence, dark shapes lit only by oncoming cars. A black wind roared in my ear. We were all bare presences – and then, at some point, absences. One by one we vanished: the girl beside me, the seat rail in front and the ponytail brushing the back of my hand; the blondes, the driver, the bus. At the terminal we came to life again, and the catcalls began. There were yelps and whistles as the blondes made their way through the crowd. Women, even young women, smiled. One man cracked up.

At the Colonial I changed my room a third time and got a shower that worked. Then there was a power failure. Nesto brought up a candle in a tumbler to light the bathroom. As I showered, a ghostly blue figure leaned through the transfer on the glass.

It was the Virgin of Guadalupe.

Orlando showed up at ten and we took a taxi to the dance. The hall stood on an open ground with a long approach on which pickups cruised, raising dust. There was a barrier at the door to keep out gate-crashers. We were frisked – sides and legs but not the front – by security men, rubber-stamped without ink and allowed through.

Inside, all the chairs had been cleared away. It was a big hall with a second stage run up on bleachers at an angle to the main stage. A Sonoran band was playing on the lesser stage, to lukewarm applause. One or two couples were dancing. On the main stage a glittering backdrop promised, in gold sequins:

EL REY
Ramón Ayala

A lady who might have been Anglo-Indian, beige but rouged and powdered, was selling coupons for the tables placed around the dance floor. It cost the price of an extra ticket to sit at one, so most people stood. Not all the men were dressed al norteño, but white sombreros ruled. Every man wore boots. The women wore short dresses or long gowns with plunging backlines. They knew they were the most beautiful women in the world.

"There's a coloured man behind us," Orlando said.

The man stood out. He was the first black man I'd seen in Mexico. He looked African, an agronomist, I imagined, at the research institute. A young blanca sat on the arm of his chair and chatted.

"How do you like that?" Orlando said. "A white girl with a coloured man!"

We did a tour of the hall. There was no food to be had inside and no drink other than one brand of beer. Already there were empty cans lying crunched on the floor, bleeding foam.

"Ladies and gentlemen, the moment you have been waiting for . . . !"

There was wild cheering. It was near midnight. Ayala's three Braves, Los Bravos del Norte, came onstage in the half dark and tinkered with their instruments. The bass guitarist, a tall, sombre man who kept to the background, sounded off a few booming notes. The mike in the centre, which I thought would be Ayala's, was taken by a big moreno who would do most of the singing. I took him for Ayala at first but then a shorter, almost podgy blanco came on in the dark and the crowd went crazy.

The accordion was a shock, like betrayal. I expected a guitar.

Ayala acknowledged the crowd with a royal wave – the forearm upright, the hand swivelling on top – and a servile ducking of the head. Long exposure had made the king a slave to applause. He ran a few riffs on the accordion, a sharp scatter of electronic coins. The crowd screeched and grovelled. He stretched his arms a couple of times – still in silhouette – and loosened up his fingers like a stage villain. The crowd liked that. Then he looked both ways at his Braves and together they slammed down three gigantic chords. The lights came on, and there in black suits and black sombreros, black boots and clouds of dry-ice vapour, stood Ramón Ayala y los Bravos del Norte.

The cheering threatened to breach the wall of speakers. But the music gathered itself up and blew a hole through the crowd clear to the back of the hall. It was an old favourite. Hats went up, waved in time and shivering in the blast from the speakers. The lights did complicated things in blue and red and then a paler blue that swelled through mauve into a burst of white. For the chorus the lights were turned on the audience and Ramón and the Braves played in the dark. The crowd knew every word, not just of the chorus but of the whole song and every song. "Wearing Her Rose Pink Dress", "Forsaken Am I", "Today, Little Mama", "My Tyrant Heart", "Come Back to Me"; they knew them at the first chord.

"They're turning this into a concert," Orlando said. We had come up close to the stage ourselves. But people were dancing, and the blast from the speakers drove us back. Others stood their ground, facing down the music; a white-haired man leaned on it, two feet from the speakers – something he could hear at last. The hats got in the way, but Orlando, who stood a head shorter than most, didn't mind. He shouted line-by-line translations right into my ear, but even at two inches the words were blown to shreds. His voice became a hoarse screaming in my ear.

Ramón sang of love and abandonment, of hardship and sorrow and abandonment, of sorrow and abandonment and love. The accordion gave the songs a lederhosen air, but the band's energy burnt up the saccharine. With his pink cheeks and chubby face Ayala looked like Santa Claus in a stetson. He dandled grown men and they trusted him; he knew from years past their list of woes and needs. He expressed exactly their delight, their yearnings, their sense of loss. And he had the showmanship they demanded: he milked the keys shamelessly, his hands fluttered on the buttons, he was master of the trill – and halfway through he changed his white accordion for a spangled green one.

There was a break. Local dignitaries came on stage to make speeches of appreciation. Ramón mopped his florid face with a handkerchief and made a speech back. The beer magnate whose goods lay strewn on the floor spoke feelingly, gave Ayala a plaque. Then the Bravos trooped offstage, a bodyguard fending off admirers. Orlando got to shake the drummer's hand. Couples danced to a second-string band; we drank more beer. I began to feel weary and there was nowhere to sit. The women began to look painted.

Ayala returned in a white suit, with a black accordion, and more old favourites. The crowd, a little more drunk, careened towards the stage, a dark human wave with a froth of hats. One young man leapt onto his friend's shoulders and rode him like a horse, waving his hat and conducting with a beer can. The beer slopped onto his horse. The floor was littered with trodden cans, wet pools forming around them. Couples danced side by side, hemmed in and hopping on the spot. A woman in electric blue wore a sash that read: AMO VAQUEROS, *I love cowboys*. Up against the stage two young vaqueros did a brisk boot-clicking dance, their fists making pistons in the air. Everyone was singing except the white-haired old man who leaned on the music unmoving, two feet from the speakers, with a quiet smile on his face. He was still there when we left.

The taxis were cheaper now, so we could afford a snack. *Exquisitos*, the hot-dog carts said in fiery red. With exquisitos you get onions fried on the spot, and a range of sauces: the American hot dog made good at last. As we stood and ate ours three cowboys were herded past in the dark, their hands behind their backs. Behind them came *their* cowboys.

"The Policía Federal," Orlando whispered.

"They don't always wear uniforms," the hot-dog man told me. "They travel in unmarked cars. They can go anywhere. They can come into your house."

The three cowboys were pushed up against a black van, spread-eagled and searched.

244

"Don't look that way," Orlando said.

A tall man in a hat tried to intervene. He was shoved aside by a man with a stengun. He cursed the cop bravely. He seemed to know the arrested men. The next time he tried he was shoved aside more roughly. Bystanders were told to move on.

"No one says anything," the hot-dog man said.

"Come away," Orlando said, and we moved aside a few steps and stood eating our hot dogs.

A uniformed man told all those around us to move along. He let us be because we were eating. I thought there'd been a brawl. The hot-dog man gave a short laugh and said nothing.

"Could be drugs," Orlando said.

"Or 'spying'," the hot-dog man said.

We finished our hot dogs and found a taxi. When we left the three white hats were still there, pushed up against the black van.

19

The Five Words

Orlando slept in the other bed and Nesto said he'd have to put me down for the double rate. At six in the morning Orlando caught the Rio Muerto bus home. Neither of us was properly awake when we said goodbye. I walked into town and bought an Ayala tape. The girl in the store preferred rap.

As I packed to leave young Marta came in. "Nesto told me to collect the extra money," she said. "He had to go to college."

"I'll pay the propr_iedora," I said. I'd seen her downstairs, a fearsome woman.

Marta hesitated. "She doesn't know," she confessed. "Don't tell her."

I gave her the money and wondered how – or if – it would be divided, and what it would buy.

The bus to Culiacán looked in at Navojoa, then the highway returned to the coast. After Navojoa the mountains came up close on the left and the plain on the right shelved gently into the sea. All around was classic Aridamerica: organpipe cactus, turpentine brush, spinifex, drifts of tumbleweed. Into that beautiful silence burst the bus driver's music. "Qué lástima!" sang the cowboy, What a pity! He sang of sadness, abandonment, a certain red dress, a horse. Trumpets sobbed, the strings were positively Bombay Talkies.

Looking out, I saw a giant Virgin Mary on the rocks. She was on a red bluff a hundred feet above the road, a painting this time, not a photograph. To get a closer look pilgrims climbed a dizzy flight of steps, with a rail for the faint of heart. The Indians venerated lofty places too, rather as Hindus and Greeks were apt to crown

246

a hill with a temple, but most modern Mexican shrines are more accessible. The roadside ones wear a familiar look, decked out in kitchen tiles like any Kali or Durga or mother-goddess sanctum in India.

There is a difference. The Virgin has a gentler face. The miracle is that she conquered Mexico at all, when one considers that the principal Aztec god was a war god, Huitzilopochtli, fed on palpitating human hearts, usually male. There were female deities that went much further back, rather in the way the fierce mother goddesses of the Hindu pantheon have deeper roots than many a Vedic god, but they too wore garlands of skulls. The Virgin's appeal was to a still older human need than blood: mothering. In India, despite a male victory in the heavens, the earth produced a softer, mother-centred ethos – where the male child rules. In Mexico, where the clash of god versus goddess seems still to echo, the resulting personality is more impervious, less yielding, except to the madrecita, the little mother. No sorrow like abandonment by her, no yearning like the yearning for her. "Abandonado Soy", wails Ramón Ayala, and every paid-up vaquero in the audience shivers in his boots.

We crossed into Sinaloa. The countryside began to look familiar. It was not just the tropical crops and trees, but the size of the fields, parcelled out to smallholders, bounded by handmade mounds, brought back down to human scale. Then, to jolt me back, huge ranches with Piper Cubs parked in front of roadside hangars. Then a cowboy on foot, herding six head of cattle.

The road entered the mountains, forest coming down to its edge. A pink antignum creeper ran wild over trees and bushes; whole wooded acres dripped its costume jewellery. Millet covered the gentler swells and hollows with a nap of rust. The Sierra Madre grew wonderfully varied, with long serene slopes, sudden spires, graceful cones. Flocks of snowy egrets made for a rare lake. Frangipani appeared, then palms, painted municipal white up to the hip. Culiacán.

I was in Culiacán to learn five words from a stranger. Riqui's index card with the man's name and address in Mariana's spare triangular script lay like a charm in my pocket.

After Obregón, Culiacán looked like a modern city. A girl went by alone, walking like a norteamericana, as if unconcerned with her body, dressed down, not up. Obregónian women carried their femininity like a chalice; they would not have dreamed of wearing glasses. (Nor would the men.) In Pueblo Yaqui I'd seen two boys on a motorcycle pretend to grab a young woman. She didn't even blink: it happened all the time. And that night the two blondes on the bus had done a kind of grabbing of their own. "My two blonde sisters are married," Riqui had said. "The one who has my colour is still waiting." This woman walked as if grabbing – as if marriage itself – were ancient history. It said more for Culiacán than the flash hotels on the palm-fringed boulevard I tramped as far as the statue of Cuauhtemoc.

Cuauhtemoc was the Aztec prince whose feet the Spaniards roasted on an open fire. When a fellow sufferer complained of the pain Cuauhtemoc replied, immortally, "I am not on a bed of roses either." I'd entered the ambit of Aztec Mexico, and felt the North slip away. I ate the first meal of the day after dark at an outdoor grill where the flames spurted high above crisping chicken legs.

The loncheria next day was blinding white. With its blue and white awning El Pipirin looked Greek, but the customers wore sombreros and huarache sandals; it was a working man's lunchhouse. A shabby teenage balloon-seller took the next table. He simply dumped his balloon-stick at the entrance and fell into a chair. Two more balloon-sellers fell into other chairs, at another table. Lastly an itinerant photographer in black suede boots that showed no trace of dust. He set his camera on the table and wiped it tenderly with a napkin, as if mopping a child's forehead. When that was done he took out his belly, unbuttoning his shirt to get a grip on it, and began to mop that. I ordered what the man ahead of me was having; he overheard and on his way out gave me a brief bow. It was a caldo, a clear meat soup with zucchini, carrots, potatoes, cabbage, corn on the cob, beans, green coriander, and chunks of tender meat floating in it. To bring such a variety of vegetables – Sinaloa's pride – to a state of perfect readiness required skill.

In the evening I took a taxi to the home of Saul Mastretta, the man with the five words. It was dark when the cabbie found the street. The house was locked. The neighbour lady came out and said Saul was away, in Mazatlán. I felt deflated. The lady registered my disappointment and invited me in while

248

she phoned a friend for Mastretta's Mazatlán address. I sat under the ceiling fan and sipped the fresh lime in sugar-water she brought me, the very drink we served guests in summer at home. The room was full of lace. At one end, in a bassinet hung with mosquito curtains, lay a newborn babe. Its young mother smiled and floated in and out of the room. The Mazatlán address was a hotel. The lady wrote down the name, the street, the city: five words.

I took the bus back to the city centre and sat in the spray of a fountain by the cathedral. Dinner at El Pipirin was a stuffed capsicum swathed in cheese. On my room TV was an early Western in which the Indians were black: D.W. Griffith's *Birth of a Nation*, a Reconstruction drama "not meant," a florid title said, "to reflect on any race now living." Before the Civil War negroes dance happily in the street for whites. Afterwards, thanks to the radical Stoneman, Lincoln's successor, they get uppity. Elected to the state legislature they take off their boots in the House, put their feet up, wriggle their toes, eat fried chicken. Their mulatto leader is a bounder — named Lynch — who wants to marry a white woman. "And so you shall!" Stoneman claps him on the back. "The woman I want to marry is your daughter." Stoneman staggers. The negroes revolt, a white family barricade themselves in. But here comes — no, not the US Cavalry — the Ku Klux Klan! On the gallop, in perfect order, robes fluttering. The black rabble fly, the barricades come down. The Klan parade with banners, there is a double white wedding.

* THE END *

It was of course a Southern, not a Western, a mulish backward look; and like the mule it had no offspring. For all that, the South kept better than the West. The West lacked the mordant of defeat to make its dye fast. Perhaps it was also too popular, and as entertainment too prolific, for its own good.

Griffith's classic, seventy-five years old and suppressed in the United States, was on the serious channel, with Satie and fancy graphics — and an advertisement for population control. Mexico's population stands at 85 million, a tenth of India's. Its growth rate is roughly the same. As I slept that night 2000 new Mexicans were born, and 20,000 Indians.

Next morning I returned to the cathedral with its Easter-egg dome. Pink canna lilies blazed against its white wall; the pilasters were painted a matching shade of pink. Old vaqueros came and went, tottering on walking sticks. Inside, a peon leaned on his string mop and threaded the pews like Odysseus in the labyrinth. People raised their feet up for him so he could mop underneath; when they did he waxed meticulous and kept them suspended.

Across the street I bought a book of maps. The book next to it was Gandhi's *My Experiments with Truth*, in Spanish. Down a lane of crumbling yellow garages, stationers, and X-ray clinics I found a tiny snack bar.

"A pretty little place, no?" said the other customer, a policeman. The owner, a grey-haired lady, bowed and smiled.

"That's why I came in," I replied, and got my bow. The policeman and I talked of chillies: whose were hotter, Mexico's or India's? Each of us conceded defeat.

At noon I checked out of my hotel and into El Pipirin to wait for my bus. This time I barged into a balloon-sellers' convention. A forest of balloon-sticks crowded the entrance. On TV was villainous laughter, and an old wide-brim chambergo on the hero. It was cruelly hot. My security vest, a pant pocket sewn onto a singlet, clung damply to me; later I had to dry out my papers. One of the plastic balloons, a Ninja turtle, had gone limp, but the pink and blue bunnies were straining at the leash.

The only bus to Mazatlán was air-conditioned, but the cooling unit failed five minutes out of Culiacán and the driver ordered all windows opened. In rushed the country air with its sweetrot cowshitty odours, making up for the swelter. The big trucks packed a wallop as they went by inches away. I felt punch-drunk and delirious. Roadside crosses, whole village cemeteries, flashed past unheeded. Great shocks of a hydra-headed daisy, a deep hot yellow, overran the verge. On one barren flat there rose a cactus with more pipes than the Mormon Tabernacle organ.

And then a cairn, the first of its kind since the Arctic Circle:

───────────── *Tropico de Cancer* ─────────────

Mazatlán lies just south of the line, on the sea. We got in after dark. Only the Nanjing restaurant was open. The owner served me and said his son preferred to speak Spanish. His own Chinese was getting rusty.

Next morning I looked out over holiday traffic at a wide blue band of sea. Little passenger jeeps whipped along the Paseo del Mar like demented hornets. A Basilica bus with San Francisco markings on the side made more sedate progress. Joggers left their tracks in the sand; a pelican skimmed the top of a swell; a butterfly with orange leadlights fluttered and glided, fluttered and glided. I let breakfast stretch out, carding the scrambled eggs for the minced hot sausage called chorizo. After nine o'clock the joggers vanished like a morning sickness.

The lofty Hotel Decima was just up the road. In there were my five words. I asked for Saul Mastretta.

"Mastretta? No, there's no Sr Mastretta at the hotel."

"Are you sure?"

"Absolutely."

"Could you check the register?"

"Certainly . . . No, no Sr Mastretta. You can see for yourself."

There were eight names on the guest list – eight in the entire hotel; I'd often wondered about occupancy in resort hotels – and Saul Mastretta was not one of them. Nor had he been there the previous night or the night before that.

I crossed the road and waited for a bus to the faro, an old lighthouse, then on an impulse crossed back and took a bus going the other way. It was the San Francisco bus again, heading north, and it seemed to get me to the United States in five minutes. *Mickey's No Name Restaurant With Home Cooked American Food. Gringo Lingo. Burger King. Dairy Queen. Donkin Donas* . . . Greenery returned. I got off at the end of the line. At one time it would have been farmland and villages; parts of it still were. On the landward side of a palm-lined boulevard, beyond slack ropes of barbed wire – tropical slack – were farmlets, huts, hedges hung with a delicate centipede creeper that wore tiny blood-red stars.

I heard English spoken. A family of gringos, mother, father,

251

and two young children, had stopped to pet a tethered calf.

"India!" the man said. "I've been there. In another life. I was there in the last century. The railways were going through, I remember that. I think I was helping build them. When was that?"

"The 1850s, 1860s on," I said.

"I have clear memories of it. And I remember being shut away from the natives as a child. I was not allowed to play with them, even in our bungalow. Later on, when I grew up, I was in the army. I was taking part in a charge when I was shot. It was a mistake. I was shot in the back, by my own side."

Naturally I agreed to a Kahlua coffee.

They were coming back from a promotional breakfast where as prospective buyers into a time-sharing holiday condominium scheme they'd got a free bottle of Kahlua. When we got to their trailer at the end of the beach, young Nathan poured beer for the adults and he and Olivia had lemonade. The coffee came later, after mangoes, cookies, a pineapple, nuts, in a random sequence, as hunters and gatherers might eat.

John worked with cars. Noni was a primary school teacher. She had a year off, with pay. They'd driven down from Vancouver Island in a camper that held everything, down to bicycles.

"Don't let John talk you into the ground," Noni said, sticking her head out of the van. "He can do."

He was doing, but I was intrigued: he was talking of Seth. I'd heard of this mystic Seth, seen books attributed to him in esoteric shops. Now I was holding one, *The Nature of Personal Reality: A Seth Book*. The book was long and life was short so I read the preface. Seth was a disembodied consciousness who spoke through his amanuensis on earth, Jane Roberts. Roberts had discovered a language called Sumari, "a psychological and psychic framework" that freed her from normal verbal shackles. In this other language Roberts was a litterateur. "I write Sumari poetry and translate what I've written . . . I sing Sumari songs." She had also written a novel, *The Education of Oversoul 7*, produced "more or less automatically". Then, rashly, she had died and not been heard from. It was dispiriting stuff, but it may have read better in the original.

John put Seth away and produced a drum. It was a ceremonial

drum, one he'd made himself during an immersion course in Native American culture. He'd done the sweat bath too. In secular hands the drum sounded trite, stripped of mystery, but the world is hard on magic. Gary Oker of Dawson Creek would have let it go; the elders might have taken a dimmer view. "Blindness, deafness, head-ache, paralysis, and insanity" were visited upon another European interloper, the translator of the sacred Navajo Night Chant, a ritual of purification by sweat baths.

There was nobody on the beach. We took a dip in the warm Pacific and lay on the sand, five bodies. For dinner John made a porridge of lentils and rice and ground beef.

"Our plan is to head south in a couple of days," he said, "if you'd like to come along."

But I was running to a tighter schedule. They walked along the beach with me towards Mazatlán. It was past Olivia and Nathan's bedtime, but they came along. They were a well-knit family. Where the lights began they turned back. I cut through an unfinished hotel, imagining vicious guard dogs as I scaled the iron gate. But dogs are not a Mexican failing.

20

Where the

Waters Divide

There were six dead pigs on the road to Guadalajara, strewn like gunny sacks. We slalomed through. Twisted trucks sprouted like Martian weeds along the verge. As night fell we ran a level crossing just ahead of a speeding train. On the bus was a femme fatale with a wide Latin face and Indian-dark eyes. Her gaze had a deathbed fire, unsettling on something so mundane as a bus. I last saw her rolled up in a ball like an armadillo, asleep or playing dead. The bus was taking her to Mexico City; I was tempted to stay on it. But then I would not have met Francisco or danced with the Indians of Jalisco. Or watched a cowboy tango with a broom.

Past Tepic, Highway 15 turns its back on the Pacific and begins a long, slow, treacherous ascent of the steps of the Sierra Madre. With every thousand feet the air grew more chill. I needed my jacket for the first time in Mexico. In the upper reaches, where the highway switches back and forth in total darkness, the edge of the abyss was lit with flaming tar barrels. Near the top a chorus of phantom coyotes set up such a howling that everyone on the bus smiled uneasily. Up on the plateau the road meandered through little night-lit towns that looked strangely low-voltage through the tinted glass. At Magdalena, the town square with its white wrought-iron benches and ghostly iron-lace pavilion very nearly charmed me off the bus. The next stop, Tequila, brought more temptation, but by then the next stop was Guadalajara.

At Guadalajara's ultramodern bus depot you pay a courtly pensioner in the city's employ and he finds you a hotel. This frail cobweb of a man drifted with me as far as the door to point out the government hotel. Government hotel it was, the rooms small, square and austere, the windows grudging, the lobbies all polished grey cement, the restaurant and bar furnished out of a clerk's head.

A row of new, hopeful shops faced my garret. The shirtseller among them began advertising his wares early, with English rock: *Let's spend the night together*. I wondered how many young Guadalajarans would.

"It's a matter of honour," Orlando said, "for a girl to have a white wedding. She takes her virginity seriously. I have friends who've dated a girl for four years without going to bed with her. I ask them, 'How do you manage!' "

"A young Mexican will be twenty-five years old before he sees a woman's sexual part," John said on the beach, as Olivia, nine, and Nathan, seven, listened with interest. The border with Latin America is also a sexual divide.

A friction amounting to hostility characterized relations between the young men and women I saw. Brought together, the sexes seemed in constant danger of exploding. They could touch but they couldn't have, a more intolerable position than in India, where even touching is taboo. Out of that frustration came a rage no different from the rage of those who covet more durable goods. The strain on demure young women must have been even greater: enough perhaps to conjure up the Virgin.

At breakfast the middle-aged man at the next table reached across and touched his wife on the cheek, then dropped his hand to her shoulder, which he gave an affectionate squeeze. She looked at him and glowed. All passion spent perhaps (it was a late breakfast) but the gesture was so simple, so merely friendly, there seemed little left of Mexico's notorious sexual machismo in middle age.

"Latin women put much more energy into their love-making," said Orlando, "more emotional and physical concentration. Gringas have a reputation here for being cold."

That was the theory. In practice TV commercials sold gringa mores, often with a gringa bait, to match the marca gringa. "It is better to marry than burn," said Paul. But early marriage is hard on the earner (and bad for the birth rate). So girls remain virgins for their families, and their families rent halls for them and stage white weddings. And young Mexico, bombarded daily by sexual invitations much stronger than those in the Asian media, burns.

And then, in middle age, that tender stroke on the cheek at breakfast.

The city bus winds lethargically through the outer barrios of Mexico's second city, then with sudden resolve speeds along a boulevard of graceful pepper trees. I got off at the chapel of Our Lady of Aranzazu and sat a while in its darkly florid womb, where candlelight twinkled on plateresque barley-sugar. Next door was the more sombre Franciscan temple, its former garden, where the monks ambulated, now run through by the busy Avenida 16 Septiembre. A cowboy sweeper in a blue sombrero and boots danced along the sidewalk with his wide-skirted broom for a partner. When I took a photograph of him he bowed deeply and held out his hat. Later I watched him steer his partner through the park, embarrassing the sitters, cleaning and clowning as he went.

The city's principal avenue is named for the day in 1810 when Father Miguel Hidalgo raised the cry for freedom from Spain. It skirts the Plaza de Armas and bustles past the cathedral with its icecream-cone towers. Facing the Plaza de Armas is the Palacio de Gobierno where, as you mount the chief stair, you get the most celebrated fright in Mexico. Jose Clemente Orozco's lurid Hidalgo bears down on you with a firebrand, eyes rolling, and mouth open in his historic shout, *El Grito*. The rest of the mural is more scream than shout: it was done just when a second world war was threatening, and its puffy clerics and choleric generals glisten like raw tonsils.

Evening was coming on when I got to the graceful neoclassical Instituto Cabañas, once a state orphanage, where Orozco spent two years up in the cupola painting his most famous mural, *Man in Flames*. The flames were less menacing this time, higher up and further away. The sun was going down, the guards were locking up. The man in flames is drawn from below, a Blakean figure (like his painter) eager for immolation. Tortured figures ring the clerestory.

From the quadrangle came the voices of girls singing. I went to listen. There was a stage, some microphones, a rehearsal underway. A light-skinned man stood by the pillar, watching. He wore glasses, and an air of refined abstraction. In his hand was a ticket. I asked him about the concert. He said he was actually going next door to a film show that started in ten minutes. We got talking.

"What did you think of the *Man in Flames*?"

"I hardly saw it. The chapel was closing."

"Have you seen all of this building? There are many cloisters and patios and yards. This is just one."

We began to walk along the chaste colonnade. A door led to a passage that opened onto another cloister, a small square with a fretted arcade topped by a second, simpler arcade. An old tree grew in the middle, spreading to fill the space allotted it. We threaded another passage, came upon another yard paved with flags laid in diamonds. In a farther patio, a fountain played.

"Simple, beautiful lines," Francisco said, sketching in the air. "There are more than twenty such patios."

"Your movie!"

"It started half an hour ago." He dropped his ticket in a bin.

We stood outside the former hospice and admired its multiple shells: a bell-tower in front of a parapet in front of the ring of columns that enclosed the chapel dome. Francisco smiled on the building, looking from it to me; he might have been Manuel Tolsa himself, the 18th-century architect. The yellow sandstone, the city's signature monochrome, glowed in the dusk. A cold wafer moon rose above the dome.

We walked down the Plaza Tapatia. "In the old days the Indians used the cocoa bean as a kind of money," Francisco said, "like your cowrie shells. Guadalajara was the centre of their exchange, and this was their marketplace."

Guadalajara was also the centre of the old slave trade in Indians. In his *Shout*, Hidalgo's voice was raised not only for independence but for emancipation. I saw many more Indian faces around me now than I'd seen up north.

Francisco was a lawyer; he pointed out the civil and family courts where he worked. Nearby was a modern fountain done by a sculptor from Mexico City, a stylized bronze serpent, the plumed serpent Quetzalcoatl, undulating into the sky. Under our feet flowed the traffic of the Calzada Independencia – in an old river bed. The river was one of the reasons why the site was chosen for a city in 1542; now it was a river of cars. Where the plaza narrowed we came to an old building, now a restaurant.

257

"Have a look in here," Francisco said and we stood among the elegant tables, the diners and waiters looking on, as he pointed out little chambers off the central hall. I saw once more the Islamic hand across the sea; southern Spain owed her most striking buildings to the Moors, and here was a transplant of a transplant. The diners themselves might be eating al-bondegas, Arabian rissoles, in an Aztec sauce.

We came to the school of music and went in. The exquisite former convent had a central patio whose upper storey spouted gargoyles from a European bestiary. Every colonial structure had its patio with deep shaded verandahs and jardinières and balconies of iron lace. It was always an effort to leave such buildings.

We sat in the Plaza de Armas. Francisco didn't care for the ornate Palacio. He pointed out a bullet-hole in the face of the clock: a cristero had made that – a pot shot at the State – when the Church went underground in the 1920s. On the balcony below, every 16 September, the governor appeared before the people as Hidalgo.

"He waves the flag and shouts *Viva Mexico!* three times, and the crowd replies *Viva Mexico! Viva Mexico! Viva Mexico!*"

Before us was an ornate bronze pavilion, with nude musicians for pillars, dating from the French infatuation of the dictator Porfirio Díaz.

"You won't find statues of Porfirio Díaz in Mexico," Francisco said of the man whose long rule ended with the Mexican revolution. "Or even streets named after him. Well, no, there *is* one here in Guadalajara, but on the outskirts, a short street. But you know, a man who is in power for thirty years in the life of a country must be important. Porfirio Díaz introduced the railway, he improved the cities, he brought in capital. And he was the cause of the revolution. I don't admire him, but a country should be able to revise its official history. There shouldn't be a hallowed past."

I asked him what he thought of Mexico's future.

"Our future is tied to the United States," he said, "and they're in a recession. Our economy can only reflect that. But I think this Tratado Libre Comercio will serve the interests of our two northern neighbours."

"Canadians say the same thing about their two southern neighbours."

"Alán, we're much more disorganized than they are." His hands sought out everyday words, words I would understand. He had studied English, but I never heard him speak it. "Our products can't really compete. I think our economy will suffer, businesses will close down, and that'll bring massive unemployment. I think new social classes will have to come into being in Mexico. We're going to need a class that can sell our products to our neighbours and to other First World countries."

"Quite a few of your unemployed go up north of the border." I wanted to direct the conversation that way, and I touched an unexpected nerve.

"There are millions of Mexicans living over there in the most degrading circumstances. They do the jobs a gringo won't touch and are treated as animals for their pains. It's the same with Guatemalans and Panamanians and the rest. There's a town up there with a sign that says: NO DOGS OR MEXICANS OR SOUTH AMERICANS."

"Why do you call them norteamericanos here? Isn't Mexico in North America?"

"We're in the middle of the *American* continent."

"What do you think of their way of life?"

He smiled forbearingly. "I think North American culture is in decay. They seem to value the very things that harm them: drugs, guns, so-called freedoms. They don't have a history as such, and besides they don't value history. Very little history is taught in their schools. They're barbarians in the literal sense: they don't know their past. So they don't have a past."

"Francisco, I've lived there. They do value their history. They have democratic institutions, civil liberties. They have a culture of knowledge. Their arts are alive."

"I've lived there too, Alán. They're nouveaux riches who make their money selling guns to countries that can't make their own. And out of their military strength they would like to dominate the world. And control its markets, and dictate peace. I tell you it was a cruel fate that made us neighbours."

On the beach the night before, John the Canadian had been just as plain. "You starve an army for months," he had said, speaking of the Gulf War, "and then shoot them in the back

259

when they're retreating. That's not civilized. They violated every rule in the book. They were itching to get in there."

It reminded me of what the Canadian novelist Hugh McLellan wrote of the Americans in another war: "I knew that they were going to bomb hell out of Germany and Japan, that they were going to wage war with loathing for its traditional aspects of infantry marches and travel in strange countries but with a cold fascination for what they could do technically."

"Do you think there's anything Mexicans can learn from Americans?" I asked Francisco.

"We can learn how to work. We tend often to be slack. I think we could live more . . . decently if we worked harder, and more systematically. I think we could learn cleanliness, and order, from them."

"What is it that keeps Mexico going? An American once called India a functioning anarchy."

"I think the vital force is unconscious. It's a sense, maybe half conscious, of Mexican history, a kind of pride. It's the tradition of many centuries that inhabits the people."

It had grown dark as we talked. We agreed to meet at noon the next day, by the same bench. I returned to the government hotel. The cook's pozole, the classic Jaliscan pork and maize soup, made up for my poky room. The waiter had a womanish plumpness that shook as he trotted up and down; he held my bill close to his chest in both hands and looked about him, daring anyone to peep.

I woke to the shirtseller's rock. In town the park bench at the Plaza de Armas was bare; then someone else, not Francisco, occupied it. I sketched the Palacio, then the cathedral; an hour passed, then two. I went for lunch and returned; he was still not there. Then, as I turned away, I realized what had happened: I was still on Pacific time! Guadalajara – and Francisco – were on Central time, an hour ahead. I rang his house but he was not there. For the rest of the afternoon the mistake weighed on me like a crime.

A drumbeat was coming from the direction of the opera house. Its relentless monotony drew me. In the Plaza de la Liberacion under the portals of the Degollado Theatre a group of dancers was performing a ceremonial dance. The drummer was a blanca in a white cotton smock. The dancers wheeled in a wide circle around her, doing the old Siberian crane dance of the American

Indian, where the body crumples, knee and backbone buckling, and springs back upright again, miraculously erect. The women wore smocks, the men were barebodied with a white cotton clout and medicine pouch about the loins. All wore white headbands and a kind of clicking anklet. In the centre of the circle a white altarcloth was spread on the flagstones. On it, arranged in a square like a mandala, were flowers and herbs, maize and squash gourds. Four blackware braziers burned copal incense at the cardinal points. Every so often a woman broke away from the ring of dancers to sprinkle more copal, sending up clouds of incense.

The dancing went on monotonously, led by a gaunt, long-haired man who carried his own drum. When he tired, the drum passed to another and then another man. A booth nearby had leaflets. The group was Atemaxak Tenamaztli, named for the last Indian defender of the Atemajac Valley in which Guadalajara sits. (*Atemaxak* means Where the Waters Divide.) The *x* and the *k* in the revised spelling stuck out, language skirmishing on behalf of the vanquished – 500 years after Columbus.

> "Further to 12 October, 1492," one pamphlet said:
> "—it was not a 'discovery', it was an accident
> —it was not an 'encounter', it was a collision
> —it was not 'colonization', it was plunder
> —it was not a 'peopling', it was a dispeopling
> —it was not a 'civilizing', it was a destruction of civilizations."

"It was a cross," said a Spanish historian, "driven into the mass grave of the aborigines."

Another pamphlet, entitled "The Sack of a Continent", quoted Columbus' own accounts of burnings at the stake, cutting off of hands, torturing, enslaving, and starving the Indians. It also rewrote in a few acid words the history of Europe.

A third pamphlet extolled the life of the indígenes before the arrival of Europe. The writer recalled a time when people lived "with other creatures, not against them . . . in a harmony that reached from the ant to the stars". In this world, "every pyramid was an open book, its inscriptions there for all to read so that knowledge might be freely disseminated. From that knowledge sprang the cultivation of maize and wild grains. The priest in his sanctuary cut open tubers and wild grains to learn their secrets, patiently experimenting with their many mutations, for neither wheat nor rice existed in nature.

"We are a solar race because the sun not only impregnates our earth, it was the architect of our cities. With its trajectories it raised our towns and houses; it showed us the proper and just orientation for our streets. Our medicine was natural medicine, and sufficient. It did not cure one malady by creating another. The ancients classified some three thousand plants. Our social organization evolved from natural laws, not out of caprice. Our calendars bound us to the cosmos, setting our lives to the rhythm of the constellations. From them we learnt not to rush, not to compete with one another. Our writing sprang from simple and symbolic drawings, and evolved through hieroglyphs to arrive at sublime abstractions. Our mathematics could pinpoint any planet in the solar system. According to learned Europeans the earth was flat, its oceans pouring incessantly into the abyss at its edge. According to other learned Europeans [actually the Hindus] it was a mountain held up by four elephants that rode on a tortoise.

"And then, on 12 October 1492, came Columbus and the nightmare began . . ."

The moon had come up. The dancers turned to the crowd and invited us to join their slowly revolving wheel. The drumbeat kept up its solemn pounding. We revolved a very long time, doing a simple syncopated sidestep, more walk than dance, but one that served its binding purpose.

The moon climbed higher, the west grew dark, the opera house was spinning, we were standing still. A woman heaped copal on the braziers. At the beat of a new, deeper drum we faced east, south, west, north. Four times, four conches were raised to the sky and sounded. The circle closed in to face the altar. The leader spoke of the meaning of the ceremony. When he had had his say the dancers chorused: *"Listen!"* Those who remained in the circle were invited to speak. After each one's say came the chorus: *"Listen!"* I said I was a traveller from India – an Indio – and that I was passing through Mexico to meet its people and learn their ways, and tonight I had done both in a manner most fortunate. I thanked the dancers and said I felt sympathy with their cause and I was sure the people of India did too.

"Listen!"

It was a bit rich but it matched the slightly trumped-up air of the proceedings. It also matched the rhetoric of the opera house, and afterwards I realized why the dancers chose that spot, under those bombastic pseudo-Roman columns.

When it was over we shared the fruit at the altar. The dancers wanted to hear about India; we peeled our oranges and talked. Before going home they did a livelier impromptu dance; they danced as if the ground were theirs. The blanca who had been heaping incense all evening gave me a piece of sticky resin.

"This is copal," she said, "from a tree out east. Use it reverently. Respect all things in nature." She spoke like the author of the idyll in the third pamphlet.

On the long bus ride back to the hotel I learnt a new word: "leucophobia". It was in yet another pamphlet, one that quoted Rudyard Kipling, "the British poet who lived in India and left us the legacy of 'Sambo' ". I braved a reverse translation:

> O little Japanese or Sioux
> O wouldn't you rather be me than you?

No! replies the leucophobe, who fears not milk but assimilation into the white world. A celebrated leucophobe, Chief Piel Roja (Red Skin) of Seattle, once asked the Chief of the Pale Faces (in the White House): "You wish to buy our land, but how can you buy the sky or the heat of the earth?"

Next morning I was back in town early. Janitors with wide-skirted brooms were sweeping up in front of the opera house. The law courts where Francisco worked were just coming to life. I waited next door in the school of music. All around the patio pianos rumbled. A soprano voice ran up and down the scales, climbing higher and higher – and ending with a loud sneeze. At the music shop opposite I bought a Bach tape for Francisco to suit his archi-tectural tastes. When I got to the civil courts his name was not on any door that I could find. I went from room to room, my chronic bureauphobia returning. No, each office assured me: they did not know Sr Francisco Marquez. A girl who worked there, seeing me terror-stricken, took me under her wing. She asked at desks and counters and windows, in Dickensian cubby-holes. "You must be in the wrong building," she said finally.

I found Francisco's work number. He picked up the phone. "Alán! Stay where you are! I'm on my way." So he was in the building! I waited the five minutes I imagined it would take him to come downstairs. The five minutes turned to ten. Half an hour passed and he still had not come. The clock said 11.30. My bus left at 1.00, the only bus to Pátzcuaro. It would take me forty-five minutes to get back to the hotel – and then I had to pack and check out. I would be lucky to catch the bus.

I waited till a quarter to twelve. Then I left feeling even more wretched than the day before. Months later when I returned home there was a letter from him. He said he would come to India some day, he did not know how or when, but come he would.

21

Crossing Over

The closest I got to a grizzly in thousands of miles along the Great North American Divide was in my hotel room at Pátzcuaro. It was on the bed, one of those counterpanes in violet and sepia and white with a furry pile. It was too far south for grizzlies, and it looked unhappy, even at that altitude.

Pátzcuaro is a mountain retreat on a lake of the same name halfway between Guadalajara and Mexico City. It was within my eight-hour limit, though the last hour seemed to last forever. You burst upon the lake from the north, spread like watered silk on the valley floor below, and just as you prepare to disembark the road jinks away and the bus goes all around the lakeshore through gloomy hamlets with blackened tile roofs and empty whitefish restaurants to limp at last into the damp colonial town at the very bottom.

It was an ancient bus, and it served all the little towns and villages on the way from Guadalajara. It was even, for part of the way, a school bus. The woman beside me was reading a pamphlet in which I glimpsed with boding the word *Lucas* in brackets followed by chapter and verse. I braced myself.

"God's word is beautiful!" she sighed.

"It is *very* beautiful." I put the stop in italics.

"Do you read it often?" She reached for a pamphlet.

"Sometimes," I said, and added meanly, "in English." My bags were already full of everyone's pamphlets.

She put her bag away. She was going to visit her parents in a village off the main road and would have to change buses at Zacapu. The old folk were now in their seventies and she visited them every month, sometimes more often. If she missed a time they were terribly distressed, although they had sons in the village.

"Why did you leave?"

"After I got married I went to live with my husband in Guadalajara. He's a mechanic. I work in a garment factory. I don't like it much but the children have to eat. There's no work in the village."

She was plainly dressed, her long straight hair touched with grey. Her face was almost Goan, dark, smooth, substantial.

"How old are you?" she said.

"Forty."

"Forty! I am too. Married?"

"Yes."

"Why doesn't your wife travel with you?"

In Guadalajara Francisco had asked, 'Alán, why do you travel alone?" It was the question the Malaysians in Wyoming asked me, a tropical question. For Canadians and Americans, travelling alone was acceptable, even laudable: the solitary venturer had his own aura. I thought of the student in Whitehorse setting out in his canoe: not a trip, he said, a *quest*.

To Francisco I said when you travelled with your wife you talked to her, not to the natives. To the evangelist I said it was too long a journey to inflict on a spouse. I showed her on the map where I'd started, omitting Canada and the US. Nogales, she said, yes, and pointed. Hermosillo, Ciudad Obregón, Culiacán, Mazatlán, Guadalajara. Her finger ran ahead of mine.

"To Yucatan?"

"Yes."

"The very east!" She said it ("the east of the east") with a fascinated smile. Then she folded the map expertly and handed it back.

"Children?"

"No."

"Ask God!"

But then forty teenage schoolgirls got on the bus and she may have had second thoughts. The girls took over the bus, packing the aisle, hanging on the rail, all chattering at once. The leader of the pack shouted at pals up and down the bus.

"Big fucker!"

My evangelist wilted and took out a hymn book. She had four children of her own, schoolgirls no doubt. She began to sing under her breath. The loud schoolgirl had a universal face – I marvelled at how few faces there really were in the world – and a rasp to match her hectoring way. Somewhere in a Michoacan school was a young macho who would be tamed by her. There was a pretty one too, with her universal face, talking avidly of her schoolmaster: Maestro Reyes says this, Maestro Reyes says that. Her beautiful fingers were covered in tin gold rings.

Zacapu came and the evangelist stood up.

"Vaya con dios," I said.

"God keep you," she smiled.

I thought I could guess at her life, her village, from the stories of the Mexican writer Juan Rulfo, a Jaliscan himself. Rulfo's characters are shadows with voices, their horizons shrunk to a handswidth, their aspirations beaten down. He writes of the dispossessed – the disembodied, almost – beings compounded of more bone than marrow, more flame than flesh. He seems to work in metal, as if hammering and welding were better suited to his harsh land than writing. Mexican Catholicism, the Catholicism of the Guadalupana, succoured that land without touching it; its promises left the landscape intact. Evangelical Christianity seems to offer palpable benefits: tongues, excitement, transformation. Its trinkets dazzle (it's a ready colonist throughout Latin America) but they fill a need. The evangelist resisted my attempt to fit her into a Rulfo tableau. She had a solid presence that appeared to have escaped the hammer. And she had a delicacy, a refinement. A poor woman, she did not say what more than one person in Canada and the United States said to me: "You must be rich."

After Zacapu the bus seemed to float up into the clouds, its toiling engine strangely muffled by the moist air. The upland pastures were filled with rags of mist and mauve cosmos. It was a country of stone huts whose broken, exhausted look stripped them of the picturesque. Only the hills, gone up and down with stone fences and great swags of buttercups, looked inviting. The campesinos wore the drab look of poverty. It had rained, and the women were wrapped in serapes. A boy hawker got on the bus with a basket of confections his mother would have made: pink and white squares, discs of sticky nuts and puffed rice, fudge. He

267

was bound for Pátzcuaro and picked at his wares all the way.

We came down to lake level. It had been raining there too. It was almost dark and the evening trees had an elongated European look, as in a painting by Corot. We passed through Tzintzuntzan, whose meaning flutters on the tongue: Place of Hummingbirds. Outside Pátzcuaro the rain returned. The streetlamps cast a jaundiced, mizzling light; we sloshed past dreary terraces, cemeteries rank with weeds. One should not enter a town at dusk.

The bear was waiting in my room under a chintz canopy whose pink net curtains were tied with twists of tinsel. I had my first hot shower in Mexico. Letícia at the desk, a short, smiling girl with the bottom-heavy build of the local Indians, gave me a town map and marked likely eating-places on it. I took an umbrella up the steep cobbled street through a wet market where even the vegetables looked tired of the rain. A woman offered damp posies of heliotrope. But the whitefish at dinner, Lake Pátzcuaro's delicacy, were crisp and melting.

Pátzcuaro is the quintessential colonial town, with its air of faded authority and its churches dating to within a generation of Cortes. It was the conquistadores' excesses that occasioned its founding when in 1534 Vasco de Quiroga was sent out to investigate certain atrocities and set up his capital here. I breakfasted in the plaza that bears his name, a spacious square lined with trees planted by the good bishop himself. I wrote a letter there to Francisco explaining what went wrong and enclosing his tape.

The other plaza in Pátzcuaro is less elegant, more popular. Its lawn is maculate, it's where the ordinary Pátzcuaran shops and sells his wares. Up the hill from it is the cathedral, on an eminence that looks out over tiled roofs to the bronze and pewter lake. Brooding at one corner of the people's plaza is the dark façade of the Gertrude Bocanegra public library, a lofty 18th-century hall lined with dismal bookcases. Misled, the eye boggles at the mural on the far wall: all Mexico in riotous assembly there. It's the work of Juan O'Gorman; the gaudy palate is his signature.

The mural moves from geologic time – scenes of elemental fury – at the top, down through Mexican history. Above are vignettes of pre-Columbian Indian life: maize is cultivated, pyramids are raised, war and sacrifices made. Below is the Conquest – scenes of torture and pillage – and the missionary work of Quiroga. At bottom right is a 19th-century corner. Gertrude Bocanegra, patriot, kneels, blood spouting from her chest. The whole painting teems, but with a static energy, obeying an older Mexican muralismo than that of the post-Revolutionary revival. O'Gorman and his wife stand on a ledge at the extreme left. He holds a page that reads:

> *The centuries have passed, but the Indians are not vanquished, despite the conquest that decimated their numbers. Exploitation, misery, disease, have not crushed them. They have endured the mines, the highways, the railway. They have worked the earth with their hands to give us to eat. Their treasure-houses were robbed, their temples laid low. Their backs were loaded with stones to raise countless churches. But their resistance is a buried force that will one day deliver them from the chains of oppression, and bring forth an extraordinary art and culture like the eruption of a mighty volcano.*

There is a volcano erupting at the top of the painting – a tornado rages off to one side – but it's a long way from the O'Gormans in 1942. She wears a cloche and a viridian dress, he a workerly blue shirt, the vivid cobalt blue that flashes all through the painting. At their feet is a grotesque dwarf in coat and tails (he has a monkey tail too) and a cobalt-blue hat stuck with a feather. He wears checked pants and two-tone shoes. A cigarette burns in his lips, he carries a cane on his arm, and in his hands is a scroll that says, with heavy bathos: *Such is Life*.

Like the innocent/evil Indians of earlier centuries, the hapless/heroic Indians of this century are partly the work of blancos; the Indians themselves will produce a plain unvarnished Indian. The mural ends where once there would have been a row of bookcases. The bookcases are now gone, leaving a bare stretch of wall with one or two of the painter's study sketches. As I was leaving, a ray of afternoon sunlight fell on one of these, a fisherwoman squatting by her basket of whitefish in the market. That at least had not changed: in the market behind the library the fisherwomen sat on, unmoved and unmoving.

In the basilica on the hill a woman and her daughter advanced by degrees up the aisle on their knees, the mother carrying a candle. I could not imagine my evangelist in that posture. The Virgin awaited them, a silver crescent moon under her feet. Beyond was a terrazzo altar, recent and ugly, where pledges were pinned and miracles recorded. One grateful drawing showed a girl in a hospital bed with an intravenous drip from a horn of the Virgin's moon. A bell clanged overhead. I recognized it as the bell that had tolled in the dark of the morning. The damped sound was comforting: a bell should clang – or better, clank – not peal.

Letícia was back at the hotel desk. She spent all morning at college, from seven to two, went home for the main meal of the day at 2.30, and then worked at the hotel from three till ten. She rose at five and breakfasted at six. At night her father, a nightwatchman, came to get her from the hotel, and she had a light supper before retiring.

"One has to work hard to survive," she said. "Mexicans work hard."

She was up against that familiar myth, the Snoozing Mexican. I could have told her about the Indolent Indian. In fact both worked long hours, when work was to be had. In India what had atrophied was not work but the idea in the work. The loss of that idea, or picture, was the essence of our drudgery.

"Mexicans want work," Letícia said. "That's why they go to the United States. But they don't like Hispanics there."

"What do you think of them?"

"Gringos?" She looked around. There was a gringo couple upstairs. "Falsos!" she said under her breath. I looked for the trace of a smile, even a bitter one, but she was serious. "Malos!"

"How, Letícia?"

"They kill Mexicans who go there. They took away half of Mexico. You should not call them Americans. We are all Americans. They are Estados Unidenses, United Statesians."

"But you call them Americanos on TV, or Norteamericanos."

"Maybe so. We are taught at college to call them Estados Unidenses."

Roberto, the Canadian from upstairs, came in. He was tall and handsome – rather like Charlton Heston as Moses – and half-Mexican himself. His Canadian father, now separated from his mother, had lived in Mexico for many years. Now Roberto had brought his American fiancée to live in Pátzcuaro. They were putting up at the hotel while their house was built.

Letícia had a chubby face, a light skin and a dumpy build. Both races had met in her.

"You must be part indígena," I said.

Roberto, with one foot on the stair, hung on her response.

"Our family are Hispanic," Letícia said. "My grandmother is pure Spanish."

"But Mexicans have indígena blood as well?"

"The Spanish married the indígenes and the Mexican race was formed, so we are Mexicans, but we are Hispanic."

"The earliest indígenes come from Asia," I said.

Roberto explained the land bridge theory. Letícia frowned. She had Siberia in her eyes, but she shook her head in confusion.

"You must talk to someone who knows more," she laughed. She was eighteen, a student of history.

Roberto went upstairs. "Come up and watch a movie with us," he called. "My fiancée would like to meet you."

I said I'd look in if I hadn't collapsed from fatigue. For dinner I bought chorizos at the mercado and two colas. Letícia was affronted.

"Do I look hungry?" she said, but took a bite to appease me.

"Buen aprovecha!" said the landlady, coming in.

At ten o'clock Letícia's father came to take her home. I fell into bed. I thought I'd left the West behind, but all night long the sound of gunfire came from the upstairs window.

In the morning we had to feed the pigs so we stopped in Saskatchewan to pick up grain. SASKATCHEWAN, the gate said, in a wrought-iron arc in front of the pink concrete middle-class house.

"My old man did that," Roberto said. Now his mother lived there and the prairie scientist lived in the next town. "I hadn't quite anticipated the Jewish mother syndrome when I first brought my fiancée home."

I imagined the scene. We took the grain up a badly potholed road. "Welcome to Mexico," Roberto said as he spun the wheel. He said it again when he talked of politicians stuffing ballot boxes and killing off opponents. "Welcome to India," I said.

The sow was a great grey siren, friendly but not disinterested. Across the road on a corner block with its own mango trees a small concrete house was coming up. There Roberto and his fiancée from Portland, Oregon would live. There were three workers on the terraced roof. Roberto urged another day in Pátzcuaro: I should see the lake, and the island with a carved tower, and a grove of ancient olives – but if I had to go I had to go. I had to go. The olives beckoned, but I had three months' leave – from home – with no extensions. At the bus depot Roberto handed me his card. It said:

CANADA PIE

He and his fiancée were going to start a bakery. They had several recipes perfected – they were working on the blueberry – and the smart hotels had already expressed an interest.

"Come back and try some!" he waved, and his muzzled dobermann skated madly on its claws on the jeep flatbed.

The bus was a chrome fun-fair mirror. One passenger arrived by wheelbarrow, her foot in plaster. An indígena woman carried a pink-cheeked child and a bunch of fresh coriander. The coriander (used green in many dishes, as in Asia) trailed its heavenly aroma; I chose the seat behind it. Yesterday's leaden lake now returned the sky's blue. White cloud towers stood on the hills roundabout, white graveyards dotted the plain. The peach orchards were turning russet. The driver's rosary was twined around a bunch of silk carnations. Once again I felt the thrill of departure like a physical vibration.

What was this vibration, deeper than the rumbling of the bus? Why did it stir me to my depths? The evangelist, the Malaysians, Francisco, had asked me why I travelled alone. The question raised another: why was I travelling at all?

To write about the travel, was the obvious answer, but not the whole truth. There had been no book in sight when I first conceived the journey. It was simply a journey, from the Yukon to the Yucatan, linking two places whose names were significant to me. Only later did I realize I would be following an earlier migration, and only after that did I see it would be a Western journey. There was after all another, prior West.

My first Western journey was determined before I was born, by that forgotten British ancestor who sowed his seed on an East Indian woman. Like Letícia I had forbears I knew nothing of. But the fact – genetic, cultural – of my Anglo-Indian heritage meant that I would, when I appeared, look West. All Anglo-Indians did, even the poorest. We were Western, the furniture of our houses, and of our minds, was Western. My mother dreamed of sending me to an English university. She even wrote off, in our blindfold way, for information about scholarships, but all that remains of her bid is the fragment of an address: Honeypot Lane, a name redolent of all my childhood storybooks.

In a sense I flew over my mother's England, the country she dreamed of but never lived to see. It was my father's map, one of a venerable series of New World maps, that won the day. Like Cortes' men, like every other man who made the journey West, I came in search of treasure. I found not riches (at forty I still lived out of a suitcase) but independence. The New World gave me learning and a profession. The learning was as much of the East as of the West: I learnt more about Asia – more about India – in North America than at my college in India. The profession too incurred a debt: I began to write – an Indian novel – in the West. My scholarship, North American money, subsidized a habit it was not designed for. North Americans completed my education; North America set me free.

It was only after the journey that I realized I'd flown over my father's map too; in a travesty of Columbus I'd discovered India while imagining myself in America. I found also I had misread my mother's journey. In her last years my mother could study Hindi, try on Indian clothes, a feat for an Anglo-Indian of her generation. She wrote at leisure a sheaf of poems on Indian birds. She was at peace with the land of her birth. She had crossed over.

Had I? The wheel looked to have come full circle, but a gap remained. Was travel a vain attempt to fill it?

I wondered about Roberto and his fiancée in their Mexican house, baking Canada pies. Would they last? Roberto's father had started it, but "SASKATCHEWAN, Mexico" epitomized an old and abiding cross-fertilization. It was why I had trouble with the nativist claims, with words like indígena. Roberto's flat-topped cement concrete house with its windowless façade broken by a single door was a late and necessary echo of a pre-Columbian style. From the bus I saw several new verandahs that used the old Indian arch, still false. The whitewashed tombs in the graveyards were stepped pyramids – topped with a cross. That was how history worked, abhorring purities.

From the start, the Conquest was a chronicle of excess. Historians of the New World collision split reactively into fabulists and moralists. The fabulists dwelt on the wonders and glossed over the horrors; the moralists had no time for feathered monkeys and men of gold, picturing instead entire villages torched, the inhabitants mown down, the survivors penned in labour camps.

Excess was built into the very notion of a New World: the novelty heightened expectations. Here, it was felt, was a special case. The actual arrival was surely an exchange of wonder. Horses, glass beads, pale-skinned men! Singing monkeys, speaking trees, copper-coloured men! Montezuma dispatched artists to the coast to paint the new arrivals; they drew the Spanish ships with sails, the horses, the cannons and cannonballs, even the greyhounds, and runners bore the film-like rolls back to a king as consumed with curiosity as Cortes.

Hunter and victim were drawing nearer, each hypnotized by the other. Then the wonder wore off and the killing began, but the killing was not new nor on an unprecedented scale. Five years before Columbus, the Aztecs sacrificed tens of thousands of captured warriors to sanctify a single temple. Spanish violence replaced Aztec violence, and temperate historians bracketed the two into a convenient category: tropical folly. It's a durable tradition, from the Evil Empire propagated by Spain's colonial rivals to the Tristes Tropiques of the anthropologist. Sad tropics! Pullulating ceaselessly amid bouts of pointless butchery. The nativists reply with vilifications of their own, and glorifications of an ideal past, and somewhere in between the truth is lost.

The banal fact that history blunders forward would not have escaped the first great historian of the Americas, Inca Garcilaso de la Vega. A man half Spanish and half Inca, he produced in his *History of Peru* a great work that was both a vindication of his royal Inca forebears and a celebration of the inevitable advance of Europe. Over the centuries Spanish royalists censored the work, and Indians revered it. It inspired the ill-fated rebellion of one Tupac Amaru II (who was hanged but could not be drawn, a clerk reports, "either because the horses were not very strong or because the Indian really was of iron"). But both nationalists and colonialists neglected a lesson the author was at pains to draw.

In a remarkable passage, Garcilaso describes how the first Incas tamed the savages of Peru. The savages, says Garcilaso, marvelled at the Inca strangers clad in "a very different dress from their own . . . and saw that their words and countenances showed them to be children of the Sun". They were put to work, some to sow and some to reap, others to cook and build, until finally, civilized, they worshipped the strangers and obeyed them as kings.

It's hard today not to see the parallel with the Spaniards, whose fair skin and curious garments, smooth words and wondrous techniques – as well as their eastern origin – made them children of the Sun. But behind the legend, behind those happy, innocent words lies the old and bloody clash of hunter-gatherers with more sophisticated peoples – *Inca* conquistadores. In just this way the invading Aryans subdued the aborigines of India: pastoralists, farmers, and finally city-dwellers driving back forest-dwellers, civilizing those they spared, mocking their gods even as they assimilated them, reserving the meanest jobs for the vanquished and inventing an inflexible hierarchy, caste, by which the primitives were attached and yet dangling, down and out.

In Mexico all the national pieties revolve around the indígenes while the eleganca continue steadfastly white. Between the Knights of Cortes and the "God is Red" nativists bulk the nation's mestizos, with their dream of a Castilian grandmother. All three groups have their demonologies; obsessed with purity and violation they mirror their opponents and lose sight – except once a year – of a painful fact. The Spanish rape was the making of Mexico as well as its unmaking; in the fever lay the cure.

The temperate view, cool and detached, sees only degradation and loss. *The Loss of El Dorado* is how V.S. Naipaul, writing of the Caribbean, titled his most affecting book. But a fellow Caribbean, Wilson Harris, takes a less finite view. Harris's writings explore a territory beyond simple loss and gain, uncovering hybrid resources that run conquistador and conquered together, rather in the way Octavio Paz sees revolutionist and reactionary accommodated by a larger Mexican dynamic. The long, survivalist view is easily obscured by horrific details of real lives and injuries that documentarists address without ever redressing. The language of absolute loss feeds both old-world orthodoxy and indígena nostalgia without resolving either. It was what Francisco meant when he looked for a less polarized view of Porfirio Díaz. It's why one is inclined to trust – if one can trust visitors – Lawrence and Malcolm Lowry on Mexico, despite their enthusiasms, and to distrust the clinical, clear-eyed, and marvellously crisp Graham Greene.

The bus droned eastward. On terraced slopes stood corn, the corn of millennia that fills Indian legend and poetry as it does Indian life: down the centuries it shoots green, glances yellow; its tassels tremble under cloud and repose in the sun. Flocks of white cosmos filled the fallow spaces, and in the villages poinsettia flared against adobe. The sky was a stonewashed blue. Towards sunset the east grew black and lightning scribbled at the horizon. The highway split in two, then four, then eight, the metropolis approaching, and we swept into Mexico City like valkyries on a thunderstorm.

At the taxi counter was a young Canadian in distress. His backpack, cumbrous armour, displayed his colours, a maple leaf patch. He spoke no Spanish; he was making little headway at the window. A middle-aged lady sized him up and decided he was genuine.

"You need money?" she said. She looked comfortable, not rich.

He fell ravening on her English. "My wallet!" he said, and his hands fluttered away from his pocket.

She produced a note and nudged her less forthcoming friend. "Poor Canadian!" she said. "God knows what trouble he's in." The two ladies scraped together a taxi fare and handed it over. The Canadian was overcome. He seized the first lady's hand and kissed it fervently. She simpered, young again, and they parted amid effusions. I couldn't help wondering how she would have responded to the Stars and Stripes.

"Hindú-*uuu*!" said my taxi driver, his voice running up high. "Aaaayy!"

"Indio," I corrected him, but of course all Indian nationals are Hindus in Spanish, and Indio is a term of abuse.

"Ayy!" he went on. "A beautiful country. I've seen it on television." He lived in the suburb of Coyoacan.

"*Coyoacan* is an Aztec word, no?"

"Not Aztec, *Nahuatl*. Aztecs are the people, Nahuatl is the language. Coyoacan means 'the place of coyotes'."

I named a cheap hotel.

"No, no!" he said. "It's frequented by low types, prostitutes and the like." And he drove me to the Hotel Cancún. "Watch out for cyclones in Veracruz!" he called as he drove off; cyclones were to be avoided like potholes.

The next morning I looked down from my tenth-floor window upon the largest city on earth. The view was of rooftops black with dust, rapidly greying washlines, a satellite dish slung like a crafty cobweb. Far below, beyond a gritty window, was a contact-lens factory where the girls wore white coats and worked standing up; the chatterbox among them was already leaning over the high table and talking down the line.

At noon I moved to the cheaper Hotel Uxmal. I picked up my mail at American Express and occupied one of the grand stone benches by the Angel, the city's Independence monument. A woman with a giant palm frond chased October leaves along the sidewalk. All along Reforma stood heavily made-up women in fatigues and bullet-proof jackets. Their red nails stroked sten-gun triggers, and yards of sexy lacing fastened their commando boots; a commando lover might flag before he got a single boot off.

Back at the Uxmal a big man was leaning over the desk and howling into the telephone. I never saw so much passion poured into an inanimate object. His voice filled the lobby; he was oblivious of the scene. He screamed accusations, he wept, he raged, he choked in some old glottal language while Jose the desk clerk looked mildly on. I tried to imagine the distant party; only a brother, I felt, would not hang up.

In the afternoon I bought a train ticket to Veracruz: Mexico City was once-trodden ground. By my own rules I should not be there at all. I bought a book of poems at the old university and rode the metro to Cortes' house. The late bus back was a mobile discothèque with flashing red and blue lights and a decor of swizzle-sticks. A young boy hung out of the door soliciting customers; a still younger boy drove, steering from time to time. The music swung like an axe, the Virgin simply smiled.

On the night train I looked at the book of poems. The author's photo showed a woman in Indian dress — my kind of Indian — but the poems were in Spanish. The name, to confuse matters further, was English, Elsa Cross.

22

The Rule

of the Knee

The night train to Veracruz thunders through whole chapters of Mexican history in viscid darkness. The ground it covers, in its descent from the capital on the plateau to the chief port on the coast, is soaked in blood that works its way into the traveller's dreams as he lies swaying in his cabin. Down this route the Aztecs and their predecessors travelled to subdue the Mayas; up it came Cortes and his conquistadores; halfway down – and up – were the formidable Tlascalans who rushed on both enemies "like mad dogs". It is also a journey back to the tropics, from the cool central plateau. In the morning you wake to the flicker of banana fronds. (Master Basho would have sat up: his pen-name meant banana leaf, to signify a sensibility green and pliant and yet frayed.)

The Pullman car, one more used car from America, itself engenders fantasies of violence and sex. The sweet steel efficiency of each cabin, the sense of closeted indulgence, the partial glimpse of arms and legs at bedtime, the hidden presence of whole bodies in other cabins a breath away: all arouse a serpent in the brain that could not survive the shared public gaze a few carriages along. As every penny-dreadful reader knows, the rites of love and death, to satisfy, require privacy.

I fondled all the cunning knobs and catches around me. A fiendish ingenuity had gone into their designing. The steel sink pulled down out of the wall and emptied automatically when you folded it away; its high curved rim was spill-proof. A full-length mirror hung on the cabin door; it showed you yourself, and your partner, when the bed came down – fully made up – at night. Steel hangers clinked in the steel hanging closet. The walls were a gothic tapestry of shutters, vents, bins, trays, sockets, and concealed recesses operated by buttons, levers, and switches at some cunning remove from their devices. When the bed was down (resting on the toilet seat) a bevelled catch popped out to lock the sink upright: you could never get accidentally wet. Nothing was left to chance. The porter button might summon God himself. Nothing could go wrong – except love and death.

In the camarin across the aisle a faded criollo couple sat in silence. For a long time I saw only their legs. When they retired I saw, through a gap in the curtains, his toupée come off. The porter brought apple cider. I turned in and wondered who would survive the night. All night I had a dim sense of swaying in a hammock. Two things the Pullman company had got wrong: the beds should have run crosswise to the train, and the car should have been called a Woodruff car. But Mr Pullman was born lucky. The real inventor, Theodore Woodruff, did everything wrong: he lost his patent, went bankrupt, and was run over by a train.

Cortes himself dug the first spadeful of earth for Veracruz, despite his velvet cloak with its loops of gold and the lordly manners he had begun to assume in Havana. It was a significant decision, the digging, as symbolic as the burning of his boats. Were they there to trade, or to settle? That was the question that plagued, and almost split, his followers. The spade was his answer: the Rich City of the True Cross was laid out by all hands, and among its first improvements were a pillory and a gallows. But for his peculiar mix of force and guile, the 1519 expedition to Mexico might have been led by one Vasco Porcallo and have come to no more than the two previous expeditions, of 1518 and 1517.

On both those expeditions was the man who would become Cortes' most celebrated chronicler, Bernal Díaz del Castillo. Bernal Díaz would not have won Mexico for Spain. He lacked Cortes' single-mindedness, his ruthlessness, his shrewd diplomacy. But he is the better traveller. "I was never tired of noticing the diversity of trees and the various scents," he writes, while Cortes has eyes only for the gold. In 1517 Bernal Díaz notices "jewish idols" in Yucatan, in 1518 he sows orange pips in a temple garden. It is on the second expedition that the word *Mexico* first scuffs in European

279

ears, but the ships turn back, weevils in the cassava bread, water in the hold, and one greyhound bitch missing. The bitch turns up for Cortes, "fat and sleek" after a year in the wilds; so do two Castilians lost in 1517.

And so the expedition sets out, in quilted cotton armour (against darts), on hempen sandals, along the road the railway will traverse in a single night. The Indians fare best against them when they fight as guerrillas; in pitched battles the ten brass cannon, the falconets and horsemen mow them down. In peaceable villages Cortes barters beads for roast fowls and baked fish and maize cakes and jugs of honey: he all but throttles one soldier who steals a fowl. Gifts of women come from canny chiefs; among them is the invaluable Doña Marina, Cortes' mistress, counsellor, and chief interpreter. Montezuma sends caciques with a gold sun "big as a cartwheel" and a silver moon; Cortes, strapped for foreign exchange, sends back a gilded cup of Florentine glass and three holland shirts. He is sent by his sovereign, he announces solemnly, to see that the people of Mexico "do not rob one another".

On they march, skirmishing, smashing idols, raising altars to Christ and the Virgin. They pause, scandalized by boy prostitutes dressed as women, revolted by sacrificial altars where the corpses of victims are splayed, the chests opened, the hearts laid out in a row. In one cue or temple Bernal Díaz counts 100,000 skulls: "I repeat that there were more than a hundred thousand." They are shown a dinosaur bone, evidence of a vanished race of giants. They release caged boys being fattened for eating. "We will eat you with chillis and tomatoes and potherbs!" shout the natives, and half the party are for going back.

Cortes goes down with tertian fever, takes a camomile purgative; Bernal Díaz and his comrades of the settling party put heart into him. The soldiers run out of salt and oil and must dress their wounds with fat from the body of "a stout Indian". They sup on small dogs and passionfruit and prickly pears; they go thirsty by salt marshes. Their horses excite wonder, they themselves are taken for teules, either gods or demons.

Then the Tlascalans take one, Moron, prisoner in a skirmish, along with his horse, and no longer fear the teules. Now they mass on the plain before the five hundred. On the eve of the impossible battle the Mercedarian priest is up all night confessing his men; he runs out of wine and wafers. But the battle goes Cortes' way and the defeated Tlascalans become, in their thousands, his staunchest allies.

In the passes beyond, there is snow; now the quilted armour, once infernally hot, is not warm enough. The four hundred make shorter marches, better progress. Montezuma shuts himself up with his gods, gets no answer. Cortes presses on. The Spaniards sight a vast lake with causeways leading to a great city.

There, before their dazzled eyes, is Mexico, and the soldiers wonder whether they are not dreaming.

In the Veracruz market I drained a coconut without a straw, a coastal rite: what the mouth misses the collar collects. Past the docks were naval cadets dangling cream paintpots from scaffolding and whistling at passing girls. In the distance swam the Isle of Sacrifices where Cortes first landed on Good Friday 1519. (That very year a descendant of Tamburlane, Babur, set out with his small band of men to found another great empire, the Mughal empire in India.) Today lottery ticket vendors peddled another dream of riches, shabby men and women who thronged the waterfront, outnumbering the buyers.

The heat drove me into a cavernous coffee house whose lightly grimed interior and frowsty waiters conjured up the India Coffee House chain popular with journalists and students and would-be-politicians; the crowd matched too. A lecturer served me my lunch, pescado à la Veracruzana, then leaned against the wall and read his paper. The fish, in a state noted for its seafood, was sad; it came with half the Atlantic in the sauce.

"India?" said the lecturer, returning. "Terremoto!"

I took the strange word for a verdict and shrugged.

"Terremoto!" he repeated, growing insistent. He took off his glasses and waved them about, he wobbled one hand like a dancer, his big shoes slid apart. I reached for my pocket dictionary and found the word. *Earthquake.*

"No, no," I reassured him, "we seldom have those."

He gave up and went for his own lunch, which he ate by his shiny patch of wall. It was only after I got back that I learnt about the earthquake in our valley. There were cracks in most roofs in Dehra Dun, but our house was spared, and I thought of this man as our guardian. Still later I learnt the Mayan hieroglyph for earthquake: *Man-Sitting-On-Ground*. It shows a figure on his rump with his knees drawn up and his weight thrown back on rigid arms, the picture of utter confusion, man confounded.

The bus left at one – not before. So the policeman at the wicket said, and he had a pistol on his hip. At one minute to one he let us through, to applause from a slow-witted woman who appeared to be the station mascot. She stared adoringly at him and giggled when he spoke. He clowned a bit for her, pretending to follow two pretty girls who went by. She laughed fit to wet herself and began to pinch his thigh. He didn't mind that either.

The bus stood a long time on the bridge over the Papaloapan River, clumps of waterlily floating by underneath. The Liard looked a long way off. From now on palm-flanked rivers sunned like yellow pythons in the mud, but whenever the road left the coast and climbed into the hills that tropic yellow shaded into blue.

The prawns in batter at dinnertime saved the state's honour. Below the wayside restaurant the Gulf of Mexico rocked in the pearly light. From this coast runners once took sea fish to Montezuma's kitchen. The hot chocolate was worthy of Monte- zuma, who took several goblets of it, unsweetened, before visiting his mistresses; Bernal Díaz preferred the cocoa froth, eaten cold. Chocolat*l* proved Mexico's most popular gift to the world, and it came from this coast, but today the chief producers are in Africa. Vanilla, another Mexican flavour (it comes from the seedpod of an orchid and costs as much per pound as cocoa does per ton), had its origin here too, and again Africa has overtaken Mexico.

Many theorists have linked the Gulf Coast with Africa, usually after seeing the negroid stone heads at La Venta, but then there are claims too of a link with Atlantis: a French antiquarian once saw telegraph wires embedded in a rock and pointing the right way. For Mexico this is a coast of origins. Here Quetzalcoatl, the once and future priest-king, came to immolate himself, pushing out to sea in a burning barge and promising to return. (The cap fitted Cortes nicely.) The sparks from the pyre rose to the heavens and his heart became the morning star, harbinger of a new day. In his gold and red shell house, spinning blue and yellow cotton, throwing green and black pots, Quetzalcoatl was the divine arti- san who gave colour and design to Mexico. In another guise he

282

brought food: he was the ant (or spider, another African link) who stole maize kernels from the food mountain. Half-bird, half-snake, this plumed serpent (surely a better candidate for the Mexican flag than the eagle) was never still. In the end, because he preached against human sacrifice his enemies hatched a plot. They made a stew of beans and corn and tomatoes and chillies and some aphrodisiac (perhaps chocolatl, yet another of his discoveries) and got him "drunk" with his sister. Filled with shame at the incest, he retired from public life and went on his last pilgrimage to this fated shore.

Long before Quetzalcoatl, before Aztec and Maya, before even the pyramids at Monte Alban and Teoteohuacan, the peoples of the Gulf Coast were evolving their own civilization. Here appear some of the only laughing figures in the Mexican plastic arts, and, in the huge stone heads of La Venta, some of the only full round sculpture. There are no Khajurahos in Mexico, and it's odd that the only pre-Columbians whose stone sculpture goes beyond bas relief should have had a reputation – among the death-intoxicated Aztecs – for excessive sexuality. (The Mayas too, in their *Chilam Balam*, despised the people of this region as great oglers and winkers and slaverers.) The Gulf Coast people had their grim sacrificial altars, but they look to have been readier to laugh and to love than their enemies.

On the great Coatzacoalcos River we were at Mexico's narrowest point, the Isthmus of Tehuantepic. If the Gulf is Mexico's mouth, this is its gullet: beyond is Maya country. As late as the mid-19th century – after the break with Spain – the Yucatan, aware of this vulnerable divide, declared its independence of Mexico. Things would have gone hard with the republic had the Yucatecans succeeded, for here, offshore and on, lie Mexico's oilfields.

Night fell. An orange bushfire became the moon and rose into the black sky straight ahead. Tarpots flamed along the road as markers, oil for the burning; more flames danced in the sky. Further out, lightning flickered over Campeche Bay. A ring of lights raced around the driver's crucifix.

"I always wanted to write," said the garment salesman beside me. "But where do you start?"

When I asked his profession he made a deprecating gesture and said, to the window, "Far removed from the world of books."

Next day I found the Parque Museo de la Venta, where I learnt that the ceiba, that majestic native of the Americas, was a cousin of our own silk-cotton tree, whose nectar left small birds in a state of helpless intoxication. The Mayas held the ceiba sacred (so did the West Africans) and such is its stature, branching where most trees end, I felt inclined to worship it myself. There was an altar snug in its buttressed roots, but it had only been installed there lately. The park was a museum, and even the great stone heads that draw people from around the world had been transported there from La Venta to escape the oil drills. I sketched the enigmatic heads with their famous pout, the trees, the altars, the racoons, a crocodile, but it was the smallest creatures that finally defeated me.

"Moschetoes" plagued the artist Frederick Catherwood, who passed that way in 1840 making a series of notable engravings. The expedition leader, John Stephens, supervised the clearing of the monuments, but it was Catherwood who had to be still and draw. He used a *camera lucida*, and made a grid on the paper for accuracy, but more than either he would have needed gloves. Stephens' *Incidents of Travel in Central America, Chiapas, and the Yucatan* records a journey of ten months by mule through dense jungle. Archeology doubled with politics: the president of the United States had himself entrusted Stephens with a "Special Confidential Mission", perhaps the negotiating of a proposed "Panama" canal – through Nicaragua. The men traversed "wildly beautiful" jungles, astonishing the local people as much by brushing their teeth as by clearing the monuments; "even the monkeys," writes Stephens, "were embarrassed and confused." They ate the monkeys, and the parrots and lizards, and when the salt ran out they sprinkled gunpowder on their hard-boiled eggs.

As late as 1938 Graham Greene had to hire a mule to get to Palenque and found the monuments overgrown. His Villahermosa had grown too, but the mercado with its labyrinth of dry-goods grocers, button-and-bow stalls, and fetid dens where humans and caged fowls squatted stunned by the heat, that cannot have changed much. The fruit and vegetable end was deep in trodden filth, but out of the muck rose sublime pyramids of oranges and vivid mounds of parrot-beak chillies. "I have live prawns!" sang one man, and his heap of green prawns shuffled obediently. His neighbour had fish skewered on sticks from mouth to tail and grilled till golden; the next man hawked needles stuck in strips of yellow cardpaper.

Our bus crawled over grassland pricked with ceiba and dotted with beef cattle; here the trees were sacred and the cows were not. A wild bird-of-paradise lily reared its showy head. A ring of white herons chaperoned a cow. The farmhouse roofs were of corrugated iron, canted and waiting: "three months of showers, three months of thundershowers, and six months of wet northerlies" is the Palenque forecast.

I struck two dry days in a row, so I planned a walk to the ruins.

RUINAS, said a sign at the crossroads, and I followed the arrow, but darkness fell, a blank, stony darkness, and I turned into La Selva for dinner instead. It says something of the pre-War British palate that Graham Greene could find no good food – not once – in all Mexico. Dinner at The Jungle was so good I asked the waiter if I could copy out the evening's menu. He brought back the card and a second candle and I wrote:

I   *Tomate relleno de ensalada de atún*
II   *Sopa de zanahoria*
III *Arroz con plátano frito*
IV   *Mojarra frita*
V   *Frutas de la estación*
VI   *Café*

Pointless to praise Mexican coffee, but the fruit platter, the fish fried whole and crusted with herbs, the plantain strips sizzling on rice, the dressing of coconut and garlic concocted merely to spike a tuna salad – these are not post-War inventions. I ate in the garden. Night birds stirred in the trees; the bushes hung out white trumpets and varnished leaves as big as cellos. It was the meal of the journey, and it cost less than a caribou burger and fries in Inuvik. I walked home by the road Greene would have taken on his mule and saw his priggishness was bound up with his colon. *The Lawless Roads*, astringent and inimitable, left its mark on the next generation of travellers, dyspeptic men whose wit and prose would be sharpened on hapless countries, men dispassionate and censorious and scrupulously honest – and no more reliable than the next man. "Tiredness and anxiety and homesickness," Greene confesses, "can turn the heart to stone."

The next day I stood in a bank queue for two hours and felt my heart petrify. I could have counted 100,000 skulls with Bernal Díaz and gone home smiling. A whole humid afternoon I simmered in the Banamex while the descendants of a people who could calculate the transit of Venus to within half a second reinvented time.

It was a comedown from the morning. At first light I'd set out on foot along the road to the ruins through a landscape of primeval beauty. Fields, farmhouses, a school, the blacktop road, had pushed back the archaic jungle, but only provisionally. Strange trees hung pickled in the vitreous light. A creeper hung sinister little bells over the sweetsop bushes like an elaborate trap. Then the sun came up, hot even at the horizon. I flagged down the bus and rode the rest of the way through dense jungle.

The present road sneaks up on the monuments from behind: a Mayan king would have approved of this tradesmen's entrance. The royal palace faces east, and nothing comes between it and the rising sun. Today's visitor happens first on the pyramid, actually an adjunct, and immediately climbs its hundred-and-some feet. The steps are so narrow, the gradient so steep, one reaches the top sweating as much from fear as from the soupy sunlight. In Stephens' time there were trees and lianas all the way up what must have been no more than a stony hill.

Considering the climate, the 7th-century surfaces are well preserved. Stephens found the stucco "hard as stone" (it still is) and a lintel of sapote wood that rang like metal. Having bought the ruins at Copan in Guatemala for $50 ("there was never any difficulty about the price") he considers $1500 a fair offer for Palenque. But there's a hitch: foreigners may not buy land in Mexico – unless married to a daughter of the soil. Nine months on the road, he confesses, "there are moments when a lonely woman might root the stranger to any spot on earth." Here too are complications: the oldest eligible lady is fourteen, the loveliest lady already married, and the two ladies in possession of the prized Temple of the Foliated Cross are "equally interesting".

He sighs and presses on. By the time he gets to the Yucatan the women are looking "really handsome".

The crypt in the pyramid was not discovered until 1949, when Dr Ruz Lhuillier, working at the top, noticed a loose flagstone with fingerholes. The flag concealed a stair packed with rubble — and seven skeletons — leading down to a chamber in the heart of the pyramid. After two years of digging Dr Lhuillier shifted the last slab and gazed on the richly ornamented tomb of a grandee who had lain undisturbed since his burial in AD 683.

The sunlight was a shock after the grave. I clambered over the ruined palace where crickets scroop and butterflies burn. The souls of Mayan sacrificial victims were said to enter butterflies; those seven slaves still flitted among the stones. The poet Elsa Cross, whose book I'd picked up in Mexico City, has this poem:

Palenque

Tall in shadow
Clear in dense thickets —
          presences.

Their footprints followed an interminable road
(yellow princess in the corridors).

The stones
Held by time
like little acid fruit between the teeth
    — sensation of water through their pores
    shock of the wind —
break their silence.

Begonias wear down the stairways.
Trees lift above the fretted crests.
No temple suffices the god,
no temple contains him.
Turned into air,
turned into stone,
he pulses strange fibres in the breast.

At noon I returned to town for breakfast, and the bank. A squad car stood outside the garden restaurant; inside were the policeman and his girlfriend. She was beautiful, he was handsome, but then there entered into their paradise the snake. He was a talker, the policeman's friend, and he sat down between them. As the talk became man to man, the policeman turning gradually until he all but faced his mate, the girl began to look around. She wanted the policeman, his crisp khakis, his gun, his squad car, but she had begun to suspect that life with him would always be like this. She gazed about her in mute appeal. *Take me away*, her gaze said, *far away!* and for a moment the waiter, bored in his own way, was tempted. Then he would have remembered the squad car and come to his senses.

On the four o'clock bus back to the ruins was an English couple, survivors of the Banamex Line; we compared wounds. At the gate a ranger stopped us and declared the ruins closed. He was unapproachable. Never, I wheedled, ever, would I get a chance to return, no, never. "No," he said, "no, no, no, no, no." Then, as I was turning away, he waved me through. The English, sounder tacticians, waited till he wandered off, then slipped in.

It was too late. Other guards were already blowing whistles, rounding up the visitors. I ducked into a passage and climbed the tower. A guard spotted me and whistled. I stalled in embrasures on the way down. The walls to the courtyard below were pierced by the T-shaped vents which for the Maya symbolized the wind. Today every T-vent framed a guard with an expressive whistle. I came down and gave myself up. They herded me out, the errant goat, walking along behind to make sure.

I had dinner with the English, expatriates from Sydney, where they worked for rival newspapers. Andrew had been in India and endured Indian Standard Time. When I told the waiter I had a night bus to catch he gave a priestly nod and disappeared into Mayan Time.

Every fifty-two years the ancient Mexicans believed the sun needed rekindling – on the breast of a chosen victim. When that time came they smashed their cooking pots, extinguished all hearths, and repaired to the cue where the papas were already

288

chanting. At the appointed moment the chief priest held down the victim with his knee (the infamous Rule of the Knee) and cut open his chest with a knife of jade. Immediately he plucked out the heart and offered it, still beating, to the imperilled sun. The sun rose. The priest relit the sacred fire. Time began anew.

I didn't wait for the knee. I left some money and ran. Back in my room I flung everything into my bags as the taxi waited. A figure came sprinting down the unlit lane: Andrew, with my change. We shook hands through the cab window and the driver sped me to the depot.

The ten o'clock bus to the Yucatan left at a quarter to eleven.

23

Sisal

On the night bus to Mérida I felt the loss of the sun as keenly as an ancient Mayan. It was the last stage of the journey and I wanted to enter the Yucatan with my eyes open, but I saw only the stars and a flat, fugitive bushscape lit by a waning moon. We traversed the whole length of the peninsula in darkness. There was still the breadth, however.

Around midnight we crossed the Champoton River, the last river of my journey. There are no rivers in the Yucatan proper. The peninsula is one gigantic limestone sill jutting into the Gulf of Mexico, as pocked and pitted as a grindstone. The pocks – cenotes is the local word – hold the region's rainwater; without them life could not exist in the Yucatan. Yet on this fragile ground there flourished, thanks to that porous quality of limestone, one of the notable civilizations of North America. In a sense the Yucatan was the apogee of the long journey south that began at the Arctic Sea. But an Eskimo would demur: not all igloos aspire to the condition of a pyramid.

The bus got in to Mérida at dawn. Across the street from the depot was a row of wretched hotels. The owner of the best among them drew himself up as I entered, a sallow, bird-like man in need of drawing up. His glasses and beaky nose gave him an owlish look, and daylight did seem to trouble him. When I turned down his best room he fetched from the depths of his being a look of aggrieved dignity.

"It's too . . . small," I said.

He nodded quickly at the wall, the beak climbing up, not down. I almost changed my mind to mollify him, but now I was counting hours, not days. And yet as time ran out the small change of brief encounters grew precious.

"*Hweesh!*" said a man who narrowly missed walking into me, and I hoped to run into him again.

"Bless you!" said two complete strangers, turning simultaneously when I sneezed.

I had even succumbed to the thumb-and-forefinger gesture for "a little" (it could mean "just a moment" or "a little further"), in universal use. Here, in the momentito or little moment, was the notorious "later" of Mexico; I'd suffered its long duress in the bank at Palenque.

I returned to the depot. The old lady at Enquiries repeated herself four times for my benefit without impatience. I found myself on an eastbound bus. The start of a new journey — by daylight — was a tonic, like sleep itself. As the sun came up I grew impervious to the rending of gears under my seat. Here at last was the flat Yucatan of my imaginings. Close up it was hummocked with limestone strewn about like lumps of crumbly cheese, but the horizon was level on all sides, as numbingly level as the Gangetic plain of my earliest years. I was ten before I saw a hill; even a hillock was a wondrous thing. To be propelled into a featureless landscape at daybreak was to re-enter that early pre-montane age. Only palm trees and windmills broke the monotonous level.

The driver was a droll Buddha in a bush shirt, with high, arching eyebrows and sleepy Mayan eyes. I never saw more than half the iris under his heavy lids. The kinks in his hair were African, a reminder of the Caribbean connection. It was from Cuba that the Spaniards launched their assault on the mainland, bringing with them negro slaves. One of these had smallpox, which spread like a bushfire among the Indians; others left a quicker legacy. "No negro, slave or mestizo shall enter any village save with his master," ran a decree of 1552, "and then stay more than a day and a night." One night had been enough for this man's ancestor. He himself seemed in an even greater hurry, using his radio as a horn, bowling through villages where children peeped over lattice gates and signboards proclaimed thatch temples: *Bethel*, *Eden*, *Galilee*. The proper churches were in the towns, pink stucco hulks in worse repair. On one ruined dome a vulture sat sunning its outstretched wings like a morbid satellite dish.

291

I saw no quetzals in Mexico — I missed my Mallee fowl after all — but all the way down I watched the vultures. They wore an aloofness almost brahminical, but it was the aloofness of outcaste brahmins, fallen priests. At times, not just on the wing, they resembled eagles, eagles gone to seed, gone to hell, eagles of the underworld, the eye just as sharp, but the palate jaded, like the Aztec papas who eventually developed a taste for human flesh. The difference between their behaviour at rest and at meals was almost schizophrenic. Their churlish hissing and shoving reminded me of my countrymen at wedding feasts. Afterwards there came a lax interval of flatulence and grumbling; then, one by one, they withdrew into themselves and sat in silent rows on ceibas and church roofs, looking steadily away from one another. In the morning they shook out their wings and faced the east, muttering like old men against the sun that thawed them. Their mockery conjured up the dying Voltaire (vultour?) cackling as a nurse brought a candle: "What? flames *already*!"

"Chichén Itzá!" the Buddha called, and left me in a cloud of dust with a cha-cha "Blue Danube" circling in my head. I hauled my bags half a mile to the ruins, resting in the scant shade. "The sun burns fiercely," warns Friar Diego de Landa on page one of his famous treatise on the Yucatan — but I didn't find the book until that evening. At the gate Ramon the gateman told me the hotels by the ruins charged $100 a night.

"Best go back to town, to Pisté," he advised.

I wilted at the thought.

"A taxi will be along shortly," he said, making the momentito sign. As he waited he told me of his stint in the army, of his growing family. They were building their home room by room, as the money came in. Right now they had two and a half rooms, but the kitchen was tiled. The taxi arrived too soon.

"Are you Mayan or mestizo?" I asked him quickly.

"We all have some Spanish links," he said, "but we are Mayan. At school we learn to speak Spanish, because we have to use it, but at home it's *Maya-Maya-Maya*."

Their language was the Maya's salvation. It was what kept them secure when all else was taken away. The 1552 decree — designed to protect them — required that the subjected race be "doctrinated" and that every town have its own church where the

Indians learn to "enjoy God". No Indian could now change his town or go missing; none could pray or fast in secret according to the old rites. Every child was to be brought for baptism and none could be given a heathen name. The very telling of dreams was denied them, as was "divination by casting grains of corn", tattooing, or any other "marks or ornaments of their heathendom". There could be no banquets or night dances, and anyone who prepared "ancient drinks" could be fined fifty pesos. All bows and arrows were to be burned excepting "two or three dozen" against attacks by tigers. Slavery, but not servitude, was prohibited, and a cattle-and-cotton economy imposed. Women were required to wear long skirts, men shirts and sandals. Both were instructed in "holy dying". The Yucatan was pacified.

In the first New World maps the Yucatecan was drawn as an island. Columbus, ever hopeful of a farther passage, thought it was one, and so did Cortes a generation later. Yet even as Cortes was tracing out his "Montezuma map" in Mexico, one Alonzo Piñeda, voyaging around the Gulf, showed a continuous coastline from Florida down past the pommel of the Yucatan. No short cut to the Pacific existed and Columbus, who kissed the unyielding mainland at the Honduras in 1502, must have envied Vasco da Gama his sensible route to India. (There was more gall on that, his last voyage: he lost all four ships he set out with. And yet it is always with three splendid caravels – the *Santa Maria*, in fact a tubby supply ship, the *Niña*, and the *Pinta* – that he streams through the imagination.)

Island or not, there was always a Yucatecan mentality, out on a limb, away from the rest ("the east of the east", as my evangelist put it), a kind of frontier, like the Yukon, but a frontier with monuments. Even in pre-Columbian times the northern or Yucatecan Maya were a folk apart. With the Spaniards there developed a further division within the Yucatan, between the settled west, around Mérida and Campeche, and the east, a *Terra Nulla* of marshland and wild turkeys and desert beaches. It was on such a beach that I saw myself ending my journey.

The taxi dropped me at the unfinished Posada Pisté. Four rooms were complete and I got one. It was new but barracks-plain, the windows merely square holes covered in mosquito mesh. At my door lay a giant snake with its jaws wide open. It was a stucco plumed serpent, Quetzalcoatl himself. At one time the land on which the posada stood had been a park at the edge of town, the Chichén Itzá edge, with small-scale pyramids and a large-scale snake; the neighbours got the pyramids, the Posada Pisté got the snake, and were building around it. It was thirty feet long and chest high, and you could fit comfortably in its jaws if you sat on the tongue between the two lower fangs.

Always restless, the Toltec's snake king visited the Yucatan and instructed its people in his many arts. They say this early missionary returned to Mexico (I imagined him going the other way, to the fatal coast) but that may only have been the Toltec conquerors going home, their Yucatecan adventure over. In time the Maya came to worship him, or his memory, as Kukulcán.

Kukulcán went home about 500 years before the Spanish conquest (he would have left about the time Leif Ericsson sailed to Newfoundland). Some 500 years before that, Palenque was at its height, and the city-states further south already in decline. The first florescence at Chichén Itzá was probably the result of a southern Mayan push northwards, the Itzá adventurers dislodging a still earlier group of Yucatecans farming the land round about the huge limestone cenote called *Chichen* or Well Mouth. So the site outside Pisté is a cross-section of the peninsula's history, one of successive waves of conquerors, of whom the package tourists on a day trip from Cancún are only the most recent.

"I'll bet the Maya were gay," said a man at the top of the Great Pyramid of Kukulcán.

"Oh yeah?" his friend said, and farted loudly. They sniggered and I stepped aside offended. Later I remembered Kukulcán was god of the wind.

"Yeah! Who else could have laid out the place with such imagination?"

They were part of a group swarming up the narrow steps. Far below us other groups ranged from temple to temple across the grounds.

"With the true God, the true *Dios*, came the beginning of our misery," says the *Book of Chilam Balam*, written by a 16th-century historian in the Roman script he learnt from the Franciscan friars. And the Yucatecan Maya endured much at the hands of the Spanish: repeated humiliations, beatings, torture, rape, lynchings, massacres. Yet they showed astonishing resilience – not just in their spirited rebellions, which continued long after the rest of New Spain was quiescent, but in their capacity to digest invasion. Their books of prophecy are full of horror: rivers of blood, of scorpions, of pus; the dead lie heaped up, there is a buzzing of flies at the crossroads; owls screech by day, frogs croak in empty wells. The fact is every invader brought misery – and the true God. The Toltecs brought their true Dios, Quetzalcoatl-Kukulcán, and one imagines the southern Maya overwhelming the primitive farmers at the great well with *their* true gods. As late as the 1900s, under Porfirio Díaz (whose god was Progress), parts of the Yucatan resembled a gigantic slave-camp. What is astonishing is that over the millennia the Yucatecans have absorbed the outsider and his customs while preserving a decided good cheer. It might be the same peninsular mentality, or a frontier spirit, but here at the fag-end of Mexico the Indian sullenness lifts and one begins to notice among the native people smiles for the stranger. It is as if the long-held aboriginal grudge melts away in the Yucatan, on that unpromising and much-abused soil. Perhaps it is because the language has kept so well, because at home it is still *Maya-Maya-Maya*.

I came down from the Great Pyramid and rambled over the grounds: the remains of a market square, a mossed bathhouse with the false Mayan arch, a nunnery, a forest of stone columns built back up into avenues. At the east end, where the governor's palace might stand on other Mayan sites, is the Temple of Warriors with its Chac-mool altar at the top of the stair, where the rain god was propitiated with human blood. Further in is a massive stone table, ten feet across, mute witness to ritual mayhem. The wall behind it has fallen down, and there in the distance, where the sun must rise over the green baize, is the flat horizon of the Yucatan. Westward lies the skull rack, an ossuary designed expressly to terrify. And beyond looms an immense pelota court, a colosseum where the Maya played their fatal team squash, the gladiators assigned astral roles and playing, with a rubber ball, the game of their lives. Grassed today like a football field, the empty court still rings with the spectators' cries. But of all echoes the most chilling hang over the great cenote: at the end of a stony path through the forest is the Mayan Well of Death.

The park authorities, with matchless insouciance, have placed a kiosk by the cenote; you sip a cola at the sacrificial site. It is a testimony to the terrible aura of the place that the kiosk fades away. It was dusk when I came on the well, a great grim hole fringed with trees. The well walls are honeycombed with limestone sockets all the way down to the green water forty feet below the surface; it is almost two hundred feet across to the other side. Here, bound and drugged, the victim was led down the narrow road from the pyramid, and ceremoniously tossed over the edge. I got no nearer than a dozen paces from the rim, and even then I had to hold on to a tree trunk. On that edge a mortal dread seizes you and compels pushing or being pushed; by twilight push and pull are one.

One day in 1927 the young adventurer Richard Halliburton came to this well, stood on the brink, and jumped in. By his account he had spent the night on its edge absorbing its terrors, and at first light felt impelled to take the leap. His notebook and travel papers (and his travellers' cheques) got wet, and he was lucky not to hit a submerged log. He was in the air a long time and even longer underwater, and he came up with a headache, but the next day he jumped in again, for a friend with a movie camera. It was the kind of feat, especially the re-run, that suited his career of climbing dormant volcanoes and charting once-charted seas. The daring jump might have been in its way epochal, a secular plunge closing off the age of the sacred, but even that glory was denied Halliburton. A generation earlier another American, the archaeologist Edward Thompson, had already set up a dredge and swept the bottom of the cenote. Thompson drew up treasure and human bones and rubber idols that were then smuggled to America. The well stood stripped of magic; Chichén Itzá had entered the age of tours and cultivated voyeurism.

The park rangers shooed me off, their whistles keen as darts. I slunk away in the half-dark and followed two hotel maids going home by a staff route. They wore the frilly dresses of the Yucatan, not unlike the cowgirl frock of Bombay curry westerns.

When the Spanish arrived, vanity appeared to be a male preserve among the Maya. "All the men wore mirrors," writes Diego de Landa, "and the women not." Men wore their hair long, coiled around a tonsure, the hair a hat. Over their shoulders they wore a cape, and in front, for modesty, a "long fillet". The women Brother Landa found "not bad looking" and better built than Spanish women, but given to excessive bathing (which he felt darkened the skin) and filing their teeth. As mothers they were responsible for the Mayan sloping forehead, which they induced in infancy by binding, as the Chinese did with feet. Their breasts, Landa decided, grew large from being unbound while they ground the corn. The long skirt which the Franciscans obliged every woman to wear, "and over them their huipiles", has metamorphosed into a third thing, the frilly frock, one more example of the Yucatecan talent for refashioning an imposition to suit themselves.

I bought a copy of Landa's *Account of the Things of Yucatan* as the bookshop was closing and it proved immediately useful, in its plastic bag, as an umbrella. The rain started as I stepped out of the Chichén Itzá gate and stopped two kilometres up the road as I stepped into Ignacio's. Landa kept my glasses dry. (Fire, not water, was his element; fire occasioned his book. In 1562 he lit a notorious one in which he burnt all the Mayan manuscripts he could find on a heap of wooden idols as "works of the Devil", an act the Maya are said to have "regretted to an amazing degree". For his excess of zeal he was summoned to Spain to explain himself, and did so in the roundabout way of his *Relación de las cosas de Yucatan*. The book was his expiation, but not enough for divine justice: the manuscript disappeared for almost 300 years. When it surfaced in the 19th century it was the richest surviving account of Yucatecan customs, and a sympathetic one at that.)

Ignacio's was the taqueria at the edge of town, a modest roadside affair burnished to mythic perfection by the owner. The tableware shone, the tablecloths dazzled, the thatch appeared to have been polished straw by straw. On a fine day the tables spilled out into the evening; tonight they were drawn back under the awning. Only two were occupied: a couple speaking German, and two young Pisteaños waiting on a takeaway order. Ignacio took my order himself. He looked Spanish, an aristocrat I would have said, in another century. The reading glasses, suspended on a chain, were for signing treaties, not for taking taco orders.

He employed a whole Mayan family — father, mother, daughter, son — and they huddled at the back in an awestruck group, awaiting orders. The boy was the waiter. He had approached as trained to take my order when Ignacio appeared from nowhere and displaced him. The order taken, Ignacio conveyed it to the mother. Then, on second thoughts, he went into the kitchen to supervise the cooking. Nothing, his manner suggested, must go wrong. The tacos, which he served himself, the boy trailing pointlessly, were excellent. The quesadillas that followed were so good I felt the mother must have smuggled some Mayan disorder into the diabolical efficiency.

I began to imagine Ignacio as Diego de Landa himself, autocrat, superman, demigod. Landa ran a tight church. He flogged those who got out of line, he burnt wicked books, he noted the habits of underlings with an eagle eye; later, when he returned as bishop, his excesses forgiven, he flogged some more. He even dug up the bones of his chief informant and scattered them about because he believed the man had practised heathen rites after turning Christian. The backslider must not go to heaven. Nothing must go wrong. Ignacio ran the perfect restaurant. The food was delicious and cheap; he didn't do it for the money. The portions were huge, his pizzas so big the German couple groaned at the sight of theirs.

"Save some for breakfast," Ignacio said, pleased. The staff in the background beamed feudally. They were proud of his perfection and registered his lightest glance, wilting or perking up by reflex. He treated them correctly, evenly, by some inner code. The waitress poured orange juice and polished the jar under his eye, then gave the lid an extra twist before she put it back into the glass-front fridge, in line. She looked bright and clean and happy, as one might who worked for God. The juice looked happy too, fresh and squeezed by hand: I saw the squeezed orange halves, scoured to the zest. A row of tightly sealed jars stood on the top shelf. Ignacio poured some for the Germans and spirited away the empty jar. (With a single clink the full jars moved across to fill the gap.) Unstarching suddenly, he sat down and chatted with the couple, then sprang up again to refill their glasses – to the brim – screwing the new lid back on tightly.

"Better you come and sit at this table," he called to them in English from under the awning. I hadn't seen him leave the room. The couple were waiting for the Cancún bus. Ignacio craned up the road, waved from the hip at a passing car. Another pair of locals came in for his pizza: all of Pisté spoke of it. The boy-waiter approached, Ignacio displaced him, then disappeared to check the

298

oven, swifting away my empty glass on the way. Café con leche appeared before me, and disappeared when I was done. A black kitten prowled about, fussed over by guests; dogs might look in, but were chased off if they crossed an invisible line.

A scruffy boy of nine or ten strolled in and sat down at the next table. Ignacio whipped off the tablecloth before he could lean on it and vanished. He returned with one even more dazzling that he spread and smoothed down in a single motion. Then he stood towering over the urchin, his pen poised above the pad.

"Hamburguesa," the urchin snapped, a regular, "y Coca." He smiled toughly at me.

Ignacio scribbled and turned to go, but the boy-waiter barred his way. There was a moment's hesitation, then Landa gave in and repeated the order. The boy fled trembling with pride and I heard him bark *Hamburguesa!* at his mother.

The burger when it came dwarfed the Great Pyramid of Kukulcán. The urchin and I exchanged an approving nod.

"Salsa!" he rapped out, and Ignacio was there with two sauces, red and green, freshly made.

I stepped out under a clear sky. The night air was fresh, almost chill after the rain, and the crickets chirruped madly. My room felt stuffy by comparison and I had begun to wedge the bed into the door when I remembered rain brought out snakes. There was already one in the garden, in stucco. In the middle of the night I woke and walked carefully on the grass under the old Mayan stars. Venus was under my feet, on its way around to come up as the morning star, but the plumed serpent lay there in the moonlight, a crumbling Quetzalcoatl with lockjaw.

The Restaurant Sayil promised TIPICAL FOOD but I got curried chicken for breakfast because the patrons before me got the last three eggs. It was mild, the pollo pibil; the cuisine too flattens out in the Yucatan. Back on the street I flagged down the Mérida bus coming from Cancún.

Cancún is about as far east as you can go in Mexico, but with its luxury hotels and its beach littered with foreign bodies it has come to symbolize Mexico without the inconvenience of Mexicans. There is an international airport that allows visitors to miss Mexico altogether, save that brush with its golden sands. "I always called that place Hell," wrote Bernal Díaz of the sacrificial temple at Tenochtitlán, a place of blood and scattered limbs and grisly cooking pots. On a more pallid journey I always thought of Cancún in that way.

The east coast tainted, I looked for another course, and during the night's pacing I had found one. Ekchuah, the North Star, Mayan god of travellers, spoke: *Leave east and west. Go North!*

For the next two hours we flew past spiky agave scrub and stone fences towards Mérida. It was a rocket, not a bus. One touch, I kept thinking, one *glance* off another vehicle and we are all dead. For no good reason survival becomes more important near the end of a journey. But Ekchuah was appeased; some unsteady Christian on board had burned copal to him the night before – I could smell it still – and he saw us through. Just short of the depot the driver, suddenly dilatory, left the engine running and sloped off to buy some onions, but no one appeared to mind. In town I found a hotel and booked a flight for the next day to Mexico City. Now all I had to do was reach the sea. Mérida, city of savants, rich capital of the Yucatan, was reduced to a staging post: the point was to get to Sisal.

Sisal. The word inhabits the very edge of consciousness – like the town itself, at Mexico's land's end – on that shore of the *mare ignotum* where lurk words such as *kapok* and *sago*, *couscous* and *Timbuctoo*. Things vaguely known but not proven, never tested, taken on faith. I knew or half-knew the thing (as I half-knew jute and hemp) before I ever knew of the place. I still cannot say when I first saw it on the map.

Sisal is a forgotten port at the northwest corner of the Yucatan peninsula. It could never hope to compete with Campeche on the west coat or Cancún on the east, but even on the barren north coast it has been outstripped by the brashly named Progreso. Progress has sidelined sisal the product too.

The product is agave fibre, for rope. The stones of the pyramids were hauled with it, but it was also used for hammocks and sandals, the way Maoris used flax, another hardy sword-leafed plant. In the late 19th century it passed in such quantities through Sisal that the port gave its name to the thing and a word to the

English language. Sisal twine bound sheaves of wheat all across North America. Then came nylon and other synthetic fibres that killed off the industry just as chemical blue spelt ruin to whole plantations of indigo. The port slipped back into obscurity. And now the word is dying too, sinking back into that shadowy sea of monsters. Most Mexicans have never heard of the port, and it is frequently omitted from maps. Sisal, like the unicorn, lives unto itself.

A modern reproduction of Catherwood's *Gateway at Labná*, printed at Mérida for the tourist trade, shows on the back the route of the explorers' Yucatan journey starting at Progreso. Untrue: Stephens and Catherwood landed at Sisal. (They had sailed across Campeche Bay for the last leg of their land journey, Stephens still sorrowing over the farewell to his mule, Macho.) The slight is typical; when I spoke of Sisal to a university lecturer she shook her head in amused puzzlement.

Not so the lady at the second-class bus terminal from where the only bus to Sisal plies. She looked out of place, a middle-class woman compelled to make a living selling tickets to campesinos. She gave me precise instructions and told me I mustn't miss the last bus back.

"Wait *there*," she said, aiming a crochet needle, and returned to her antimacassar, one more piece of Yucatan lace. (Lace in Mexico was like the cinnamon bun in the Deep North: wherever ladies still made it was the frontier.)

I had just missed the two o'clock bus; the next one was the last. I got on it annoyed at myself. I would get to Sisal late and see nothing of it. *Due North!* Ekchuah urged, and in fact the sea at Progreso, straight up from Mérida, is an hour closer. But Sisal lay northwest and northwest the bus went, past pumpkin-plain churches whose façades were stained a deeper yellow by the late afternoon sun. After Hunucma, the halfway point, the bus emptied out. I saw we would reach Sisal after dark and cursed, but looking back, I was spared the embarrassment of a sunset ending. My last photograph was of a campesino on horseback riding at a canter towards Sisal, but it was too dark and the slide shows a ghostly rider wreathed in ectoplasm.

I began to think of endings. Sailors kiss the earth at the end of a voyage; what would I do? I could walk fully clothed into the

301

sea, the End Cinematic. I could scoop up a handful of the Gulf of Mexico and taste a drop, the End Ceremonial. I felt still the wonderment of standing on the pebble beach at Tuktoyaktuk and looking towards the pole, the exhilaration of setting out in the first bus, Fabio's van. It had been a long journey, the longest I would make, and I felt it. But it was not the journey of my life.

The journey of my life was to the other West, the Occident, at twenty. My carrier was Kuwait Airways, who offered the best deal out of India. I had never been abroad; I had never been in a plane before; I had seven dollars in my pocket. It was hard on this later journey to match that exaltation.

Still, something had to be done. I had some American money left, the once-strange greenbacks. I decided to return those seven original dollars to the continent. I would make a Columbus fleet of paper boats – a five-dollar-bill *Santa Maria* and two one-dollar caravels – and float it at Sisal, pushing the nosy discovery back into the sea. In fact the admiral never sailed as far as Sisal, but Cortes did, coasting around the Yucatan in search of rivers that did not exist.

We got into Sisal at dusk. The street lights had come on but there was still a little colour in the western sky. I made straight for the beach. There was a pier at the end of the main street where two anglers fished on in the twilight. A few gulls kept them company, circling whitely overhead. I headed along the beach for a bit before dipping my hand into the water. It was warm, by Arctic standards. Then I began to look for pebbles to set beside my Arctic ones. There were none. I combed the sand in the failing light but kept finding shells that glowed the same luminous blue-white as the gulls. In the end, as darkness settled, I began to gather shells; some one or two might be nibs of porous limestone.

There were fishing boats drawn up along the shore, side by side, their prows pointing out to sea. They were moored with taut rough hawsers – of sisal rope. The prows were fitted with bamboo fishing poles, their nylon lines drawn back and secured in the boat. The tide was in; every seventh wave nudged and lifted a prow that sighed and settled back into the sand. Where the beach narrowed the boats rode on water and the hawsers strained and trembled. I tripped over one, the first of many. Beyond the swells, white breakers blossomed in the dark and flattened out as they came in, piling up like rows of knitting. The sea breeze came out of the east, over the pier, a cool steady stream on my back. The palms, higher up, got rougher treatment. Wisps of cloud were blown about the sky.

I passed the lighthouse and a row of concrete houses. At an upstairs window a woman framed in yellow light looked out to sea. Two slender radio towers rose beyond the houses. I decided to walk along the beach until I was clear of the town. It was a steeplechase, over and under the mooring ropes, some at thigh height, others buried in the sand and snapping taut without warning. If the Mayan heaven is a place of ceiba trees and abundant corn, and hell a Cancún beach at noon, then limbo is a gauntlet of sisal hawsers run in the dark, ropes that might be bruised nylon after all.

Every three seconds the lighthouse glare swept the shore. Three neon street lights stood at the head of their streets. Now and then a car turned up a street and its beam shone out to sea. I passed the last of the street lights, then a few houses scattered among vacant lots. I imagined a point up ahead where the shoreline turned south, the peninsula falling away, and made for that point.

The lights of Sisal dropped back. Now I was past the boats and houses, walking on white sand, shells crunching under my boots. An oystercatcher cried in the dark. The stars were out in force but a low ledge of cloud was building on the southern horizon where lightning flickered.

I trod in something soft and stepped back. The beach had taken on a marshy look, the white sand stained black and appearing to ooze. The darkness conjured up a vision of quicksand. I was a long way from town: there would be no help even if my cries weren't blown clear across Campeche Bay. The ooze stuck to my boots. Buck McLeod's word *oilpatch* popped up – or it might be the town's sewage discharge. I turned back.

In the south a tower of cloud had built up. When the lightning flashed behind it it looked like a second lighthouse. The wind had risen; it now struck me full in the face. If I wanted to launch my flotilla I had better set about it. The first dollar bill simply flew away. I had pictured three paper boats sailing together, and already the *Niña* was gone. There was no solid surface on which to fold the bills. I put the next note straight into the water. I was now back

303

among the last of the fishing boats. There was one boat buried in the sand with a pool of water collected in it, a tranquil little sea undisturbed by the wind. I made the *Santa Maria* on the gunwale and left it floating in its own cove.

After miles of sand the solid ground of the foreshore came like a reprieve. It was still the edge of town. What looked like a high cemetery wall, with a colonial coping, made an angle where I came up from the beach. There was a gate with a stone arch, and just inside the enclosure, a dead tree. The lightning threw the tree and the cloud tower into sharp black-and-white relief. It was a scene flat and stark, from an old witchcraft movie. I took out my sketchbook and drew the apocalypse on the endpaper, working by touch in the dark. (I had to bring the book up to my nose to tell the back from the front.) Then I crept back to civilization, entering town from the wrong end, a rough beast risen from the sea, or the sewage, or the grave.

House lights appeared, and a car beam that I instinctively dodged. I walked back east along the first cross street. One block from the sea the wind had dropped to a breeze again. All the houses had their doors and windows open, with TVs and radios playing. Under one streetlight a fisherman sat and darned a tarpaulin. A family sat around a cleared table talking. A woman sat at a sewing machine running up some lime-green fabric. Across the unpaved road at intervals lay what looked like pythons. I reached down and stroked one. It was a great fat rope of sisal – genuine sisal – laid, with a kind of pathos, as a speed-breaker.

The street brought me back to the town square, a place of simple concrete benches and a garden. At one seaward corner was the lighthouse; at the other, off by itself, was a tiny food stall, another sort of beacon, bright only in the general gloom. Rosita was warming a row of cleft buns; shredded meat and cabbage crowded a tiny chopping board, spilling over onto the grim counter. I bought a packet of corn chips and a shocking pink soda.

"Sure tourists come to Sisal," Rosita said. "We had some just last month."

I asked what Sisal had to offer them.

"You must go and see the Swordsman," she said. "It's just a block away. At the corner there's an old house with a statue on top. A man with a sword raised up like this."

304

Her imitation was so dramatic I felt I didn't need to see the original. A man entered her little stall from behind and picked intimately at the food on the counter. "Gaspar caught them in the act," he tittered. Rosita made him a special sandwich.

"*Sisal*," the man beside me said, "means a place of sweet water, in the old tongue."

At the foot of the zócalo stood a church in the failed-modern style of new churches in Mexico and India. It faced the sea, its three doors thrown open. From where I sat across the street waiting for the last bus I could see straight up the aisle. On the next bench sat two old men who could look in one of the side doors. The church was brilliantly lit and full of women. It must have been sweltering in there.

"Alleluia, brothers and sisters!" shouted the minister. He was almost the only man in the church.

"Sing!" called a woman with a microphone. The women sang, an organ played. Groans of ecstasy, of surrender, rose as far as the ceiling fans and revolved there: the ceiling had an echo.

"Clap your hands, brothers and sisters!"

"*—manos y —manas!*" came the muffled echo.

But the brothers, the men of Sisal, were playing volleyball on a floodlit court outside. Their cries went straight to heaven, a black sky stuck with stars. A whistle skidded like chalk on a blackboard: the referee, a manic grammarian, wanted to put exclamation marks on every sentence. On the other side of the church, in a park with swings and seesaws, were the children, loudest of all.

"Alleluia! Alleluia!" the minister called, clapping his hands.

"*—luia! —luia! —luia!* . . ."

One of the old men beside me, who had stood up to watch the worship, laughed and spat and sat down again. A couple of push rickshaws went by on the street, father pedalling, mother and children on the boards facing forward. All Sisal appeared to be there, the women in the church, the children on the swings, the young men playing volleyball, the old men in the park.

My bus arrived, I climbed on, we turned the corner into sudden darkness. But the sounds persisted: the shouts of the children and the muffled singing, and the referee's shrill whistle, and the meaty walloping of the ball.

24

The Right Eye
of the Virgin

Are we dreaming, Cortes' soldiers asked themselves as they stood on
the threshold of Mexico City. What they saw was a city that rode on
water, with causeways and pyramids and gardens and houses washed
with silver that turned out to be lime. As a moment of wonder it has
few equals in the New World. For centuries Mexico City was the
metropolis of the Americas; it remained so till New York came of
age. Bernal Díaz, the chronicler, who stood with Cortes on the chief
causeway, was for once at a loss. "It was all so wonderful that I do
not know how to describe this first glimpse of things never heard
of, seen or dreamt of before." It was a brief dream. At the bottom
of the page comes Bernal Díaz's lament. "But today all that I
then saw is overthrown and destroyed; nothing is left standing."

The dream city was a Spanish creation; the destruction of
Mexico, only too real, was the end also of the figment. In
between came an almost pathetic idyll. Montezuma, "in every
way a great prince", lodged the foreigners in palaces, showed
them his treasure-house. The Spanish doffed their caps in his
presence. They took him sailing on the lake. It was his special
pleasure, scudding along in their fastest sloop, his last, and perhaps first, taste of freedom. Then suddenly, almost inadvertently,
he died, and a less fey prince, Cuauhtemoc, took his place. The
Spanish were driven from the city and returned the following
year in greater force. Cuauhtemoc was taken and tortured until
he confessed he'd thrown the treasure into the lake. The Great
Pyramid was razed, a church built on the site: a Spanish city
had begun where the dream city stood. At the end of the 19th
century the lake was drained. There was not much treasure at the

bottom. The great city began to sink under its own weight. It is still sinking.

America, said a Mexican historian, is "an invention of the European spirit". Europe's American dream (the nightmare from which the Indians of the Americas have been trying for centuries to awake) was both the epiphany on the causeway and the bombardment with ten brass guns. Bernal Díaz's orange pips (in Pisté a Mayan woman sold me the late fruit of those pips, very sweet) and Cortes' cannon set the tone of Mexican development, but it was not all one way. The Indians, too, did some inventing of Europe. They reinvented the Spanish God, or rather, and better still, the Mother of God.

To see the cult of the Virgin of Guadalupe as a Franciscan trick is to patronize her followers. The Guadalupana was an Indian dream, or vision, to set beside Bernal Díaz's, an attempt to come to grips with a foreign apparition, "things never heard of, seen or dreamed of before". At the top of the Way of Mysteries, aligned with the very causeway on which Cortes and Bernal Díaz stood, are the hill and the shrine of the Indian Mary. She looks back down the old thoroughfare, returning as it were the invader's gaze. (In 1847 the Americans too entered Mexico City by that southern route.) At the shrine you can buy postcards of that celebrated gaze. There is even one that isolates the right eye.

It is a dark eye, an Indian eye, and one wonders what it sees. I bought it for a few pesos and it watched over the writing of a book with no appreciable result. The faults that remain are my own. But it was a reminder that the Mexico I saw was my invention, my private dream. My enthusiasms did not deceive it, or trouble it, nor did my reservations or my earnest enquiries.

"It's very simple," said José, the desk clerk at the Uxmal. I'd gone straight there on getting back from Mérida. He took up a sheet of Uxmal letterhead and drew four fluid lines across it.

"This is Reforma," he said frowning. Already he was in trouble. Why four lines? I wondered, until I remembered it was a boulevard. He turned the page over and continued the lines.

"Here is Reforma, and we are here." He drew a big box. "This is the Uxmal." It was too close to the corner so he made a rapid extension to the box. "*This* is the Uxmal. Here is Independencia.

307

Here is the statue of Cuauhtemoc." Cuauhtemocs abound in Mexico, while Montezuma gets a short street a long way from the centre.

"You take a bus from here. Go all the way up Reforma, up – up – up –" But again he'd run out of room. His Reforma threatened, like the equator, to join up on the other side. He took a second sheet of paper. I grew impatient. Here was a man who would never cut his coat to fit his cloth.

"Now. Here is the top of the calzada that joins Reforma. *Don't* go this way." He drew a grand loop where the bus turned around. "*Don't* get off here, *or* here." Two fat roads fanned out, neither to be taken. "Get off here." He drew a wide overbridge that swept perilously close to the top of the page. His improvidence was ingrained. "Go over this and follow it up – up – up – and *here*" (he drew a minute hill and shrine in the very corner) "is the Villa de Guadalupe. Simple!"

I got there in the afternoon. The morning I had spent with the poet Elsa Cross.

I found her in the Mexico City phone book, and we met at Sanborn's, the coffee house by the Angel. Sanborn's waitresses wear a tiny square kerchief on the head and on their shoulders sweeping V-shaped wings. I stood at the entrance brandishing her orange book of poems. It was part of a university series, No. 160; her predecessors were Giacomo Leopardi and Walt Whitman.

Cross appeared, at shoulder-level, and greeted me with her hands pressed together in a namaste. She was small and prepossessing, with a wide, worried smile. We ordered and poured coffee, but after an hour and a half I found I had not touched my cup.

Elsa Cross was born in 1946. A part-time professor of philosophy at the University of Mexico, and a full-time publisher at the Diplomatic Archives, she was the mother, "happily divorced", of two children. Her job at the archives was recent. It meant driving across the city twice a day and left her with little free time. "But I feel," she said, "that whenever I have something to write it will come, no matter how." In this way she'd written ten books of verse. She had just finished a doctoral thesis on a 13th-century Hindu poet, Gyaneshwar.

I had read some of Cross's poems and thought I saw in their impassioned transcendentalism a parallel with the 17th-century Mexican poet Sor Juana (also, incidentally, named "of the Cross"), a complex personality: scholar, lover, feminist, and nun — there in gold wash on the 1000-peso coin. But Elsa Cross's inspiration came from further east. Drawn to India by Swami Muktananda, she wrote many of her poems there. "Sri Nityananda Mandir" describes a Siddha temple:

> Smiling from his statue
> On his black chest are reflected
> the flames of the lamps
>   waving in circles.
>
> Incense,
>   camphor.
> And the rain brings a scent of jasmine
> to the window
>   guarded by a clay cobra.
>
> (More fragrance in his hands.)
>
> The chant begins.
> Sparrows in the temple,
> salamanders slide along the wall —
> and the sparrows quiet
>   as if listening

Vande jagat karanam

> Cause of the world,
> lord of the world
> form of the world
>   destroyer —
>
> Smiling from his statue.
> In the nocturnal ablution
> his head receives
> rosewater,
> perfumes,
>   rivers of milk and honey.
>
> The curve of his shoulders trembles,
> his eyes stare

> *and his dark skin is warm.*
> *His closeness,*
> > *rapture.*

After two years in India Cross returned to Mexico. There followed a book of Mexican landscapes, *Jaguar*, which included poems from the Yucatan. Was this, I suggested, a return to the outside?

"You come to a point," she said, "where you cannot separate the outside from the inside. Meditation is a discipline that teaches you not to disconnect from the outer world but to bring to the outer what you have found inside. The division is arbitrary anyway. Object and subject break down, just as in modern physics."

"Once you break down object and subject, can't you choose any system you please?"

"I happen to like this one."

She'd dealt with sceptics before. I asked her how she came to learn meditation.

"One block from my house here in Mexico they happened to open a centre. I would pass by every day, and one day I went in. I didn't like anything, because they would simply chant and then meditate. But I just kept looking at Swami Muktananda's portrait because I felt a lot of strength and a lot of love in that photograph. When I went home I had an incredible experience. I did not know how to meditate even but I just happened to think of him and to invoke his help somehow. In a matter of seconds I began to feel a very soft rain of . . . energy – I don't know how to explain it – this water kept falling on me and entering me and after a while I was just filled with a tremendous energy that kept building till I attained an incredible ecstatic state. I felt myself completely drowned in this ecstasy, I felt something open in the middle of my eyebrows and a very sweet smell came from there . . ."

"It filled the room where you were?"

"I don't know – it filled me. I was just completely gone. I don't know how long that lasted, and then I heard some Sanskrit words and then I had a vision. There is a poem, a simple poem in there."

"You had never felt that way before?"

"No."

"As a child?"

"I had a longing, a tremendous longing . . . for God. I went to a convent school. But I couldn't find the way. Strangely enough, after meditation I could experience what Christianity was meant to be. Many people from different religions gathered around Swami Muktananda, and now his successor Gurumayi, to experience the essence of their own faith. I don't think religion matters. I don't think God, an abstract God, matters."

"How much does poetry matter?"

"It can matter nothing at all — no thing can matter really — and it can matter totally, but poetry is an approximation of the experience, a way of expressing the inexpressible."

"Is it more important to convey that experience of otherness or to create a poem that is true and beautiful?"

"I would say that poetry is independent from anything. I try to make a poem the best way I can, not to slip in any messages, no matter what they are. But a poet speaks out of her own experience, and if your experience happens to be meditation you write about that."

The talk turned to religion.

"What's distinctive about Mexican Catholicism as opposed to Spanish Catholicism?"

"Nothing in particular, at the deepest level."

"So the Virgin of Guadalupe . . . ?"

"It was a real apparition, as you find also in India. They say the Devi, the Goddess, manifested herself on a rock and they worship the rock. Here it's the same phenomenon: the Devi manifested herself."

"I find many parallels with popular religion in India: the roadside shrines, the readiness to project a Mother —"

"Now that must be a very distinctive trait, this cult of the Mother. Spain has much more patriarchal values."

"Is that phenomenon an original Mexican creation?"

"Yes. The indígenes say the apparition took place twelve years after the conquest, on a hill here. She appeared to an Indian, not to a Spaniard, and she was dark. She was not a Spanish-looking lady. And in her robe she had secret emblems that were meaningful to the Indians but not to the Spanish."

"Was this a kind of syncretism in the mind of a conquered

311

people? It looks like an unconscious desire to absorb and tame the conqueror."

"That's what happened. It's a very perfect phenomenon, the fusing of two religions."

I went to La Villa de Guadalupe to see for myself. It's a surreal landscape: a vast stone chessboard strewn with Escher-like pieces, buildings so crazily tilted from the city's subsidence that the visitor is thrown out of plumb. The colonial churches, straight ahead, lean towards one another; both are fissured, one is declared unsafe. A smaller chapel leans a third way. The new and ugly basilica is off to the left, a concrete circus tent. On the hill behind the old churches is the original shrine of the apparition, but most people were making for the circus, the mark of a living faith, so I abandoned the hill and followed them. And there, the focus of an interior that looked like the general assembly of the United Nations (the flags of the world, microphones, curving pews), is the picture most Mexicans know by heart long before they make their pilgrimage to it. The Guadalupana, in an attitude of musing.

Behind the altar is a viewing well where the devout can make a nearer inspection, from below. People stand and gaze, their lips moving silently as they offer her their lives, or perhaps just their ailments. I watched a shabby family: a father, his sweater much darned, a mother in cheap yellow slacks, their four children in grubby castoffs. All stood rapt. Life for many who came was harsh, sometimes violent, often perplexing. That was why they came – much as they go to the smiling Shiva – for a glimpse of serenity.

AM I NOT HERE AS YOUR MOTHER? ARE YOU NOT HAPLY IN MY BOSOM?
WHAT MORE NEED YOU? DO NOT FRET,
NOR LET ANYTHING TROUBLE YOU.

So the Virgin, to Juan Diego, indígeno, on the hill. Beyond the ramps was a miracle. In such and such a year a man tried to vandalize the painting: mark how the steel here buckled to protect the Virgin! Further in were the trinkets: Guadalupana keyrings, ballpens, statuettes, holy pictures. I bought my postcard and stepped out into the night. It was drizzling and I felt only depression.

312

The next day was the Day of the Dead. Marzipan skulls, dead chocolate babies, candy skeletons, filled confectioners' windows, death sugared over. It was also the day of the President's state-of-the-nation speech, and the living were out to make a point too. As a run-up to it, the Independent Proletarian Movement staged a demonstration the night before in the zócalo, the great square of Mexico, with loudspeakers aimed at the Palacio de Gobierno. One man addressed the powers in the building – "if they are listening" – but apart from a gingerly parted curtain at an upstairs window the Palacio made no reply. Every time Salinas' name was used there was whistling and jeering laughter. Five truckloads of soldiers in their anonymous green helmets waited in the wings, then vanished unaccountably. There was a spontaneous charge towards the Palacio entrance. Fists beat on the massive doors, women and children chanted and cheered. Every age and condition was there except the blond; in Mexico the poor are still the dark. The speakers restrained the crowd; they were union leaders and politicians and party ideologues. (Months later I took a walk in a leafy suburb of my hometown and chanced on the house of the man who helped found Mexico's Communist Party, Lenin's Bengali comrade, M.N. Roy.)

It was the rain that dispersed the crowd. It fell like judgment and the great zócalo emptied in minutes. Instantly there appeared capitalists hawking cheap plastic capes. Damp and chilled, I stood in a corridor by a vendor and ate a pottle of stewed corn, tart with lime. A woman with the Guadalupana's face looked hard at me. I had thought she was with her family, but the man and boy beside her moved off and she remained. I spooned my sour corn. The look intensified. The man beside me whispered something to his friend. The woman took out a packet of mouth-freshening gum. I bought two newspapers and walked back to the metro at Bellas Artes.

Next day I had lunch with Cross and her son, Juan, at their home on Calle Milton. (The taxi backed all the way up one-way Calle Victor Hugo.) I could find no wine to take, and recalled the tribute Prescott lists as customary in Aztec Mexico: 20 chests of ground chocolate, 8000 reams of paper, 2000 loaves of white salt, 400 baskets of refined copal, gold tiles the size of an oyster, 40 bags of cochineal, 100 pots of liquidambar, 8000 handfuls of rich scarlet feathers, two quilts of hummingbird down, 40 tigerskins, and any number of quetzal quills filled with gold dust. Instead I took one of those round blue tins of Danish butter cookies and felt a fool. (Later I found comfort in an old letter: writing to their Royal Majesties, Columbus offers them all the chewing-gum they wish.)

The Cross flat was elegant with fine old furniture and wall hangings from distant parts. A copy of Derek Walcott's *Omeros* lay open on the divan. After lunch Cross and I took her Volkswagen on a tour of the city. She showed me where she worked in Tlatelolco, the square where Cortes and Cuauhtemoc fought their bloodiest – and decisive – engagement, and where in 1968 the army shot down hundreds of students. Cross, then a student, and carrying her first child, was called away that day. Today there is a monument to the first, but not the second, encounter. There is an old church by the ruins of the Aztec cue, and a new shrine to a pair of skeletons recently found entwined in a crypt. People have begun to place flowers there for The Lovers of Tlatelolco.

"There's something else I would like to show you," Cross said.

We drove back along Reforma as far as the park at Chapultepec. There was something I too wanted to see there. It was another hill, Grasshopper Hill, above the old King's Mill, where in 1847 the invading US Army staged an execution of its own troops, the deserters of the St Patrick's regiment. The captured men were led to a long gallows erected on the hill, from where they witnessed the fall of the city they had chosen to defend in a fit of Catholic solidarity. They watched the capture of Chapultepec Castle, the military academy where a boy cadet wrapped himself in the Mexican flag and leapt to his death. Then, as the triumphal army marched into the city, the San Patricios were hanged.

The Volkswagen shot through and I was reluctant to ask Cross to stop. On a likely hill stood a grand guarded mansion behind high walls.

"Los Pinos," Cross said. The Pines, the presidential palace, standing perhaps on the unhappy spot. Cross drove to another part of Chapultepec and parked the car.

"This way." She led me across the lot and up a walk that came out on a treed avenue. "There."

On a black pedestal against two white flags stood a famil-iar ascetic figure, as instantly recognizable to an Indian as the

314

Guadalupana is to a Mexican. There is a statue of him in every town in India (one reason why the man has become invisible) and now there was one in Mexico City. The street on which it stands, once called The Mile, has been renamed Mahatma Gandhi Avenue.

"I have a meeting I must go to now," Cross said, "but perhaps you would like to come along?"

We drove to a stone-faced building that opened directly onto the sidewalk. Inside, Cross left me with a poet and went upstairs.

"Ninety per cent of the people who meditate here are Catholics," the poet said. "No, ninety-five per cent," he corrected himself. "No, ninety-nine point something. And some Jews." He had been a seminarian himself. "But there was no fire to my faith, no force. *This* is different."

He led me down to this, a podgy man with ironical eyes, but didn't go into the meditation room with me. The chanting had begun. The music filled the entire building, not just the basement where the chanters were; there were speakers at all three levels. I left my shoes on the shoe rack and padded in. An usher in a suit and tie and socks led me to a seat in a row of upright chairs along the wall. The more seasoned chanters were seated on the carpet cross-legged, the men to one side, women to the other. The room smelt of incense. The lights were low, so one's eyes were drawn at once to a spotlight. It fell on a photograph of Swami Muktananda, picking out his face. This was the portrait Cross had seen in 1978. It was an extraordinary gaze, grave and dispassionate, in a face without an attitude. Below the swami's photograph was another, also spotlit, on a gilded chair. This was Gurumayi, the swami's successor, the woman he chose before he took samadhi, or died. Her gaze too (unlike the Virgin of Guadalupe's) was fixed on the viewer. It followed you wherever you chose to sit. Dismayed by another portrait of hers I'd seen on the stair, a sidelong, almost pert glance, I concentrated on the swami.

As my eyes grew accustomed to the gloom I began to look around. In a semicircle at Gurumayi's feet were the musicians and singers: a tanpura girl, stringy as her instrument, two chanteuses, the harmonium player, the tabla, the fingerbells. In the middle was a two-tier brass oil lamp; after the white spotlights its gentle yellow flames were soothing to the eye. At the centre of the ceiling

315

was a plaster lotus that recalled the stylized sunflower in the igloo church at Inuvik. At either end of the hall were niches with effigies and pictures of goddesses and saints: the two I could make out faced each other across the hall. One was Lakshmi, white bringer of light and wealth to Hindus, her four arms confidently raised up. The other, her hands folded in diffident prayer, was the dark Virgin of Guadalupe.

The chanting, in Sanskrit, built slowly from a measured mantra to a romp. At the end of a verse the harmonium maundered on as a new line in roman script was projected onto a screen. The lead singers took it up slowly and the congregation answered. The line went back and forth until the pace built up again.

It was a young, slightly built, East-Indian-looking man who loosened up first. Cross-legged, he began to rock forward onto his heels as he clapped, working in a spinal twist at the same time. His head bobbed on the melodic line, and when the tabla fluttered in the intervals, he raised his right arm and bent the hand back, the classic gesture of singers in ecstasy. This gesture, so utterly Indian, I found repeated increasingly among the congregation.

For half an hour harmonium and tabla courted. Then the tabla, after long and patient pacing, thrilled and broke loose. In a concert this frisson is always a moment of release – and anticipation: the courting is over, the stroking begins. The kartal, a set of jingling discs, started in; more urgency. A stocky young man in a business suit (he had come in late and pressed his forehead to the carpet before Gurumayi's portrait) took them over from the boy in front of him (who took up a pair of fingerbells) and slipped into the stream with a long shivering shake. A man in a grey suit swung a censer. A girl in a sari – she looked blondely foreign to it – made an offering of flowers and oil lamps. The lights came up a little, the chant died down. A woman spoke from a lectern. We bowed our heads in silent meditation for ten minutes (the lights going down again), and then the harmonium stole up and returned us to the present. We stood and chanted a benediction, a collective salute to Gurumayi. The lights came up high and harsh and the congregation lined up to make their obeisance at Gurumayi's feet.

Upstairs, Cross had finished her committee meeting. The cafeteria where we had Indian vegetarian snacks was decorated for the Day of the Dead. When I admired the macabre kite-paper doilies at

316

the counter (a skeleton smoking a cigar, another driving a Model-T) a serving lady pressed two on the visitor from India. I bought four marzipan skulls to take home. She packed them for me and handed over the plate with both hands. On the cellophane she had placed a marigold.

Cross dropped me back at the Plaza Madrid. There was still traffic on the streets and the street people of Mexico City, windscreen washers, tired clowns and fire-eaters, wandered in bizarre chiaroscuro among the cars at stoplights like their counterparts in Delhi.

The next day, Sunday, I strolled to Alameda, the peaceful garden square where once the Inquisition burned heretics. In the market nearby I did the first shopping of my journey: a rug, a clown puppet, a folk doll, a bark painting. A man peeling cactus for his lunch offered me a taste and expounded the virtues of nopal. It was like a water chestnut but not as sweet. I spent an hour in the Franz Mayer museum nearby.

"I like things like that," breathed an elderly American going up close to a painting called *Jardin Interior* where a fountain played in the shade of orange trees. It was his fantasy refuge – and, oddly, mine too – just as *The Death of the Virgin*, a quiet 17th-century panel, was for its painter. After the frontier journey a walled garden had a special appeal: *do* fence me in.

At noon I checked out of my room and hid my bags behind the Uxmal's unmanned desk. José had the day off. I spent the afternoon wandering along the lesser streets off the Revolucion monument. The half-made sidewalks had an Asiatic feel but I envied the throng their Western city. The Revolucion arch was one more beetling, bullying Aztec monument, but typically the Mexicans turned it, after dark, into a trysting ground. *More time, more time!* I repeated, feeling the sweet misery of leaving behind something cherished. The city began to draw back from me. I gave chase up Reforma on the Villa bus. Mexico City turned on its notorious pollution, but on that last ride the blue fumes were benign. What was intolerable at home had become a colour away; I was a tourist again. But blue was the Mexican colour. It was the colour of the Virgin's robe, of half of Mexico's longings. It helped bury the old dark red.

A Volkswagen taxi, a "yellow" (the other kind cost more),

took me to the airport in heavy traffic. At the boarding gate the Mexicana airlines steward scolded me like a child for making a wrong turn.

Gandhi in
Disneyland

Halfway to Los Angeles I realize I've lost my Arctic pebbles and with them my dinosaur bones. It's a cruel blow. I have my Sisal shells, but the rocks from the other end of the journey are gone. I last saw them in Pisté in their small black film canister. I imagine the propriedora tipping them out — some old stones.

The loss sets off a train of reminiscence along the route of my journey. Already it has become a line on the map with lights at intervals. The people too have begun to haunt me. It's like an illustration I remember from childhood: Dickens dreaming at his desk, surrounded by a lifetime's characters, only these faces are real.

The lights of LA come up to meet us, the wheels go down whingeing. When we touch down the fat Guatemalan boy beside me wakes up with a start and crosses himself. In the air he had refused dinner, steak.

At the terminal I step into another world. The corridors are American-perfect, the carpet-rails beautifully joined, the seams invisible, every angle true. The clarity — sharp focus after an age in the Blurred World — is almost painful.

The bag I left unticketed at the Venice Share-tel, years ago it seems, is still there. In it, as a bonus, are the rocks and bones in their film canister. They didn't go to Mexico at all. Now I pack them carefully, penitently, with my Yucatan shells and limestone nibs, the Jaliscan copal nugget, and Mariana's black ruby.

Next day I take the city bus to Disneyland. As a student I scorned to go, but there's an older, truer, pre-adult self to satisfy. One hour, I calculate, to get there. Two hours later I'm still on the bus. The signs outside are in familiar Spanish — Roca

319

de Salvacion pentecostal chapel, Chihuahua Café — but they have clean, hard, Protestant edges. We enter the freeway. We leave the freeway, enter suburbia: small square houses, small square lawns. *Happy Miles!* says a sticker by the driver's seat. I begin to feel trapped. "You *do* go to Disneyland?" I ask the driver. "Yup. Last stop." Back onto the freeway. Off again. I thought I'd finished the longest journey of my life, but this bus has become life itself. Then I spot the blue dunce-cap towers, just as they looked on my lost Viewmaster slide. The bus is moving in diminishing circles.

Disneyland is tiny. The first thing that strikes an adult is its scale. It could fit on a large dinner-plate. Like the past revisited, it's smaller than life. And like the past, it's getting on. It hides its age by deft surgery, but repeated surgery only makes it tighter — and smaller. As something old and small it's an oddity in a land that worships youth and size, but Disney's genius was to shrink adults, to make of all the world a toy.

The bus has cheated me of half a day. I now have one hour to spare for Disneyland. I put it to the hostess at the gate.

"One hour in *Dis*-neyland!"

I feel like a thief. She gives me a map and circles the Must Sees. "But, *really* . . ." her look says.

I take the map and make for the train. Frontierland I cross off. Been there. Fantasyland is the next to go: the queue winds all around the castle. The train goes around the rim of the park: through the trees I glimpse Adventureland, New Orleans Square, Critter Country. I stay on the train; Mowgli was not the draw for a boy in India. I get off in Tomorrowland.

There's a man handing out 3-D glasses for *Captain EO*, starring Michael Jackson. It's the nearest I've got to a 3-D show since the day Nehru died. They were handing out the glasses at the Dehra Dun Odeon when the death was announced. At once the theatre was closed and the glasses taken back. It couldn't happen here: there is no death in Disneyland.

In *Captain EO*, music draws the sting of the universe. Jackson, in a white space suit, tracks down the evil queen (white, in a black suit) and wins her over with a song. The special effects work well: with the glasses the alien blobs come right at you. Without the glasses they're a blur. I play with the glasses: blur, focus, blur. It's the only place in Disneyland where you need special lenses.

320

Outside the theatre the dream comes focused. The fuzzy edges of real dreams (night dreams, ragged with possibility) have been corrected.

I slip out just before the end. It's four o'clock. There's just time for lunch.

"Good man, Gandy!" says a white-haired man on my bench.

"He should be here," I reply. I bolt my hot dog and run. If I miss the 4.20 shuttle I miss my flight.

Gandhi would have enjoyed Disneyland, I think as the monorail skims over a vast car park. He would have had his picture taken with Mickey (they had the same ears), ridden the Huck Finn raft. The child in him was not a long way down. At the Bengal Barbecue he would have had the fresh fruit box with yoghurt-raspberry dressing (and goggled at the price and recommended guavas, "cheap and nutritious"). He would have sat with Goofy at the *Captain EO* première and played with his 3-D spectacles. (Nehru would have stiffened, begun to clown.) Afterwards he would have shaken Michael Jackson's hand, for the cameras, for world peace, and raised up Ben Kingsley, blubbing at his feet. Leaving, he would have turned down the President's limousine and suggested the train. "There's no Third class," the Mayor whispers, but the Disney staff — there are 10,000 — have seen to that. The entourage leave by monorail, the paint still fresh on the yellow numeral III outside Mr Gandy's carriage. He refuses to sleep at the Disneyland Hotel. The shuttle bus takes him to a tenement in Watts.

Mine takes me to the airport, where I catch another shuttle to Venice to pick up my bags. Directly I get there I phone for a shuttle back to the airport. The bus is late. Insanely I run one block to the beach and across the sand to dip my hand in the Pacific. When I get back the bus driver is waiting. We haven't far to go. Six planes circle over the airport waiting their turn. The counter is closed. "If I check your bags in they won't reach the plane in time," the Continental clerk explains. "Run to Gate 68B."

I race down shining corridors pushing my trolley. They let me on, but store my gear bag — with the rocks — up front. At 7.42 we take off. Immediately Venice beach appears below, a string of yellow lights. Then black water, as the plane climbs steeply, heading west into the east.

Acknowledgements

I read Matsuo Basho's *Narrow Road to the Deep North* in the translation by Nobuyuki Yuasa (Penguin, 1966). The Eskimo poem, "Here I stand", is from the collection *Anerca*, translated by Knut Rasmussen and others (Dent, 1959); the *Beowulf* lines are from M. Alexander's translation (Penguin, 1973), with minor emendations. John Bierhorst's translations in *Four Masterworks of American Indian Literature* (Farrar, 1974) introduced me to the Navajo Night Chant and the Mayan book of prophecy, *Cuceb*. For Indian writing from the West I turned to N. Scott Momaday's *Way to Rainy Mountain* (University of New Mexico, 1969) and Vine Deloria's *Custer Died for Your Sins* (University of Oklahoma Press, 1988). The Inca prince Garcilaso de la Vega's account of the Incas' taming of Peru is from *The Borzoi Anthology of Latin American Literature*, ed. Emir Rodriguez Monegal (Alfred A. Knopf, 1977). Quotations from Bernal Díaz del Castillo's *History of the Conquest of New Spain* are from the translation by J. M. Cohen (Penguin, 1963); those from Friar Diego de Landa's *Relación de las Cosas de Yucatan* are from William Gates' translation, *Yucatan Before and After the Conquest* (San Fernando, n.d.). I have ventured some small changes to John Oliver Simon's unpublished translation of Elsa Cross's *Jaguar*.

I am grateful to all my informants along the road from the Yukon to the Yucatan. Among those who didn't go I would like to thank Kay and Brent McLaine for advice with books; John Cline for the unfailing despatch of reference materials to Dehra Dun; and my wife Cushla for her patience.

Further Non-Fiction Titles Available from Minerva

While every effort is made to keep prices low, it is sometimes necessary to increase prices at short notice. Mandarin Paperbacks reserves the right to show new retail prices on covers which may differ from those previously advertised in the text or elsewhere.

The prices shown below were correct at the time of going to press.

☐	7493 9815 9	**Neither Here Nor There**	Bill Bryson	£5.99
☐	7493 9761 6	**The Crystal Desert**	David G. Campbell	£6.99
☐	7493 9070 0	**Lost in Translation**	Eva Hoffmann	£5.99
☐	7493 9100 6	**Moscow! Moscow!**	Christopher Hope	£4.99
☐	7493 9944 9	**Diaries**	Franz Kafka	£9.99
☐	7493 9881 7	**Blue Highways**	William Least Heat-Moon	£6.99
☐	7493 9174 X	**The Mirror Maker**	Primo Levi	£5.99
☐	7493 9906 6	**Between Two Seas**	Charles Lister	£5.99
☐	7493 9171 5	**The Colossus of Maroussi**	Henri Miller	£5.99
☐	7493 9920 1	**India**	V. S. Naipaul	£6.99
☐	7493 9047 6	**Friends of Promise**	Michael Shelden	£6.99
☐	7493 9707 1	**Race**	Studs Terkel	£6.99

All these books are available at your bookshop or newsagent, or can be ordered direct from the address below. Just tick the titles you want and fill in the form below.

Cash Sales Department, PO Box 5, Rushden, Northants NN10 6YX.
Fax: 0933 410321   Phone: 0933 410511.

Please send cheque, payable to 'Reed Book Services Ltd.', or postal order for purchase price quoted and allow the following for postage and packing:

£1.00 for the first book, 50p for the second; **FREE POSTAGE AND PACKING FOR THREE BOOKS OR MORE PER ORDER.**

NAME (Block letters) ....

ADDRESS ....

....

☐ I enclose my remittance for ....

☐ I wish to pay by Access/Visa Card Number [ ][ ][ ][ ][ ][ ][ ][ ][ ][ ][ ][ ][ ][ ][ ][ ]

Expiry Date [ ][ ][ ][ ]

Signature ....

Please quote our reference: MAND